THE LANDSCAPE & ARCHITECTURE OF WELLESLEY COLLEGE

THE LANDSCAPE & ARCHITECTURE OF WELLESLEY COLLEGE

Peter Fergusson

PETER FERGUSSON

JAMES F. O'GORMAN

JOHN RHODES

In Commemoration of the 125th Anniversary of Wellesley College

FRONTISPIECE

A view across the Alexandra Botanic Garden toward Norumbega Hill, 1949

Published by Wellesley College, Wellesley, Massachusetts 02481-8203
on the occasion of the 125th anniversary of the College.
Copies of this publication may be purchased by writing to the publisher.

ISBN 1–881894–09–6
Library of Congress Control Number 00-111267

Graphic design by Matthew Monk, Providence, Rhode Island
Text editing by Julia Collins, Somerville, Massachusetts
Research assistance by Elizabeth Wax DS '97
Production coordination by Susan McNally, Cambridge, Massachusetts
Printing and binding by Cantz, Stuttgart

Color photographs on pages 4, 14, 17, 21, 24, 27, 45, 49,
74, 79, 83, 98, 99, 101, 106, 125, 126, 132, 135, 136, 139,
155, 156, 160, 167, 172, 187, 209, 223, 226, 228, 233, 237,
242, 246, 250, 254, 273, and 280 by Cervin Robinson
Photographs on pages 256 and 257 by David Stansbury
Photograph on page 150 courtesy of Boston Public Library
All other photographs from the Wellesley College Archives

Printed and bound in Germany

To the students—past, present, and future—of Wellesley College

The division of the book's eleven chapters reflects our teaching and research interests. Our different voices will, we hope, provide the reader with variety. Peter Fergusson wrote chapters 1, 5, 6, 7, and 11. James F. O'Gorman wrote chapters 2, 3, and 4. John Rhodes wrote chapters 8, 9, and 10.

CONTENTS

Among the daunting, yet inspiring, aspects of leading a great institution, the certainty that tomorrow's scholars will judge today's decisions ranks high. Standing as we now do in a remarkable space, at the pivot point between millennia, our obligations to an unknowable future seem all the more palpable. At such times, one is grateful for the lessons of history: the wisdom and expectations embodied in voices from the past.

When I returned to Wellesley as the 12th president of my alma mater, I came with a rich store of my own memories, many rooted in physical space. I have the most vivid recollection of arriving as a freshman at Severance Hall, walking down the entrance path with my brother who had driven me to college, opening the door and being greeted by a "vil" junior who knew my name. I remember sitting on the stone wall in the courtyard behind Bates Hall on sophomore fathers' weekend, and standing in the grass quadrangle in front of Beebe Hall on graduation day. I have the sharpest memories, still, of walking along the paved path through the Science Center meadow from Pendleton back to Bates, the carillon tolling in the background just after we had learned that President Kennedy had been shot, and of sitting with other students under the trees in the Academic Quad in a circle around Mme. Chiang Kai-shek, amazed to see her stretch limousine parked on the grass.

I remember looking at the sky over Wellesley and thinking it was bluer than I'd ever seen, riding my bike across the campus and feeling freer than I'd ever felt, sitting on the lawn with a friend and experiencing an intimacy I'd never known, walking back from a class with my mind in overdrive, more alive with ideas than I had ever been. I remember often being reminded by a visual cue—the tower, the lake, the street lamps, the rhododendron dell, a class tree, stone steps worn down in the middle, other evocations of the past

—how privileged I was to be calling Wellesley *my* college, how grateful to be joining the long line of amazing women who had set the intellectual standards that allowed me to believe that I might actually make a meaningful contribution, somewhere, some day.

Anyone who has lived, studied, or worked at Wellesley College for any period of time carries experiences of the campus that are vivid and visceral. Every Wellesley alumna knows that her education was greatly enriched by the special beauty of the campus. And I certainly brought such experiences and such knowledge to my presidency. But I never imagined—as I was making the transition back to Wellesley or settling in during the first hectic months—that the landscape would become the focus of energy and attention it has become for me and for many of my colleagues in the administration, the faculty, and the Board of Trustees.

The stimulus for my dawning awareness of the landscape I owe in large measure to two of the authors of this book, Professors Fergusson and O'Gorman. I want to add a bit of that story to the historical record they so ably present here; they are too modest to accord themselves the credit they are due. My first encounter with this interesting pair of professors was a walking tour of the campus they offered the new president quite soon after I arrived on campus. When I finally managed to clear my calendar to accept their intriguing offer, I had scant idea of what to expect. But they knew what they were doing.

They conveyed to me in that brief encounter the crucial things I needed to know: that we have one of the great college campuses in the world and with it a special responsibility of stewardship; that it has evolved over more than 120 years, as an expression of the hard work and visions of individuals (often members of the faculty, alumnae, and some of the leading architects and landscape architects of their eras), sometimes influenced by fashions of times, sometimes defying them; that the president and the Board of Trustees have been crucial at every step (selecting consultants and architects, guiding investment decisions, acting as champions); and that the story of the campus is a lens through which we can read the story of the College's mission, culture, and values.

They impressed on me the importance of a long time horizon, tracing the history from the Durants' original idea of a picturesque English landscape, through the Olmsted letter, the great fire, and Caroline Hazard's development of a ten- to twenty-year plan that was implemented incrementally over time. They pointed out critical incidents along the way, decisive moments in the formation of the campus that made all the difference. And they planted a worry that simply had not occurred to me, the possibility that the College had arrived at such a moment again, that we would be called to change our course or do irreparable harm.

The brunt of their message was that the landscape and grounds warranted a high-priority slot on the strategic agenda of the College. But, meanwhile, we had a whole universe of equally pressing agenda items— inadequate faculty resources, gaps in the curriculum, huge costs for financial aid, needed improvements in the quality of student life, growing pressure to moderate our costs and the rate of increase in tuition, the potential impact of information technology and the Internet on higher education, and the question of how we should respond to the forces of globalization and multiculturalism, to name a few of the most obvious. Each concern had a vocal constituency and a real resonance. And on the question of whether we should divert limited resources to reinvest in the landscape, most faculty, staff, and students thought the campus looked just fine. Do we really need more rhododendrons? people would ask rhetorically when the landscape was seen to threaten one of their priorities.

But Margaret Jewett Greer '51, chair of the board's committee on landscape and grounds, saw the campus as Professors Fergusson and O'Gorman did. It was her suggestion that we bring in a visiting committee to help us resolve the question of how serious a problem we really had. Professor Fergusson supplied a proposed list of potential visitors, tapping (as we're so often able to do) the deep reservoir of talent among our own alumnae and faculty. Chaired by Elizabeth Barlow Rogers '57, the committee was commissioned over the summer of 1996 and came to campus in early October for two days, to review the condition of the grounds and meet with key staff and with other concerned members of the College community. They gave me an oral report at the end of their visit and followed it with a frank, tough, pragmatic, and visionary written report.

Some of what made that report so valuable to me was that it placed the landscape in the larger context of the history and mission of Wellesley College, resonated with deep feelings all of us have about the beauty of the campus, and highlighted the importance of those feelings to our institutional loyalty. It reminded us that the Wellesley landscape and grounds are a precious asset, which require strong and steady advocacy over time, and it also conveyed a sense of urgency. As beautiful as the campus appears on the surface, Betsy Rogers wrote, we are "living off our inheritance." The report highlighted actions we needed to take right away and others that would require more time. One recommendation for the short term was that we recruit a horticulturist to the Wellesley grounds staff, and this we did in the person of J. Patrick Willoughby, who came to Wellesley from fifteen years at Harvard's Arnold Arboretum.

For the longer term, the chief focus of the report was a call for an integrated and comprehensive restoration and maintenance plan. The word restoration was used deliberately to raise an alarm. Such a plan, the committee wrote, would serve as a management and decision-making tool. It would guide the placement of any future new buildings or additional uses of the landscape, systematically address the vexing problem of automobiles, create priorities for campus improvements, and project long-term budgetary needs. It should grow out of extensive consultations with all constituencies, in a process designed to "build understanding for the campus as a work of landscape art as well as an educational and recreational resource," the committee wrote.

The next step was the selection of a firm to develop such a plan. Professor O'Gorman sat on that selection committee, which I chaired. After hearing presentations from leading landscape architects, we selected the firm of Michael Van Valkenburgh Associates. The final chapter of this book tells the story of the 1998 Master Plan. All who participated in the process—a protracted, intense, and inclusive one led by Ellen Gill Miller '73—learned a great deal about our campus.

We commenced our first meeting with an open invitation to anyone with a perspective s/he wanted the committee to hear. The session drew a sizable turnout of students, faculty, staff, alumnae, neighbors, and retired faculty and staff. One participant cited a Will Rogers quotation that summed up our basic challenge: "Real estate ... They ain't making any more of that stuff."

The most powerful messages we heard at that session, and at many others in subsequent months, spoke of and from the "soul" of the College and to the "genius" of the campus: how lucky students feel to be studying "in a park"; the sense of calm, repose, and privacy afforded by the lake; the human scale and balance of the campus and its many distinctive components;

the seamless reciprocity between buildings and grounds, "gesturing" to each other and backward and forward in time; the wide-ranging opportunities, not yet fully realized, for capitalizing on the campus as a rich learning laboratory.

Perhaps the most telling lesson was captured in the closing words of the landscape history prepared as part of the master plan, in which Elizabeth Meyer wrote:

> Wellesley's landscape is not simply a background, is more than an open space, does more than buffer, and cannot be relegated to the role of nice amenity. To reduce [it] to these terms is to deny the long struggle to construct a campus that embodied the aspirations of a group of pioneering women scholars and students, and to provide for landscape places that instructed, inspired, challenged, cajoled, and consoled…. The beauty [of the campus] is anything but natural. It has been cultivated and tended. As such, it is a legacy easily lost, despite the best of individual intentions.

Making sure we honor that legacy to the best of our ability is a high priority for us now, even as we balance it against the many competing claims on our resources and attention. This book, which represents the individual scholarly perspectives of three of our faculty, should help us keep that important goal in focus, now and, I hope, far into the future.

DIANA CHAPMAN WALSH '66
President of Wellesley College

When I came to Wellesley in 1959, no one told me that I was about to experience a landscape. It was an earlier era before parents who lived at a distance took their children for college visits. My first sight of the campus—and New England—was from the car that took me from the Boston airport. Yes, in some ways Wellesley looked like the pictures the College had sent me. But in critical ways it was altogether different.

I had lived my childhood years within the grid of a flat Southern city. At Wellesley there were no straight lines anywhere. Nor could I necessarily see my destination—trees were often in the way. Used to moving around by car, I was at first exhausted by the campus. To get from one place to another required needless roundabout walking. And then there were the hills, including the steep incline to the Quad that initially threatened to do me in. Why were the buildings so far apart? Why were routes indirect and sites shrouded? And why, oh why, was my Shafer home in the Quad placed on such a hill?

The first snowfall is an unforgettable moment for any Southerner. On that evening a cousin in graduate school in Cambridge came out to introduce me to snow and snowballs, and, I think, to see the surprise on my face. Over time, I began to love the snow-covered ground filtered through the lights at night and the immense quiet surrounding the walk from the library to my dorm. I think it was at those moments that the magic of the Wellesley landscape began to speak to me.

Spring hit me hard. Somehow in Louisiana, where lawns stayed green, trees were evergreen, and camellias bloomed all winter, I had managed never to notice spring. In New England how could I not notice a seemingly dormant world suddenly coming to life? Spring was the metaphor for my own state, as my mind awakened under wonderful teaching and as I fell in love with the man who remains my life's companion. How different was everything around me. Lake Waban was suddenly there, and it was so beautiful! Dormitories that had looked like stern castles in the gray light of winter took on a friendly, picturesque air against the blue sky. Walking up the stairs of Jewett became a daily processional with each step revealing a bit more of the Galen Stone Tower of Green Hall. And the trees—the handsome skeletons I had admired in the lamplit snow—were now taking on leafy green flesh. By the time I left for a Louisiana summer the rhododendrons were in bloom, and Wellesley was now home. In the years since college, I have carried this intense experience of Wellesley as a part of my living consciousness.

To an outsider, it would appear that Wellesley College shares many of its strengths with other great liberal arts colleges. It offers an excellent education. It provides a community in which its students find friendship. The College prods a person to grow at a critical moment of life. Such an observer would say that this is what many good colleges do. But for we who lived it, we know that our experience is like no other. The most tangible aspect of our retort is that such generalizations may be "correct," but at Wellesley all of this takes a different shape. What makes the experience of Wellesley's daughters different from that of the daughters of other alma maters is that it is framed in the glories of the College's landscape.

As a student, once I came to love the campus, I merely accepted it as the gift that was mine. It was a fact, like the Boston world that stretched at the end of the transit line. I never asked who planted the rhododendrons or why, nor did I ask who designed the buildings and landscape, nor why the College was in a western suburb along a commuter rail line. But I became a cultural historian, and such questions became my meat and drink.

In the late 1970s I began to use my training to study women's spaces. After a series of peregrinations I gravitated to a key source of my own consciousness and began to explore the landscape and built environment of women's colleges. I returned to Wellesley as a researcher into the College's past. I retread familiar paths but with a new intent: I would *understand* what had transformed my life. Moving among the Seven Sisters, I began to see Wellesley within a larger pattern of women's colleges. I explored both what I had known and buildings long lost, through fire or reconstruction. I took time for the long walks around the lake that had been all too infrequent during my own pressured college days. Seeing on the lake side of the Tower Court quadrangle the resurrected columns that before the 1914 fire had adorned College Hall gave me an acute thrill—the past come to life.

Although I was interested in buildings and landscapes—design—I came to them with questions about how their occupants dwelled in them and shaped them to their own purposes and experiences. How did students live in this world not of their own making? How did they transform it by their own collective college culture? I had my own individual recollections to draw on, but my college years were a curious time of transition immediately before the world of "gracious living" cracked under the strain of youthful rebellion. The most valuable part of my awareness was that this world of students was not immutable, that it developed and changed.

As I worked in the College Archives with original documents and walked the campus in the early evening, I began to see everything on the land as intention. Each walk became a way to test out what I was learning and to experience each design. Exploring the back of Green Hall I saw the way that the stones of construction blended into the stony hillside, the "medieval" effect desired by its architects and celebrated at the time by its faculty. Though without my dog, I tried to walk the campus as many faculty women had done earlier in the century; sometimes this brought an acute sense of the changes that had altered the lay of the land. Perhaps my greatest moment of connection with the past came when considerate owners of the house that had been built by Vida Scudder, a professor of English at the College early in the twentieth century, showed me the wildflower garden that she had planted and lovingly described in her memoir.

Scudder was one of the first faculty women to move out of College Hall to her own house. Her garden—and those of her colleagues—created a world of privacy out of doors to be shared with close friends. The unique society of Wellesley faculty women, carefully delineated in Patricia Ann Palmieri's *In Adamless Eden,* imparted to the College its special vision, a remarkably effective force on generations of students. Ultimately the independence and relative power of these faculty women led to the preservation of Wellesley's landscape glory, its hills of dramatic buildings and its protected valleys and meadows. These women constituted themselves the guardians of the land. Their intimate knowledge of its "every rock and rill" enabled them to fight successfully against the combined force of landscape planners, architects, and trustees who would have recreated Wellesley after the 1914 fire into a formal composition on leveled ground.

Although I began with my own web of memories, I eagerly reached out to new awareness and knowledge. The writing and researching of a work of history involves a conversation with documents. One begins with certain hopes and expectations about what the material might say. One reads and sometimes finds confirmation and refinement of the argument in one's head; but the more usual experience is that the pages in the archives trace out a different pattern that leads down unforeseen paths. As I traveled to some of the Seven Sisters, I had few preconceptions about what I might find. But Wellesley, of course, was different. And thus, it was Wellesley that gave me some of my greatest surprises of discovery.

The Wellesley reader of this marvelous book can anticipate just this kind of pleasure. Each brings her own memories of the landscape and her experience within it. She has in her mind if not conscious questions, then the unconscious nub of questions about a world that once was her home. She will quickly find that this book will reveal all sorts of wonderful information. Its authors are ideal guides. To their exploration of the College's landscape and buildings they bring intimate knowledge of the campus, skills as scholarly sleuths, a wealth of learning, and fine writing. Whereas I could only sketch in broad strokes some of the basic patterns and could bore down in only a few places, these writers can draw the entirety in lines bold and fine. As I read, I found myself fascinated by all the new information the book revealed and delighted by the admirable prose that conveys it.

For the non-Wellesley reader, this book should be a revelation, for it will introduce the College's extraordinary campus as well as provide its detailed history. The book is a first. No college in the United States has been so carefully delineated by landscape and architectural historians. And no college more deserves to be.

The landscape writer J. B. Jackson once wrote, "To the naturalist the whole world of beasts and plants is worth studying. The common and familiar specimens are no less instructive than the rare. How much more rewarding is the world which we ourselves have helped to make!" To Jackson, all of the human-made landscape was part of the design, awaiting our discovery. As he put it, "A rich and beautiful book is always open before us. We have but to learn to read it." In *The Landscape and Architecture of Wellesley College*, Peter Fergusson, James O'Gorman, and John Rhodes have given us a splendid study about the "rich and beautiful book" of Wellesley. Reading the pages that follow will teach all of us—friends of the College and strangers to its gates—how to read the landscape of Wellesley College.

In a 1902 letter, Frederick Law Olmsted, Jr. wrote to President Caroline Hazard that Wellesley was blessed with a "landscape not merely beautiful, but with a marked individual character." Its land was "a delicate and intricate bas-relief," possessed of "intricate beauty." The College, Olmsted wrote, has a particular duty "to treasure it for future generations." What lies before us in this book is the record of the ways in which the College has creatively attended to this duty in the past. As the present begins to shape the future, the College must return to the work in the days ahead. This book will serve as the perfect guide as Wellesley takes up the tasks of renewing its uniquely beautiful landscape.

HELEN LEFKOWITZ HOROWITZ '63

CHAPTER ONE

THE LANDSCAPE ESTABLISHED

I will give Wellesley the beautiful; others will give her the useful.

Henry Fowle Durant

THE TRANSFORMATION of the Wellesley landscape from a group of subsistence farms into one of the masterpieces of campus design in North America constitutes a defining event in the College's history. Effected through the vision and hard work of the founders of the College, Henry Fowle Durant and Pauline Durant, the transformation took place in the seven years prior to the arrival of the first students in 1875. The Durants' design served their conviction that beauty formed a necessary component of personal and spiritual growth and would thus be central to a Wellesley education. The resulting landscape validated these goals, shaping the character of the College and contributing to the experiences and memories of its students.

The Durants' conception of beauty developed slowly. It coalesced as their needs and circumstances changed and in response to a number of influences. Central to the process was their acceptance of the preexisting topography and their enhancement of it by landscaping. The Durants' attitude stands in sharp contrast to the radical intervention in land form that had occurred on the estate of their distinguished neighbour, Horatio Hollis Hunnewell, or in the large contemporary park designs of Frederick Law Omsted such as New York's Central Park. Faced with the glaciated terrain consisting of kettles (hollows), eskers (gravel ridges), kames (isolated mounds and ridges), and drumlins (rounded gravel formations) dating back more than ten thousand years, the Durants chose to accentuate them by introducing green valleys, tree-sided hills, wooded groves, planted dells, greensward, and open meadows. Substituted for the derelict farmsteads, these features resulted

A view of the College's original entry road in a photograph of c. 1876, taken near where McAfee dormitory now stands with Simpson Cottage on the right. Planted in the late 1870s with evergreens, it formed part of Christmas Tree Alley.

Model of the Wellesley campus topography showing the glaciated terrain consisting of eskers (the gravel ridges that run along the top of the model), drumlins (oval gravel hills or ridges), and kettles (dell-like depressions) that give the College its variegated, irregular topography and break the landscape into a series of discrete valleys, hillsides, and meadow areas. (Courtesy of Elizabeth Meyer)

in a landscape for the College consisting of discrete rather than large spaces, of multiple rather than uniform parts, of fullness rather than openness, of irregularity rather than formality.

The Durants acquired their Wellesley lands not as the result of family inheritance or a single purchase. They pieced them together lot by lot over a period of twenty years prior to the founding of the College. The lands' assembly was adjusted, however, to the Durants' changing family and social goals and identities. Insofar as it can be reconstructed the Durants started with the ideal of a farm-based country retreat. They then turned towards a rural estate commensurate with their rising wealth and status. Finally, in a third phase, they adapted their lands to institutional needs. By the time of Henry Durant's death in 1881, the property only partly resembled what it had been when the first lots were purchased in 1855. During the same twenty-six year period, Americans came to appreciate a new ideal of nature. An understanding of the College landscape, therefore, needs to take account of both the developing local and national contexts, each of which, in turn, twine together a variety of ideas and influences.

The Durants' first phase of land acquisition extended from 1855 to the early 1860s. It began the year after their marriage with the decision to acquire a country place to which they could withdraw from urban life in Boston as time or season allowed. Henry Durant acquired money for the purchases through his skills as one of Boston's preeminent trial lawyers and through shrewd investment in iron mines for the making of Bessemer steel, in the manufacture of rubber belts and hoses for machinery, and in railroads and oil. The choice of land bordering the north and west shores of Lake Waban (then named Bullard's Pond) in West Needham (renamed Wellesley in 1881) was probably swayed by Pauline Durant's knowledge of the area through her first cousins, the Hunnewells, whose family owned extensive lands on the south and east sides of the lake. On May 29, 1855, Henry Durant signed deeds for the purchase of three tracts of land totaling 105 acres for $9,450. These comprised Lot 1, the first of the more than twenty-one land parcels purchased by the Durants. Lot 1 included the farm of the Bullard family,

Pauline Adeline Fowle Durant and Henry Fowle Durant

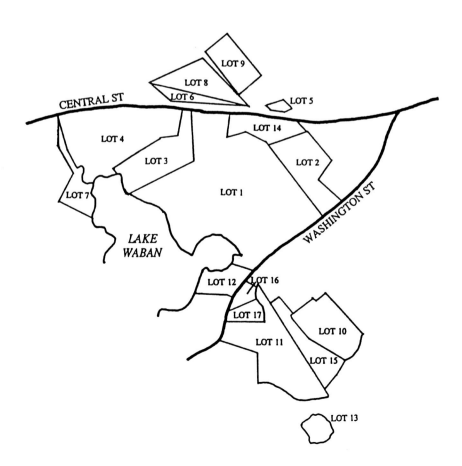

Schematic plan of the campus showing the location of land acquisitions made by the Durants between 1855 and 1881, Lots 1–17

*The Durants' Homestead. The central
part of the building with its balcony,
bay window, and gable (and chimney pot)
remain from the Bullard farmhouse.
Liquidated in 1845, the farm was bought
by the Durants ten years later. The Durants
used Homestead for eight years when not
occupying their handsome townhouse on
Marlborough Street in Back Bay, Boston.*

which had suffered bankruptcy ten years earlier. A broadside advertising the liquidation of the Bullard assets in March 1845 described a "Dwelling House, Barn, and other out Buildings, with about 55 acres of land, divided as follows, viz., about 20 acres of Mowing and Tillage, with many valuable Fruit Trees, about 20 acres of Pasture and Meadow, and about 15 acres covered with a handsome growth of wood, suitable for the market."

Purchased for $1,819 in 1845, sold six years later for $2,500, enlarged, and finally sold again to the Durants, much of the Bullard Farm survived in 1855. The Durants' first impulse was restoration, to bring back into working order the different components of the farm. They had the former farmhouse spruced up for the family and renamed it Homestead. To make the farming operation viable an increase in size was deemed necessary, and the year after their initial purchase the Durants extended their property on its north side through the purchase of forty additional acres (Lot 2), an area of high wooded hillside that today is known as Water Tower Hill.

Henry Durant's lucrative career in the law suggests that the appeal of the farm lay only partly in the commercial return of farming for its own sake and had as much to do with the ideal of a rural retreat from city life. The role of gentleman farmer drew on patriotic models such as George Washington and Thomas Jefferson, and the value of rural retreats had been praised by influential writers on landscapes and estates in the 1840s such as Andrew Jackson Downing. Durant also maintained a passionate interest in English eighteenth-century literature from his Harvard days and collected volumes of restoration poetry, which praised the arcadian ideals of rural pursuits. Like other well-to-do gentlemen of his generation, Durant equated leisure far more with productive enterprise and intellectual stimulus than with rest and diversion.

A second phase of the Durants' land acquisitions can be dated from 1862 to 1867. It corresponded to their increasing wealth acquired supplying the Union Army in the Civil War, and their changing family ambitions. Two children had been born and although their daughter had died at seven months, their son, Harry, was being groomed as family heir. The modest farm residence that served the Durants for mainly summer use no longer accommodated their needs. Instead, they envisaged a mansion overlooking Lake Waban for year-round occupation and accumulated further lands to surround it. The Durants' choice of acreage offering a greater variety of topography and generous lakeside frontage indicates a shift in their intentions away from a working farm pure and simple towards an estate that incorporated a farm.

The East Entry road to the College c. 1936 (Stone–Davis dormitory is visible on the left, the tower of Green Hall left of center). Originally, this formed the entry road to the Durants' planned estate house (intended for a site more or less where Oakwoods now sits) and was planted with an allée of American elms. These survived until the 1938 hurricane, which overturned or damaged the elms along with nearly two thousand other trees on the campus. What remained of the allée succumbed to disease in the 1960s.

The first indication of the change in purpose of the lands were additions to the Durants' holdings to the west and northwest; five lots were acquired from as many owners, Lots 3–7. The Durants' lands now totalled 243 acres; they had been purchased from seven former owners for a total outlay of $20,405. For their new mansion the Durants chose a site with commanding views of the lake. Located 300 feet west of the modest Bullard farmhouse, on a site now occupied by Oakwoods (the present dean of students' house), the Durants' house was approached by a curving driveway lined with American elms (this remains as the east entry to the College). For their house, the Durants began with the service buildings. They engaged the Boston architect Theodore Voelckers, whose 1862 drawing shows three barns arranged in a U-plan with a gateway and fence enclosing the open side. The west barn survives as Dower dormitory (its built form bulkier than it appears in Voelckers's drawing); the old cart way and retaining wall to the hayloft also survive. Pauline Durant's interest in horticulture prompted construction of a sizeable greenhouse on the eastern side of the hill at right angles to the present College Club. The new character the Durants gave their lands is reflected in the phrasing of the their Indenture with Wellesley College drawn up two years before the first students arrived, which described the property as "farm lands, pasture, woodlots, mowing fields, as well as pleasure grounds and cultivated land."

A further clue to the Durants' changing attitude to their land comes from place names, such as their successful campaign to change the name of the lake from Bullard's Pond to Lake Waban. The word "waban" meant "wind" in the language of the local native American Indians, the Algonquins. Henry Durant was prompted to select the name by the prevailing breeze off the pond's waters and by the bicentennial in 1863 of the evangelist John Eliot's translation of the Bible into Algonquin. Eliot had ministered to the Massachusetts Indians in this area around 1650 after colonists had driven them from their lands in modern-day Newton, and he settled some two thousand of them in the vicinity of what is now South Natick ("the place of hills"). The name Waban honored the Algonquins' chief of the same name, and was used by Eliot when he hunted for the Algonquin language equivalent for the Holy Spirit. The Durants' name change to Lake Waban illustrates their familiarity with local history, and their romanticization of American Indian culture (shared by many easterners in the mid-nineteenth century). It also suggests their accord with Transcendentalists like Ralph Waldo Emerson and Henry David Thoreau in nearby Concord who saw nature as sacred.

The year of the lake's rechristening, the Durants abruptly halted all work on their estate. Their precocious and handsome eight-year-old son, Harry, sickened of diptheria and died. The tragedy devastated the parents. The death led to Henry Durant's religious conversion (Pauline's faith had never wavered from childhood). Declaring the law and the Gospel irreconcilable, he abandoned his successful practice as a partner of Rufus Choate, sold his law library, and destroyed valuable volumes of Restoration drama (on account of their levity, presumably). Scrapping plans for their hillside mansion, the Durants moved to a new home in New York City in 1864. For the next five years the couple immersed themselves in a variety of Christian charitable causes. Some brought them back to Massachusetts where Henry Durant found a new role as an evangelical lay preacher, proselytizing mainly in rural western Massachusetts. Durant's stops included several at Mary Lyon's seminary for teachers, Mount Holyoke in South Hadley, which she had founded in 1837.

During this period the Durants cast around for a suitable use for their lands at Wellesley. They considered various ideas including an orphanage and a boys' school. Their decision to found what they termed a female seminary needs some explanation. At least two meanings of the word "seminary" should be borne in mind. The first, more restricted meaning, had to do with

Theodore Voelckers's 1862 design for the Durants' horse barn and other buildings. These were somewhat modified when constructed. The only surviving building is the second on the left, Dower, now a dormitory and considerably bulkier than Voelckers envisioned.

Pauline Durant's greenhouse, c. 1876, from a stereopticon photograph. The building lay at a right angle to what is now the College Club and its foundations are visible in dry summers still. The roadway is Route 16, and the wall survives. The building was used by the botany department but demolished in 1922 when the Ferguson Greenhouses were constructed across from the Whitin Observatory.

East Lodge where the carriage drive turns around the base of Water Tower Hill, c. 1880. On the College's earliest map (1875) this is designated as the principal entrance. The driveway was formally planted by the Durants (as the entry road to their intended estate). East Lodge survives as do the inner gate pylons; road widening in the 1950s eliminated the forecourt area.

teaching. In the 1860s "seminary" usually referred to institutions for teachers. Their need had been made particularly acute in the social convulsions surrounding the Civil War. The Union Army's call to arms summoned teachers from their New England schoolhouses and women served as substitutes, virtually all of whom lacked adequate education. To provide women teachers, first Mount Holyoke had been founded in 1837, and then Vassar in 1865. A second meaning emerged in the 1860s that was closer to the word "college." It addressed women's determination for liberal learning equivalent to that offered men. At Wellesley the two meanings may be seen in transition. In 1870 the Durants had obtained authorization from the Massachusetts legislature to incorporate what was called the "Wellesley Female Seminary" and this title appears on the first architectural plans, discussed in Chapter 2. The Durants returned to the same body in 1873 (still two years before the first students arrived) to change the name to Wellesley College. That the early graduates nonetheless pursued careers in teaching emerges from an 1892 survey, which revealed that of 734 graduates at that date, 540 had become teachers, 12 physicians, 15 librarians, and 20 missionaries. The result does not determine the cause, however, as Helen Lefkowitz Horowitz '63 has pointed out. The number of opportunities open to women between 1860 and 1900 was very limited; there were few other career choices.

The third phase of the development of the Durant lands extended from 1867 to the death of Henry Durant in 1881. During this period the Durants again adjusted the landscape to match the needs of their newly founded college. If beauty led the list of the land's desired effects, the campus was also designed to serve the students' health, physical and mental, and to provide them through nature with spiritual nourishment.

In this stage the Durants conceived of their lands as falling into two parts: the western was to provide for their new college, the eastern for their family needs. To serve each purpose, additional lands were purchased. On the western side, Lots 8 and 9 added forty-nine acres purchased between August 1868 and March 1869; they are marked on the earliest map as "College Grounds" despite their separation from the main campus by the Boston & Albany railway. On the eastern side (to the south of the present College golf course) a forty-acre woodlot was acquired in 1868 and a further seventy-seven acres in adjacent lots were added two years later, Lots 10 through 13; the latter were enlarged again in the same area a decade later with the acquisitions of Lots 15 through 17. The Durant sphere was now centered (with the purchase of Lot 12) on a new residence, the former Webber house (now the President's House). A pre-Civil War, clapboard Federal style house set on rising land, the new Durant home offered fine views over the horseshoe-shaped cove at the southeast end of Lake Waban. Equally important, it provided easy access to the Durants' new institution, essential since they intended to direct its construction and operation.

In setting out the landscape for their college Henry Durant served as both patron and designer. There was nothing unusual about this. His neighbor, Horatio Hollis Hunnewell, and countless others did the same. As a profession, landscape architecture did not exist until a good thirty years later: The American Society of Landscape Architects was founded in 1899, and the following year saw the first degree programs in the profession instituted at Harvard and M.I.T.

To monitor entry and exit to the 300 acres comprising the lands of the new institution, Durant had constructed two gate lodges, East and West Lodge, which still stand today. The East Lodge, labeled "Principal Entrance" on the 1875 map, was fronted by four imposing pylons, the inner two intended to receive elaborate gates (the hinges of which may still be seen). An allée of American elms backed by English copper beeches (three remain) framed the initial approach of the three-quarter mile carriage drive from East Lodge to College Hall. Serpentine and shaded for much of the way, the carriage drive rose in a wide arc around the base of Water Tower Hill, then turned to the south to run down the evergreen-massed hillside (near

An 1880s photo of the College grounds, probably the hill on which Clapp Library now stands. The relative immaturity of the plantings (as scaled by the woman posed in the middle distance) suggests that these were some of Henry Durant's plantings. The duckboard walks were a feature of the College's footpaths until World War I.

Christmas Tree Alley), crossed the wide hillock-humped meadows of the valley (where the meadows now exist), rose again to run along the flatter land (where Houghton Memorial Chapel now stands), cut through a forested belt of trees with a long depressed hollow filled with rhododendrons (still growing in front of Clapp Library), and only then emerged into a large open lawn framed by hills (known then as College Hall Green and as Severance Green since 1927) to give the visitor a first, dramatic panorama of College Hall crowning the opposing hillside. Finally, the driveway wound around the north side of College Hall Hill to arrive at the formal entrance to the five-story center through a porte-cochère. Traversing the campus along this road, students encountered rolling contours, hillsides massed with trees, pastures and meadows, hillocks and dells, shrub-lined paths, and cultivated greensward. Absent was any view of the lake or any sign of a building until they reached College Hall Green. All was variegated, rolling, alternately forest and meadow, tree-covered and open, valley and dell, wild and tended.

The landscape's overall effect was the consequence of considerable construction on the land by the Durants. Work to transform the old farms had begun in 1868. The earliest description of the landscape came from Edward Abbott, a College trustee and well-published author, in the fall issue of *Harper's New Monthly Magazine* in 1876. Abbott remarked that the "scars of engineering surgery" on the landscape were "mostly healed," and noted approvingly the topography's absence of "rawness and immaturity." He mentioned drainage of the more northerly meadows, and the regularization of the ground at the foot of the hill crowned by College Hall. Three preeminent qualities were singled out for praise. The first was the beautiful diversity of the land, how it rises "occasionally into picturesque summits, and as often sinks away into wild and retired dells." Next Abbott highlighted the manner in which "miniature forests dispute with carefully nourished lawns for supremacy." And third, he commended the blending of old and new plantings, of "established evergreens and ancients oaks joining with the flowering shrub and the young oak fresh from the nursery."

The landscape and lake fulfilled varied functions for the students. Should they grow weary in their studies, Abbott continued, "all the beautiful grounds without are before them. They ramble at will through all the broad domain." The observation is backed by a stereopticon photograph used by the engraver to illustrate Abbott's article. This shows a winding duckboard walkway leading through woodland composed largely of young trees.

Stereopticon photograph of 1876 showing Wellesley students visiting the Hunnewell Italian topiary gardens. College Hall is in the distance, to the left.

The landscape thus created by the Durants for their new institution stood in marked contrast to that of their prominent neighbors, the Hunnewells. The Hunnewell estate, created twenty years earlier than the College, was one of the most famous in the northeast, paraded in twelve pages with three full-page illustrations in the sixth edition (1859) of America's foremost book on landscape design, Andrew Jackson Downing's *A Treatise on the Theory and Practice of Landscape Gardening Adapted to North America* (1841). The Hunnewell estate had begun as a farm, as had the Durants' land. But the Hunnewells radically altered their topography, first by creating a massive flat area for the house with a wide expanse of lawn to the east. The latter was encircled by a gravel drive that approached a formal terrace with sculpted urns, statuary, and stone stairs. Towards the lake, the eighty-foot-high hillside was drastically reshaped with a series of escarped terraces planted in contrasting European garden designs—an Italian garden to the north, and a French garden to the south (now lost). Adjacent to the

Hunnewell house were laid out an English garden, an azalea garden, and to one side a large pinetum, the Hunnewells' collection of rare evergreens. This eclectic scheme constructed on a forty-six-acre site reflected the influential ideas of the British landscape architect Humphrey Repton. Working in the early 1800s, Repton modified the picturesque landscape schemes of Capability Brown (c. 1750–1790), replacing Brown's notion of gardening as extending beyond a fenced enclosure to include all of nature with Repton's innovation, a series of differently landscaped areas. Most visible today at the Hunnewell estate are the pinetum to the north (now a forest of more than three hundred varieties of cone-bearing pine trees), and the Italian garden with its terraces, topiary trees, belvedere, statuary, and granite stairways. A two-story classicizing boat house built to shelter Hunnewell vessels, including a gondola imported from Venice, burned in the 1940s.

The landscape constructed by the Durants in the late 1860s did not compete with or replicate the Hunnewells' impressive scheme. Set out during the decade after the end of the Civil War, the Durants' landscape reflected different interests, intentions, and a fundamentally contrasting interpretation of nature. The Durants left the topography largely unaltered, not for want of money or will but from philosophy. The Durants' landscape scheme called for the enhancement rather than the reshaping of the existing topography. Thus tree plantings would enrich and heighten the hillsides and form a firmer contrast with the valleys; drainage of the meadows would achieve a richer, fuller pasture; dells would be water-coursed or shrub-filled. Variety, irregularity, and a degree of roughness would dramatize the differences between one area and another. Only in front of College Hall on the green was an exception made with the construction of lawn, the "pleasure grounds" mentioned in the indenture quoted above.

In their approach to landscaping, the Durants did more than distance themselves from the Hunnewells. They asserted a different concept of nature. It began with the idea of locating their new institution in a "park," the term used to describe the Wellesley campus for the first thirty years of its history (the word "campus" appears only in the early 1900s). The concept of the park had a long history associated in particular with the picturesque movement in eighteenth-century England. There it assumed notions linked to nature and liberty, in contrast to the formality of French gardens and their association with royal tyranny. Entering the United States in the late 1830s, the term park

This view of Franklin Park, Boston, c. 1916, depicts the rural scenery Frederick Law Olmsted favored in his park designs, intending to calm the harassed urban dweller with soothing views of pastoral life. The shepherd and flock fell victim to shifts in the park's purpose a year or two after the photograph was taken. So too did the lush meadow, which disappeared with the advent of mechanized mowing in the 1920s.

was adapted to both public and private use by Downing. He defined a "landscape garden or park" as a designed space that improves on nature through "harmonious imitation" or enhancements rather than drastic intervention. Such harmonious imitation was not to be confused with nature itself and was to be recognizable as art. Downing differentiated types of landscape, singling out the "beautiful" and "picturesque." These he characterized respectively by a "spirited irregularity [with] surfaces comparatively abrupt and broken, and growth of a somewhat wild and bold character"; and by occasional smoothness contrasted with "sudden variations" that were allowed to run into "dingles, rock groups, and broken banks." As in wild nature, Downing argued, "thickets, glades, and underwoods are indispensable."

Just as influential on the Durants were the emerging park ideas of Frederick Law Olmsted, America's greatest landscape architect. The Durants encountered Olmsted's ideas at Central Park (built 1858–1875) on their move to New York in 1864, and also on their return to Wellesley in the late 1860s, where the planning of Boston's Emerald Necklace had begun in 1869. At the same time Olmsted's ideas were being adapted to campus landscaping. He served as consultant to the University of California at Berkeley and the Massachusetts agricultural school at Amherst in 1866, and the latter campus design by Olmsted was widely showcased in the *Nation* that October. The following year Olmsted advised the University of Maine and Cornell University, and in the late 1860s other Land Grant colleges on their campus layouts.

Longfellow Pond, c. 1885. One of the most prized areas at the center of the College, the pond was named after the poet Henry Wadsworth Longfellow who was a friend of the Durants and a visitor to Wellesley. Longfellow Pond formed the southern side of the green, creating a dense wooded boundary and obscuring any panorama of Lake Waban. Much of the hollow is now taken up with the extension to Clapp Library. A pale memory of this feature remains in the semicircular concrete basin and fountain at the west end of the library.

Although Olmsted's park ideas derived in part from Downing, they gave a distinctive emphasis to the creation of rural scenery. This was to be experienced sequentially in a harmonious succession of views as one moved through the landscape (the direct opposite of the single viewpoint displayed in Beaux-Arts schemes determined by symmetry and aligned axes). In addition to the aesthetic benefits, Olmsted's landscape offered its users a range of social benefits: contemplating rural scenery would impart a sense of mental well-being, strengthen individuals' health, and lay the foundation for a new sense of community.

Olmsted's ideas carried resonance for a women's college embarking on what was, for the period, still a largely untried experiment. Like others promoting educational innovation, the Durants worried that women's weak physique would make them vulnerable to collapse when faced with the rigors of higher education. To strengthen them, an hour of daily exercise in the landscape, quickly nicknamed "tramps" by the students, was prescribed; on occasion Henry Durant would accompany the women and urge greater exertion. The early circulars sent by the College to the parents of prospective students claimed that Wellesley's location "is known as the most healthy in the healthy state of Massachusetts." Frailty was frowned on as vigor was praised. The same circulars urged parents to provide dresses for their daughters "several sizes larger" than those they came with to accommodate their strengthened bodies.

ON THE FACING PAGE
Pathway leading to Tupelo Point with the Plympton "spooner" on the right. This area has hardly changed in the past 125 years. Characteristic of the Durants' handling of the lake shore, trees screen the water and obscure any panoramic views.

View, c. 1914, of the south side of Norumbega Hill. Severance Green, then College Hall Green, lies on the right with Clapp Library on the far-right edge. The hillside on the left is occupied now by Jewett Arts Center. Note the dense tree planting of the hillside and flourishing understory, both of which provided a greater sense of wooded enclosure for the green (in the present the trees have thinned drastically and the understory has vanished). The serpentine old main road may be seen at the base of the slope separating hillside from green.

The Durants were equally troubled about women's minds. The mental stresses of college life were the subject of wide discussion in the late 1860s, and it was no coincidence that the typology chosen by the Durants for the architecture of College Hall derived from the asylum (see Chapter 2). Olmsted's views were directly relevant. As noted, the landscape architect believed his parks would calm the human psyche by contemplating consciously, or at a level below conscious thought, scenery such as the pastoral or that composed of rocks, forests, calm water, and greensward. Furthermore, again in keeping with Olmsted's ideas, Durant accepted the notion that certain parts of the landscape affirmed community by providing the setting for bonding outdoor ceremonies. For Durant, then, the notion of the park celebrated themes for his college of liberty, freedom, health, mental well-being, and community.

For community functions, Durant developed one area of the landscape with particular attention. On the east side of College Hall Hill, he ordered that the irregular hollows be leveled to form a broad lawn, called College Hall Green. Constructed with deliberation, the space resembled a valley

*Severance Green in the present day. The
east (or left) boundary, although thinned
through losses from disease and storms,
formed a "miniature forest," part of the
Durants' "constructed nature."*

View from the Power Plant smokestack (1904) over what is now Munger Meadow and the Alexandra Botanic Garden. On the left the foundations for Shafer are in the process of being dug; at center, bottom, lies the Chemistry Building (demolished in the 1930s when Pendleton was finished). The road snaking across the meadow is the old North Road that joined Route 135 to the north of present-day Munger.

The just-completed Whitin Observatory lies center right; the footpath at its base is still in place. The north corner of Norumbega Cottage is on the right and may be connected with the following image to create a continuous panorama. The photo predates the introduction of the botanic gardens (including Paramecian Pond), also of the evergreens that flank the roadway Route 135.

View from the Power Plant smokestack (1904) showing the south side of Norumbega Hill. The photograph depicts present-day Severance Green on the right with Rhododendron Hollow. The chapel is the only building still standing today; it is visible (right of center) just below old Stone dormitory, which was destroyed by fire in 1927. On the hill itself Farnsworth Art Building lies in the center with the straight road running more or less where Jewett Road is today.

Norumbega Cottage is on the left with Freeman and Wood Cottages behind. Wilder Hall is the brick Federal dormitory located where Green Hall now stands. Water Tower Hill lies at the top left. The photograph is a valuable document of the College landscape as well as the buildings. Many of the closely planted trees in the foreground and middle ground that form the northern boundary of the green appear to be about thirty to forty years old, presumably planted by the Durants.

closed in by tree-covered hillsides on three sides with the fourth crowned by the cliff-like backdrop of College Hall. To the north, Norumbega Hill (site of the present Academic Quadrangle) was planted densely with trees and an understory of fern and blueberry. These were drawn around the east side of the green in a similarly extensive wooded plantation, the "miniature forests" described by Trustee Edward Abbott. On the lake side where Clapp Library now sits, a large and irregular-sided, water-filled hollow, named Longfellow Pond, was ringed with newly planted trees that screened the lake, admitting only a bare glint of its waters.

According to the Durants' plan, this hill- and tree-enclosed green became Wellesley's public center. Over the years assemblies, presentations, graduations, concerts, sports, entertainments, protests, and picnics have filled the area, known since 1927 as Severance Green. More important, it formed the setting for the College's ceremonial events that defined the institution in its early decades: Tree Day, Flower Sunday, Field Day, Class Day, May Day and the annual Hoop Rolling competition, Forensic Burning (of required first-year English papers), Float Day, and Greek Play Day. The most famous of these rituals, Tree Day became so popular at the turn of the century that it was reenacted for each class annually.

Documentation for the College Hall Green scheme emerges from photographs in the 1880s and three full-plate photographs taken from the top of the newly completed Power Plant smokestack in 1904. They show the campus in winter after a light snow, revealing the land form and plantings in their elemental clarity. The extent of the Durants' tree plantings can be seen from the photographs; arborists estimate many of the trees at about thirty to forty years old. Pruned and well tended, their close spacing best expresses the forest and valley character imposed by Durant on the area, creating the "Arcadian woodland" described by Katharine Lee Bates 1880 (the author of the hymn "America the Beautiful" who entered Wellesley in its second year and spent her career at the College as a professor of English).

The woodlands around the green were remarked on by Edward Abbott, as noted above, who termed them "miniature forests" disputing for supremacy with "carefully nourished lawns." This distinctive characterization and his image of disputation were more than figures of speech. Forests carried particular meanings in the mid-nineteenth century. Earlier, to the Puritans forests were not the kind of feature suited for imitation in a landscape; rather, they were deemed places of intimidation, not least for providing shelter for

The meadow below the Whitin Observatory. One of the least changed areas of the campus, it resembles the Durants' conception of landscape with its irregular tree-delineated boundaries, and meadows of tall grasses.

Tree Day 1919, celebrated on what is now Severance Green with Norumbega Hill in the background. Norumbega Cottage is at the upper left, Farnsworth Art Building, upper right. The left part of the hillside is now occupied by Jewett Arts Center.

Indians, to be rapidly subdued by the woodsman's axe into arable land. In the 1860s, however, the forest assumed a wholly new value. With the opening of the West, Americans were stunned by the revelation of free, unmediated nature they encountered in its forests and rivers. As Simon Schama has observed, educated opinion in these years marvelled at the great California forests where the giant sequoia—two thousand years old and three hundred feet high—came to symbolize national pride, and provided a focus for efforts aimed at preserving the wonders of the West. Olmsted had worked in the early 1860s for the Mariposa Mining Company in California near the site where the sequoias were discovered, and had visited Yosemite (made a nature preserve by Congressional act in 1864) and written convincingly of its awesome splendor (legislation to establish the first national parks came in 1872).

Similar associations attached to the three-quarter mile meadow scheme that originally formed an uninterrupted arc from the Durant barns (now Dower dormitory) around Norumbega Hill, then advanced south to where Alumnae Hall now stands, to finally descend through the present-day Service Lot to the shores of Lake Waban. The valleys were preexisting, bounded by eskers on the western and northern sides, and with hillocks of varying scale at intervals on the southern side. Drained by Durant to encourage meadow grass to grow on the valley floor, the sides were given clearer definition with plantings of trees and shrubs to form an understory, thereby amplifying the sense of enclosure. The effect of the meadows was certainly pastoral but it evoked associations, like the forests, in this case with the grasslands of the West. The Durants combined the meadows with wildflowers (see below) to suggest the variety and richness of America's heartland. Early students sang verses: "I'm a little prairie flower/Growing wilder every hour."

The Durants' interest in both forests and meadows reflected ideas about nature around 1870. As they imposed a distinctive constructed nature on the former farmlands, they intended it to be rich in association. That the forests were "miniature," as Abbott told his readers, or the meadows likewise, in no way lessened their attraction. Miniaturization as a prompter of memory had long been a standard device of the landscape and garden arts. In the early 1800s the dramatic power of the Alps could be re-memorized by gardeners in miniaturized rockeries, or, in a different cultural context, gardens in Japan could conjure oceans and mountains with their artfully raked gravel and rocks.

A similar impulse marked Olmsted's creation of urban parks whose history parallels that of the Durants' Wellesley campus. Olmsted's enduring genius lay in devising means to unite two powerful and contrasting landscape ideals, the park and the wilderness. The park was an eighteenth-century creation for private patrons, which Olmsted democratized to serve the enjoyment and health of the immigrant-swelled city populations. The wilderness embodied deeply held beliefs about America's history, its lands, ideals, and identity.

What the College's students experienced outdoors through the landscapers' arts, they had re-presented to them indoors through the art of painters. The Durants hung the corridors and parlors of College Hall with landscape paintings of the Hudson River School. These depicted subjects with frequent analogies to the landscape constructed by the Durants, as Assistant Professor Rebecca Bedell '80 has shown. Long explanatory labels under each painting extolled the beauties of nature depicted by artists like Asher B. Durand and Worthington Whitteridge. These same beauties the women of Wellesley experienced in the constructed forests, irregular hillsides, and waist-high meadows that the Durants had set out for them in a park setting redolent of freedom and health.

Two further influences merged with those of Downing and Olmsted to shape the Durants' lands. Accounts of the early landscape describe the bountiful wildflowers that gave color and variety to the grounds. Particularly notable in spring time when many visitors would journey to admire them

Part of the Great Meadow scheme, Daisy Meadow reflected the wildflower movement that spread from England to the United States in the 1860s. The movement's founder, William Robinson, was visiting Wellesley in 1870 while on a promotional tour. This part of the meadow vanished in 1918 and now lies under Founders Parking Lot.

were the perennial wildflowers in the great meadows and the legions of bulbs—scyllas, jonquils, crocuses, and snowdrops—that Henry Durant had planted "by the seven thousand" according to Katharine Lee Bates. These flowers reflected the influence of the wildflower movement of 1870, promoted by the prolific English writer William Robinson, in opposition to Victorian tastes for bedding out hothouse-raised annuals in precise geometric patterns. To popularize his ideas Robinson toured the United States, visiting the Hunnewells in 1870 to view their Wellesley gardens. Whether the Durants met him on this occasion is unrecorded, but Robinson's influence must have been known to them and found its place in the Wellesley landscape. This emphasis on flowers also accounts for the place names given to College landscape elements in the late nineteenth century that have mostly vanished since: Lupine Path, Daisy Meadow, Tanglewood Path, Violet Lawn, and Cowslip Farm, along with woodland names like Chestnut Hill and the Pines.

Lake-edge path below Claflin with "spooners" on right. The lake's border paths are all screened. Continuous fragmented views result and these provide a shoreline where trees and water merge, giving Lake Waban its characteristic sense of enclosure.

Clearly the Durants' bulbs were imports, non-native flowers planted to match an ideal with a distinctly English origin. As such they would not have pleased Olmsted, whose horticultural tastes were predominantly nativist. This interest in imported plants and flowers indicates the fourth influence on Durant. On the earliest maps of the College, the kettle or dell to the south of the main road bed (in front of Clapp Library) is shown planted with rhododendrons. The prominence of this location needs to be restored in the imagination. In the context of the original circulation system, it was shrewdly placed next to what is now Severance Green, thereby forming a penultimate accent before the arriving student first glimpsed the massive pile of College Hall. An exotic import from China, these varieties of rhododendron had entered the United States in the late 1850s through the efforts of Horatio Hollis Hunnewell, who had hybridized the shrub to make it winter-hardy in the harsh northeast. An ardent promoter of the rhododendron, Hunnewell pressed the new shrubs on the Durants, who received them with enthusiasm. Katharine Lee Bates is once again witness to Durant's planting of them "by the thousand." To the early students, many drawn from modest farming families in the western part of the Commonwealth of Massachusetts, where Durant had proselytized, the rhododendrons would have appeared sensational exotica.

In establishing the lands for their new College, the Durants' orchestration of nature combined the influences of Downing, Olmsted, Robinson, and Hunnewell along with varied geological interests. Their definition of the

"College beautiful" laid a central emphasis on place, which they saw as providing for "the intellectual, moral, and spiritual aspirations an education was designed to foster." Considered in context, the Durants' view of nature was just as contrived as that of the Hunnewells. But it was shaped by different influences and a different ideology. The twenty years that separated the two neighbors' landscape schemes encompassed a major change in taste. To Horatio Hunnewell, Europe was the source of ideas on the landscape, and his superb gardens replicated a range of forms from Italy, France, England, and elsewhere. In the 1860s a similarly passionate view of land form and landscape determined the Durants' choice of ideas, only it was to America that they looked for inspiration. A further element lay in the use of an institutional as opposed to a private estate typology. Although the College landscape may strike us today as more "natural" than do the Hunnewells' terraces and topiaried trees across the Lake, it was no less the consequence of intellectualization and hard work, and no less the carrier of conscious meanings and associations.

Rhododendron Hollow is an original feature of the College landscape. The shrubs were presented to the Durants by their neighbors the Hunnewells, who in the 1850s had succeeded in hybridizing the rhododendrons to make them winter-hardy.

CHAPTER TWO

THE DURANT ENDOWMENT

THE 314 YOUNG WOMEN who arrived on September 8, 1875 to open Wellesley College must have been as overawed by the architecture of the building (and its plumbing) as by the boldness of their venture. College Hall—where during the next four years they were to live, work, pray, play, and create an unprecedented community of female scholars under the guidance of an all-female faculty—had to be the most imposing and technologically advanced structure the majority of them had ever seen.

Sited on a rise above Lake Waban, in the center of a landscaped park, College Hall stretched 475 feet end to end, rose four and five stories of red brick and freestone trim beneath slate-covered mansard roofs, and was "set off at various points with towers, bays, porches, pavilions, and spires," according to one contemporary account. The interior was equally awe-inspiring. Beyond the main entrance, the "Centre" opened the interior from ground floor to skylight, "story rising above story, column ranging upon column," through five richly ornamented tiers to a glazed ceiling. If the grand exterior had not overwhelmed them, the Centre—which was to become the indoor spatial, social, and emotional core of the community—certainly did.

As they came to inspect this "rare achievement of architectural skill" the newcomers found the two-room suites where they would live, many of them with light-shot views south across the lake to the Hunnewell topiary garden, as well as the main indoor spaces: the richly appointed library, the austere chapel, the dining room, the recitation rooms, the science labs, the novel gymnasium, the natural history collection, and the art gallery. The students would not have seen the building's service systems—the plumbing, ventilation, and power generation—but they must have appreciated their efficiency.

Wellesley College as it appeared in the 1880s as seen from the Webber (President's) house: College Hall on the left, Music Hall in the middle, and Stone Hall on the right. This is the campus as Henry Durant left it, with the buildings on sites that rise and fall along the northern edge of Lake Waban. Hammatt Billings and Ware and Van Brunt designed richly wrought buildings whose splintered skylines echoed one another and the arboreal crown of the Durants' park.

Henry Fowle Durant commissioned the first buildings at Wellesley College from Bostonian Hammatt Billings, shown here in a photograph taken about the time he laid out College Hall. Billings was an architect, book illustrator, and jack-of-all-designs who joined his brother Joseph in providing the College with cutting-edge planning and building technology. Sadly, he did not live to see the opening of his "chiefest work" in September 1875. (Photo courtesy of the Pilgrim Society, Plymouth, Massachusetts)

Within the molded brick walls beneath the series of mansard roofs they would become members of an "academical village" of a kind never envisioned by Thomas Jefferson. These fledglings were to fill this picturesque shell with pioneering achievements in women's higher education.

Women's higher education was a social experiment in the middle of the nineteenth century. Born in part from the need to train female teachers at the beginning of mandated universal education, women's institutions such as Mount Holyoke, Vassar, Wellesley, Smith, and Bryn Mawr each in its own way gradually evolved into a real liberal arts college whose intellectual standards were equal to those of the older male schools. As an experiment the education of women drew criticism and misunderstanding. The nineteenth-century "cult of domesticity" ordained that women belonged in the home; the new colleges were dedicated to the principle that they could join the world, however tentatively at first. It took strength, determination, and brains to break with the dominant social pattern, to attend Wellesley College in the 1870s.

Winston Churchill once said that "we shape our buildings; thereafter they shape us." Architecture responds to human need, but it also molds human activity. At Wellesley as at Jefferson's University of Virginia and every other seat of higher learning, architecture plays an active role in the pedagogical and social mission of the institution. College Hall not only provided shelter; it shaped Wellesley students' lives and their intellectual, moral, and physical development. College Hall as well as the educational program it contained opened new vistas of possibility—architectural and otherwise—to the majority of entering women—Henry Fowle Durant's "calico girls"—who had left a circumscribed domestic milieu in modest rural communities of small, thin-walled, wooden buildings served by rudimentary technology. Their new lives began at Wellesley in dramatically different surroundings.

The couple who made all this possible, Pauline and Henry Durant, who had conceived the institution and donated this most visible of its assets, stood ready to greet the first Wellesley class, but the primary member of the architectural team that had made the Durants' vision come to life, the brothers Hammatt and Joseph Billings, did not. Hammatt had died the previous year. College Hall had been a collaboration chiefly between Henry Durant, the client who created the program and oversaw every detail of the construction, and Hammatt Billings, the designer who had translated the Durants' dream into an architectural event. Supported by Pauline Durant and Joseph Billings

these two men planned and directed the work of the scores of skilled and unskilled men who labored at the site to erect this educational and architectural landmark.

The Durants called the institution at its inception in 1867 a "Female Seminary," but renamed it "Wellesley College" in 1871, a change that indicated the transitional character of Henry Durant's thinking about his foundation. It took conceptual shape in the Durants' minds during the mid 1860s, assumed definitive form on the Billingses' drafting boards at the turn of the decade, and became a three-dimensional reality between 1871 and 1875.

As founder, Henry Durant radiated an heroic aura that belied his physical size. One early faculty member described him as short, erect, "with a face as delicately cut as a cameo, framed by grey hair worn rather long, looking out upon the world with keen, flashing eyes, combining at once the urbanity of a gentleman with the astute mind and powerful will of a trained lawyer and a man of the world." She also remembered him as "both artistic and scholarly, loving beauty, honoring learning." This combination of eye and intellect, or taste and scholarship, formed the basis for the college he founded and the building that housed it.

With the death of his son, Harry, Henry Durant had abandoned the law and his early Unitarian influences to become an evangelical lay preacher. This led him into the realm of women's education, to preach at and join the

Wellesley's first building, College Hall, rose above the waters of Lake Waban. The immense structure embodied Henry and Pauline Durant's vision of an institution of higher learning for women, and it formed the capstone of the architectural careers of Hammatt and Joseph Billings. Erected between 1871 and 1875 to house every aspect of the College, which huddled within its pavilions and beneath its mansards, College Hall not only incorporated the latest French and English architectural forms but cutting-edge technology as well. It was destroyed by fire on St. Patrick's Day, 1914.

board of trustees of Mount Holyoke Seminary (now College) at South Hadley, Massachusetts. One of the earliest of the female seminaries, Mount Holyoke quickly became the object of the Durants' new philanthropic interests and a source of inspiration for the institution they were beginning to consider raising on their own lands west of Boston. When Mount Holyoke decided to add a library to its original building, Pauline donated $10,000 for books, and Henry accepted the chair of the building committee. We can only assume that he picked the Billings brothers as architects of the new library. They produced the drawings in 1868 and the building opened two years later.

While the original design for the interior of the Mount Holyoke library formed the precedent for that in Wellesley's College Hall, what we learn more importantly from this commission concerns the character of Durant as client. In this, apparently his first, association with the Billingses, he proved himself to be as exacting a partner as he would later be at College Hall. Durant not only chaired the building committee for the Mount Holyoke library, he dominated it. Surviving correspondence concerning the building flows between Durant and the Billingses, and it contains Durant's "wishes," "desires," and decisions about details as small as trim color, window panes, and flooring. All this preceded his active role in the creation of College Hall, which was beginning to take shape in Hammatt Billings's sketches as Mount Holyoke dedicated its new library.

In the fall of 1869 Henry Durant wrote to William Claflin, himself a Billings client, telling the Massachusetts governor of his plan to incorporate a female seminary and asking him to join the board. Durant also wrote that he did not expect to build for two years at least. In this he was accurate, for the cornerstones of College Hall were laid in 1871, but he had already engaged the Billingses for architectural work on the grounds. Hammatt's study for what is now East Lodge survives on a sheet dated March 1869, so the concept of a country estate that the Durants had envisioned for Harry, complete with the gate lodges commonly prescribed in current English publications on gentlemen's estates, was adapted for the original layout of the campus. East and West Lodges held visitors at bay, and College Hall took the place of the landed mansion.

In choosing Hammatt Billings as his architect, Henry Durant hired a figure whose reputation has dimmed over time, but who was one of the most prominent members of the world of design in nineteenth-century Boston. In his youth he apprenticed in both art and architecture. Book illustrations, such as those for the original editions of *Uncle Tom's Cabin* (1852) and *Little*

The "Centre" occupied the heart of College Hall. It rose from a ground-floor granite arcade to four tiers of open cast-iron colonnades and variously patterned balustrades to reach an overhead skylight. It acted as a light snorkel that brought natural illumination from above and the sides deep into the interior of the building. It was also, alas, a giant flue that hastened the spread of flames at the building's destruction in 1914.

Women (1869); periodical illustrations, such as those for *Ballou's Pictorial* in the 1850s; monuments, such as the original design of the colossal National Monument to the Forefathers at Plymouth (1854–1889); as well as paintings and drawings that found their way into public and private collections; and projects for festivals, fireworks, and furniture: these and his long career as designer of buildings stretching from the mid-1840s to his crowning work at Wellesley—buildings his brother Joseph often engineered—all earned him comparison with Michelangelo as "accomplished in all departments of art." His undoubted gifts—his contemporaries often called him a genius—plus his mild, almost self-effacing disposition made him a perfect foil for the strong-willed, demanding Henry Durant.

Hammatt Billings came from old New England stock but was separated by low financial resources and lack of higher education from the elite who were his frequent clients. Like Henry Durant he stood outside the inner circle of Boston Brahmins. A little above average height, with light hair and complexion, he had what one observer called "farseeing, deep-set grey eyes" set into a finely cut bearded face. Contemporaries remembered him as the most modest and sympathetic of individuals, kindly, "nobel and large-hearted," and generous. Henry Wadsworth Longfellow thought him a "charming fellow." He and Durant seem as unlike as two men could be, but this collaboration of opposites resulted in an architectural triumph for Wellesley College.

The Durants' college evolved specifically from the models of Mount Holyoke and Vassar. Mary Lyon's school at South Hadley took the form of one building that imposed upon the students a common existence based upon the hierarchical ordering of the patriarchal family usual in the layout of asylums upon which it was based. Its simple shape and two-story porch recalled the domesticity then thought to be women's proper sphere. By the time Durant conceived his institution Matthew Vassar had erected his own, rather different foundation at Poughkeepsie. Wishing to build as much a monument to himself and his wealth as an experiment in women's education, he hired a fashionable New York architect, James Renwick, Jr., to design an impressive pile closely related to the complex asylums and hospitals Renwick had been recently building in New York City and elsewhere. Vassar College, larger and architecturally richer than Mount Holyoke, shaped its student body into a patriarchal hierarchy. Its male president worked and lived in the ornate central pavilion, male faculty lived in the somewhat less elaborate outer pavilions, and the female students huddled securely in rooms lining the halls of the plain wings between them.

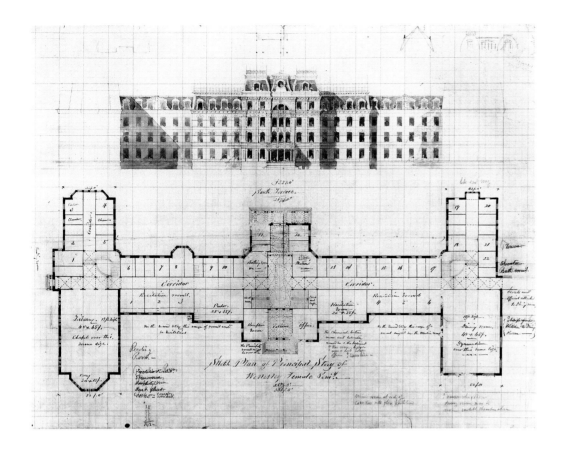

Hammatt Billings drew this preliminary scheme for College Hall about 1871. The building's long spine and transepts are present in plan, and the pavilions and mansards show up in elevation. Jottings seem to track a conversation between architect and client Henry Durant concerning such matters as circulation and sunlight. The final building grew in length, the Centre appeared at a later stage, and the exterior eventually lost some of its Gallic flavor as Billings consulted the works by John Ruskin in his library.

Durant's Wellesley followed the lead of Mount Holyoke and Vassar in secluding its students behind guarded gates in a rural retreat far from the supposed evils of city life, and in gathering them all safely under one series of roofs, but Durant, "loving beauty" as well as "honoring learning," had something else in mind too. While it is highly likely that he told his architect to remember Mount Holyoke and study Vassar, the pair evolved an architectural work distinct from these models.

That a close collaboration existed between Durant and Billings cannot be doubted. It is generally the case that the client envisions the building program, then turns to an architect to give it perceptible form in plan, structure, mechanical systems, and three dimensions. Wellesley was the Durants' in conception and aims, the Billingses' in its architectural manifestation. There is preserved, for example, a sheet with a preliminary plan and an unfinished preliminary elevation for College Hall that can probably be dated 1870 or 1871. The Second Empire style of the proposed building links the scheme to the francophile forms of Renwick's Vassar. (This was an era in which American architecture borrowed heavily from contemporary work in both Second-Empire France and Victorian-Gothic England.) The drawing is covered with scribbled notes. Although they appear to be in Hammatt's hand, they suggest a brainstorming session between client and architect in which they put the proposal through its paces. Various laconic notes, penciled then inked on the sheet, such as "Reading Room," "Tower," "Hospital," "Store Rooms," and "Bath Rooms," clearly refer to requested changes and additions to the plan. There are also notes about the location of the principal's room and the music room, and queries such as how one would reach the dining room from the kitchen, and the location of the chemistry lab and lecture room in the basement. The latter provoked the terse "?Sunshine." Discussions about patterns of use, illumination, ventilation, design, and other details have their residue in these jottings. They fully agree with what we know of Durant as the client at the Mount Holyoke library and the man who would supervise every detail of College Hall while under construction.

The plan shown on this sheet is a rudimentary version of the final arrangement. It did propose the long narrow spine and cross axial wings of the building as erected, but it lacked the Centre in the main pavilion, stopped many feet short of the length of the final version, and barely suggested the fully articulated footprint of the exterior. In the building as built a broad corridor running from the east entrance through the Centre and on to the dining room on the west occupied the four-story spine. Billings located stairways, recitation rooms, and student and faculty suites along this double-loaded passageway. Main spaces such as the library, chapel, science labs, and dining room could be found on various levels of the five-story transepts, while the kitchen and other service areas, plus the music department and gymnasium,

The definitive plan of College Hall, signed by both Hammatt and J. E. Billings and dated 1875, shows the spinal corridor, the Centre, the fully articulated transepts, and the utility building to the northwest (lower right). From east to west it stretched 475 feet. Students were initially housed in two-room suites, the majority of which looked toward the sunny south over Lake Waban. The main areas of assembly—the chapel, library, dining room—occupied the northern ends of the transepts.

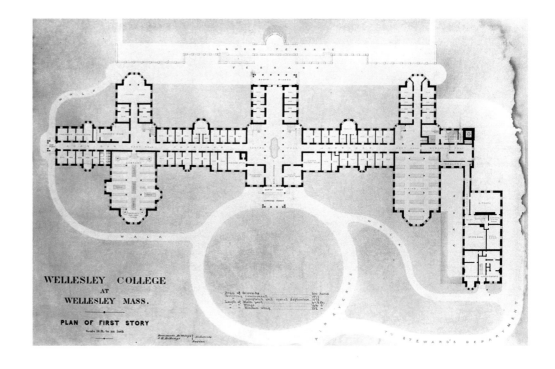

occupied a semi-detached two-story dependency to the west. Were it not for Durant's insistence that students exercise by walking the grounds and rowing on the lake as well as stretching muscles in the gymnasium, it would have been theoretically possible for the life of the College to take place entirely beneath its mansards.

Once the kinks in the arrangement of the program had been worked out in consultation with the Durants, Billings was presumably free to pull away from Renwick's francophile design at Vassar. This is made evident by an advanced watercolor study of College Hall's south elevation, probably executed during 1871. While he retained the pavilions, mansards, and the combination of external building materials of the Vassar building, Billings significantly "Englished" his design to create a more eclectic, more picturesque effect in keeping with the hilltop site above Lake Waban. As early as his 1859 lecture on "The Influences of Rural Life," Durant had championed such elevation in a statement at once straightforward and double-edged: "the landscape widens as we climb the hill, the air is purer, and the vision more clear." To Billings the site offered the opportunity to break up the rigidity of Renwick's example. While the masses of the main façades appeared symmetrical when seen head-on, from every other point of view the building rose asymmetrically from its site to splinter into assorted shapes. Variations in the fenestration and in the design of rooftop terminals in order to distinguish one internal function from another (two-story bifurcated windows in the chapel and a spire above it; a clerestory monitor above the art gallery), as well as the Italianate campanile probably inspired by the writings of John Ruskin in Billings's library added to the west end of the building (a fanciful form for a

Hammatt Billings's watercolor rendering of the nearly final design for the south, or lakeside, front of College Hall, probably drawn in 1871. As is often the case with even highly finished architectural drawings, second thoughts were cavalierly scribbled on this rendering as the architect studied a terminal above the pavilion housing the chapel (that to the right). The design is symmetrical except for the campanile to the left, not a bell tower as it is in Venice, but a necessary smokestack and foul air exhaust for the building's advanced mechanical systems.

The boldness and vigor of College Hall is apparent even in this black-and-white photograph. This view from the northeast shows walls of brick laid in black mortar, emphatically articulated beltcourses, arches of constructional polychromy, vertical pavilions, and high mansard roofs. The direct inspiration for the building was James Renwick, Jr.'s Vassar College building which opened in 1865, but Durant and Billings introduced many variations in planning and details.

necessary foul air vent and smokestack!), produced a dynamic scattering of discrete units. Billings's creation became in the end the "massive accumulation of wings and porches, towers and gables" of contemporary account.

This era's architects emphasized irregular shapes and exuberant surfaces. Billings's exterior was an eclectic, visually animated pile of red brick set in black mortar with brownstone trim. The brickwork of projecting quoins and beltcourses and recessed rectangles formed a three-ply wall related to the paneled brick style currently used by Ware and Van Brunt and other architects in Boston's fashionable Bay Back area. The dominant pattern of fenestration reflected Renwick's combination at Vassar of half-round and segmental arches. Those of the bottom two stories were laid up of alternating brick and stone voussoirs in a pattern known as "constructional polychromy"; that is, a pattern in which every unit of the assembly is discretely visible. The dormers sported segmental caps in some areas, and pointed ones in others. Billings composed solid walls and window voids into a counterbalance of straight and curved lines, of bays, turrets, and pavilions. The ground story sprouted north, south, and east one-story porches framed by unfluted granite Corinthian colonnades. All this resulted in a work the critic Montgomery Schuyler thought had a scattering effect. College Hall was a bombastic building that burst into the visitor's view as she traveled the carriage drive lined with elm, hemlock, and oak leading from one or the other of the gate lodges.

By the 1870s it had become fairly common practice for building construction to be contracted for on the basis of competitive bidding by several would-be builders and the erection to be supervised by the architect. Durant would have none of that. He acted in effect as his own contractor and clerk of the works, hiring laborers at daily wages and watching them like a hawk. He was at the building site before breakfast "looking after the minutest details of gravel, excavation, stonework, and iron-work." The construction of College Hall typified the era. The building was erected with load-bearing masonry exterior walls and an interior structure of iron columns supporting iron girders upholding iron beams upon which rested brick arches. "Everything even the locks and carving of banisters was supervised by him," according to another observer. (Nor was Pauline entirely left out, for it is reported that she tested many stairs and chairs looking for just the right dimensions to fit the female body.) Just as he intended to supervise the daily lives of his students, so Durant sought to oversee the execution of every detail of Hammatt Billings's design.

The interior of that design focused on a five-story, top-lighted Centre that both announced the lavish character of the building and—like some vertical piazza at the core of an Italian town or, as one contemporary saw it, the cloister of a medieval convent—acted as the indoor gathering place for the community. Above ground-floor Hallowell granite columns, exposed cast-iron fluted Corinthian columns supported the superimposed tiers whose parapets varied in decorative pattern from story to story. The tall narrow space acted as a light snorkel, bringing natural illumination deep into the core of the building. And serving as the focal point was a massive marble palmery, which sat at the ground-floor intersection of the long east-west corridor and the short north-south axis. The era doted upon such exotic, hothouse vegetation.

Art and its history have been an integral part of a Wellesley College education since its inception. Billings placed a studio up under the mansard of the western transept of College Hall, with painting alcoves lighted by a roof monitor. Budding artists worked among paintings, prints, Eastlake-inspired furniture, and casts of antique sculpture.

Since there was no need to provide for separate quarters for male faculty, as had been the case at Vassar, Billings scattered student suites and faculty living quarters, as well as classrooms, over four floors. He also distributed the formal gathering areas, from library to laboratories, evenly throughout the interior. The east-west corridor formed the building's main thoroughfare at each level, a long tunnel for circulation and mobile socializing. Unlike the broad corridor at Vassar, in which the students exercised, the College Hall hallway was an extension of the Centre, with works of art dotting its walls. As the main spine of the plan, with rooms opening off each side, it also exercised a form of control over the inhabitants, requiring the public passage of each student as she moved from her room to classes, the library, or meals. With residency in double accommodations, no student was ever completely alone while she attended Henry Durant's college.

The Durants' vision of women's education embraced the whole woman: her physical health, her intellectual life, her spiritual state, and her aesthetic enrichment. College Hall housed a gymnasium, then a rare feature of women's education, because Durant preached a "new evangel of health" through exercise. Located on the upper floor of the two-story kitchen wing, the gymnasium began as an open space beneath wooden trusses that gradually filled with the latest in exercise equipment. A library, an art gallery, a chapel, and other spaces devoted to developing women's "every power and faculty, of the kingly reason, the beautiful imagination, the sensitive emotional nature, the religious aspirations" formed the principal rooms. The chapel above the library seemed a rather austere two-story space only slightly relieved by faintly medieval accents in the wooden trusswork above the octagonal dias and a pair of figured stained-glass windows designed by Christian Heinrich Burkhardt of Munich and donated by Governor Claflin. The room reflected Durant's Evangelical conversion. In the spare dining room, iron Corinthian columns like those in the Centre punctuated a space filled with tables and black walnut chairs made expressly for it, perhaps from Hammatt Billings's design. The physics and chemistry labs were all business, too, but that business—individual experimental research—stood at the cutting edge of scientific education, whether for women or men.

Other rooms more handsomely treated augmented these largely prosaic spaces in College Hall. The Durants saw no conflict in pursuing Christian learning within a beautiful natural and architectural setting enhanced by works of art. Over time they lined the light-filled Centre and handsomely wainscotted corridors with paintings, prints, and drawings (some by Hammatt Billings himself) and dotted the interior with sculpture. Many of the paintings were landscapes, echoing those of the Hudson River School, with long didactic labels extolling the virtues of nature. Billings located the art gallery on the fourth floor of the western transept, and shaped it as a loft-like space with painting stalls or alcoves flanking a wide-open central area beneath the roof monitor. This the College furnished with prints, paintings, decorative arts, and statues, some of them reproductions after the antique.

The library on the ground floor of the eastern transept formed—after the Centre—the building's most impressive space. Typical of the era before libraries included isolated metallic stacks, the long rectangular room was divided into a central aisle defined by piers (the structural iron columns boxed in wooden paneling) that separated it from side alcoves of shelving on two levels, and, following a practice that descends from classical antiquity, punctuated with busts of famous authors. For its walls Billings chose Pompeian red. To a nearly contemporary eye "the great bay windows, the cozy alcoves, the book-cases in black walnut, with their glass doors, the large library-tables ... the rare engravings, the beautifully bound books—all unite to producing [sic] the harmonious effect." Although documents report its planned capacity as a whopping 120,000 volumes, by 1897 it sagged beneath 47,000. The earliest books included some from the library of Rufus Choate, with whom Durant had been associated in his lawyering days, and 10,000

The library in College Hall was the intellectual center of the building. It was directly inspired by the library the Durants donated to and Hammatt Billings designed for Mount Holyoke College. As was usual before the advent of isolated metallic book stacks, the room was divided into central hall and double-decker alcoves, with spiral stairs giving access to the upper tiers. Wood paneling hid the structural iron columns, gas fixtures illuminated the room at night, and works of art hung from every available surface.

The Elizabeth Barrett Browning Room was one of two areas of College Hall updated in the 1880s to conform to the dictates of the English Aesthetic Movement. Layers of decorative patterns, richly wrought furniture, and objets d'art added up to a fine example of late nineteenth-century eclecticism. Ellen Robbins executed the floral patterns, and Donald McDonald designed the art-glass windows. Paintings by or after Muziano and Mazzuoli, a bust of the poet by William Wetmore Story, and John Adams Jackson's statue of The Reading Girl *completed the setting.*

from Durant's own collection. In the Centre, the art gallery, and the library especially, Billings embodied the artistic and scholarly aspects of Durant's character, and of the educational institution he endowed.

Two rooms redecorated after the opening of Wellesley College further enhanced the artistic ambience. They exemplified the Aesthetic Movement imported from England. In 1880 the Durants paid for the lavish redoing of a room dedicated to the memory of Elizabeth Barrett Browning. In his youth Durant aspired to be a poet, and he championed this literary pursuit in his educational program. The ceiling of the Browning Room was divided by ash frames into panels of Venetian leather the color of old gold embossed with rosebuds. Ellen Robbins painted the frieze of flowers, beneath which the leather wall covering was a dull red embossed with birds, flowers, and foliage in bronze and gold. Windows designed by Donald McDonald illustrated Browning's poetry, while the frame of the great mirror showed more foliage by Robbins. Along the walls stood a medieval German cabinet and a seventeenth-century German marriage chest. The other furniture on the "Turkey" carpet was oriental and ornate, as was much of the bric-a-brac that rested on it. Paintings by or after Girolamo Muziano and Annibale Mazzuoli leaned on easels, and statues of Augustus, of the poet by William Wetmore Story, and the centerpiece, *The Reading Girl* by John Adams Jackson, peopled the room. It was a monument not only to Browning but to the era of over-heated eclecticism that created it. Its designer's name seems not to have survived.

Eight years later Professor Eben Horsford of Harvard, a longstanding friend and trustee of the College, paid for decorating a faculty parlor by his nephew, the little-known New York architect Thomas Tryon. The College newspaper, the *Courant*, described the finished product as a "richly-wrought and luxuriously-furnished interior with mellow and harmonious hues." Tryon said at the dedication that he leaned toward the Renaissance rather than the Gothic. The effect here was less ponderous and more colorful than in the Browning Room. Using gold for background, Tyron said, he "endeavoured to blend reds, yellows, blues, and greens so that the general effect shall … be … rather subdued." Thomas Edison's new electric lighting, added to College Hall a decade after its opening, created his chief design problem. Here again a statue focused the space beneath an ornamental ceiling. In this case it was a bust of one of the contrasting Elaines of Arthurian legend. Stained-glass transoms enriched the lightly draped windows. Wicker furniture and what appears in old photographs to be a frosted-glass-and-wood screen rested on a patterned carpet. Horsford's portrait surveyed his gift. With their wicker furniture, layering of ornamental patterns, paintings resting on easels, and art-glass windows, these eclectic, artfully composed rooms were characteristic of the Aesthetic Movement that swept from England to the United States in the 1870s and 1880s.

All this artistic luxury did not preclude concern for basic necessities. In 1877 Henry Durant wrote that "all beauty is the flower of use." He and his architects were primarily concerned to create a fit environment. Health and physical comfort dictated many of College Hall's features, and the founders paid for and got the latest in mechanical systems and building technology. It was originally lighted with gas and heated by steam distributed by convection from the boilers into brick chases serving every room. Steam also powered the elevator. Sunshine, a fundamental requirement as we learned from the notes on the preliminary plan, poured through the many windows, especially those facing south over the lake. Fresh air also rose high on the list of Henry Durant's wants as it did in the building programs of many public and educational buildings of the era. Durant early stated a preference for elevated building sites where the air was pure. He carried that concern into College Hall. "They seem to have pure air 'on the brain' at Wellesley," wrote one observer in 1880, who also noted that the building was "perfectly ventilated" with outside air cleansed by steam and charcoal. Fresh water came from an artesian well. Contemporary accounts describe the drainage as faultless.

Only the provisions for fire security, alas, ultimately proved inadequate. Iron construction, relatively new in the 1870s, was thought to be fireproof, but the experience of the great city fires of Boston, Chicago, and elsewhere soon taught otherwise. Photographs taken after the College Hall fire of 1914 show twisted iron members strewn across the smoldering rubble. Iron would not burn but it did soften like boiled spaghetti in the intense heat and lose its structural strength. The fire left only fragments and memories of Durant and Billings's great building.

The destruction of College Hall means that only the East and West Lodges stand from Hammatt Billings's work at Wellesley. Although both have been internally altered, both bear precious witness to the original layout and architecture of the Durants' institution. The lodges originally gave restricted access (but never on Sunday) to a winding carriage drive that led through the grounds to the great school building on the hill. West Lodge, shown on the 1875 plan of the College but with the designer undocumented, is a picturesque English cottage of particolored granite walls. Hammatt Billings's preliminary sketch for East Lodge shows an elevation reversed and somewhat different from what was built. T-shaped in plan, its polychromatic random ashlar granite walls rise to Flemish gables only slightly less ornate than those that architects Ware and Van Brunt were soon to create for Music and Stone Halls. The lodges were the first buildings of this experiment in women's education to greet arriving students or turn away the idly curious.

The Durants and the Billingses provided a sturdy foundation for the architectural development of Wellesley College. When students first reached Wellesley in 1875 they found a colossal, picturesque College Hall set into a gated landscaped park that expressed Durant's belief that the "meaning of life is education," as he had said in his lecture on "The Influences of Rural Life," and that the best education took place in the country, not the city. Billings created for him a sprawling rural building in which he could direct the moral and intellectual development of women within healthy and beautiful surroundings. At its opening in September 1875 Wellesley joined Mount Holyoke, Vassar, and Smith as a leading institution devoted to the higher education of women. College Hall represented the ideal architectural setting for that endeavor in the years after the Civil War. But it was not long to stand isolated and aloof on its hilltop site, for that ideal was changing as College Hall rose, and the founder himself harbored greater ambitions for his fledgling institution.

East Lodge and its gate posts are the oldest surviving fragments of the Durants' college. Hammatt Billings's original sketch is dated 1869. Particolored stone walls, Flemish gables, and (originally) cast-iron ridge crestings present a delightful face to the world, but the little building existed to control the movement of outsiders onto the restricted campus.

Sometime after the opening of College Hall, Henry Durant took a walk through the College grounds with Louise Hodgkins, a member of his faculty. He eyed the rolling landscape surrounding the building and described for her his vision of the future: "On that hill an Art School, down there a Musical Conservatory, on the elevation yonder a Scientific School, at the farthest height a Medical College, and just there in the centre a new stone Chapel." Durant's ambition embraced not just a college but a university, not just a multipart educational philosophy but its architectural embodiment, not just the grand building on the rise above Lake Waban but a series of specialized educational structures. He lived only long enough to see a fragment of his dream come true, but his concept of a decentralized campus with buildings crowning the hills and nestling in the valleys became reality in coming years under the guidance of his successors.

Even during Henry Durant's brief six-year tenure as *de facto* head of Wellesley College (Ada Howard was nominally "President of the Faculty"), the process of dispersal began. In 1878 he founded a College of Music and in 1880 gave it its own building (now part of the Schneider College Center). At the same time Wellesley created a school for "Teacher Specials," or mature women without degrees who came to the College for advanced training. To house them the College's first outside donor, Mrs. Daniel P. Stone, funded a building situated on a rise above the lake to the east of College Hall, while, as Durant had envisioned, his "Musical Conservatory" rose "down there" on a low spot along the path between Stone and College Halls. These additions to Wellesley, like College Hall itself, nudged the shore of Lake Waban well away from the public thoroughfares that defined its northern and southern borders. Since both Billingses were dead by this time, the College turned to another pair of architects to give these facilities shape: the Boston firm of Ware and Van Brunt.

William Robert Ware and Henry Van Brunt, both Boston-born graduates of Harvard, had trained in architecture with Richard Morris Hunt, the leading American practitioner of the mid-nineteenth century. Sketches made during trips to Italy by William Ware show historical architectural details that would form the inspiration for the buildings that would later appear at Wellesley and elsewhere. A college football injury left Van Brunt, the firm's leading designer, lame for life, and constant pain left him on edge, impatient, and arrogant, according to one contemporary, or, on the contrary, "courtly, dignified, and gentle," according to another. Like Ware he was bookish and scholarly, with a literary career that paralleled his design of buildings, and he looked the type: a lean, buttoned-up figure with a walrus moustache drooping beneath a tethered pince-nez.

By 1880 Ware and Van Brunt enjoyed a reputation as one of the leading architectural firms of the day. Between 1863 and the dissolution of the partnership in 1881, with Ware increasingly preoccupied with founding America's first school of architecture at M.I.T. in 1865, and Van Brunt taking on more responsibility for design, the firm turned out a series of eclectic works in francophile, English Gothic, Flemish Renaissance, Queen Anne, and other currently fashionable styles. Among their chief works were the Episcopal Theological Seminary in Cambridge (1868–1880) and St. Stephen's Church in Lynn, Massachusetts (1881–1882), but the partnership also produced a series of important buildings for Harvard: Weld Hall (1870–1871), Memorial Hall (1865–1878), and the bookstack addition to the Gore Hall library (1876–1877). With such prestigious educational buildings coming to completion at the end of the 1870s, the firm must have seemed the ideal one to design the first additions to the Wellesley campus.

Henry Durant uncharacteristically distanced himself from the erection of these additions. Although he paid for the music conservatory, there is no evidence that he took an active role in the design or building of it, or of Stone, perhaps because of illness as he neared the end of his life. College Hall had been his baby, but these children he treated like foundlings. The contracting firm of A. E. and O. L. Giddings of Exeter, Massachusetts, erected them, not entirely satisfactorily it seems, and Van Brunt's office supervised the lot.

The smaller of the two new structures was Music Hall (now Billings, but not through any relationship to Hammatt, and, with additions and altered first-floor interior, the oldest standing College building other than the lodges). It originally stood isolated on the flat between its heftier neighbors, Stone and College Halls. Like them it had entrances on the north and south that gave access to a stairhall from which a corridor ran east and west. The symmetrical block contained thirty-eight rooms for vocal and instrumental instruction, all designed with an ear for acoustical isolation.

On the exterior of Music the protruding entrance bay, of stacked windows after the model of French Renaissance chateaux Ware had visited in Europe, emerges from between round towers. The walls of red brick rise from the relatively plain lower story to projecting diaper patterns within the actively profiled Flemish gables. Molded terra cotta (a revived building material

Music Hall, now called Billings (but unrelated to the first architect of the College), originally sat isolated along the path between College and Stone Halls. It was the 1880 design of the Boston architectural firm of Ware and Van Brunt. Now the oldest building on campus except for Homestead and the gate lodges, it too was the gift of the Durants. The decoration of the brick and terra cotta exterior of Music becomes more elaborate as it rises from the plain water table to the curvilinear Flemish gables, its picturesque skyline echoing those of its larger (and now vanished) neighbors.

that had begun to find common employment in the Boston area in the decade since the design of College Hall) forms keys, balustrades, spandrels, window heads, and other decorative accents, all of classical derivation. The three-and-one-half-story building rises to a multi-pointed silhouette of tall, slated candle-snuffer cones and high-pitched roof planes. These originally seemed less exotic as they added their own pointed silhouettes to the bold roofscapes and arboreal canopy of the campus. Like Stone and College Halls—and most other buildings of the period—eclectic in design, Music seemed the little sister of its larger siblings.

When Daniel Perkins Stone died in 1878 his widow Valeria, much to the disgust of her potential heirs, dispersed her $2 million inheritance to worthy causes. She was persuaded by her friend, Rev. William H. Wilcox, a College trustee, to include among her many donations $100,000 to Wellesley for the erection of a building dedicated to her husband to be used for "the Christian education of women for their efficient service of the world and of God." Her bequest contained the restriction that, should the $100,000 be exceeded, the College would lose the entire amount. The trustees laid the cornerstone of the new "Normal College at Wellesley" in May 1880, and the building opened its doors in the fall of 1881.

Henry Durant championed the education of Christian teachers, and had early on begun to accept special students, but he was dismayed that many arrived ill-prepared for college work. Still, here they were and they had to be housed. Since the demand for entrance into the College proper grew during these years as well, expansion was necessary. Stone Hall rose during Durant's last days, but the Board of Trustees acted as client, and the Teacher Specials and their building long took a back seat. The executive committee of the trustees in May 1887 ordered that preference be given to entering college students, even if that "excluded new Teacher specials." The distance between the older women and the regular students manifested itself, in the architectural terms of the original concept of the College as an integrated institution, by the long path between College Hall, where the specials took instruction, and Stone, where they lived.

Durant spent lavishly on College Hall, but Valeria Stone provided a fixed budget. According to the architects, the restricted funds affected the final result because the building contract fell to "coarse-handed people." In 1886 Henry Van Brunt wrote to Trustee Eben Horsford that Ware and Van Brunt "were betrayed by the cheap builders (Messrs. Giddings) whom we

were compelled to employ under the extreme pressure of economy." Since Van Brunt wrote the letter at a time he was angling to land for his firm the design of the new art building, he obviously felt the need to excuse earlier shoddy work at the College by blaming it on the circumstances of the budget, so his statement might not stand at full face value. But tight money is a recurring factor in the architectural history of the College. Not until 1885, when Valeria Stone's estate did donate an additional $5,000, could the building be called finished.

The design of Stone Hall furnished by Ware and Van Brunt called for a larger version of Music and a reduced and more economical version of College Hall, with the latter's monumental Centre subtracted and the firm's own personal touches added. The plan stretched east and west along a double-loaded corridor running from the reception hall left and right to stairhalls. One hundred mature women could be housed in single accommodations. Rather than one large dining room as at College Hall, here Ware and Van Brunt located four smaller rooms on the first floor in the east wing.

Compared to College Hall Stone housed a rather plain interior. Only the Great Parlor at the west end of the second floor received special treatment. It contained a monumental wood-framed round-arched fireplace facing a

The original Stone Hall was the last building Henry Durant saw rising from his hilly park, and the first to be funded by someone else. It housed 100 "Teacher Specials," older women who came to Wellesley to improve their deficient educational training. Stone too was the design of Ware and Van Brunt. Although nearly symmetrical in plan, this three-quarter view emphasizes the building's asymmetrically picturesque silhouette—a silhouette that marked all the first buildings of Wellesley College.

Although the tight budget restricted the design of Stone Hall, and according to architect Henry Van Brunt the building contract was awarded to "coarse-handed people," there was one outstanding and richly appointed room in the dormitory. The Great Parlor on the second floor of the western apse sported a monumental fireplace frame that rose to a cathedral ceiling supported by curved pointed arches. The decoration smacked of Eastlake and the English Aesthetic Movement.

polygonal apse beneath a cathedral ceiling. Wooden pilasters divided the wainscotted walls into bays and reached up to wooden corbels that supported the curved pointed arches of the ceiling. A spindle gallery that looks as if it had been borrowed from contemporary furniture inspired by the fashionable English designer, Charles Locke Eastlake, created a frieze at the top of the wall and crossed in front of the windows to hide a curtain rod. The transoms in those windows bore ornamental patterns.

Although the plan looked symmetrical on the lake side, the apse of the parlor found no echo on the east and closer inspection found other compromises with axial rigidity. The east-west spine showed four stories, the stair towers rose five, and the east and west wings three. Like College and Music Halls, then, when seen from most parts of the campus Stone Hall reached up in asymmetrical disarray, its red-brick, terra cotta, and slated shapes a three-dimensional counterpoise of straight, curved, and angled; its many chimneys, towers, high conical roofs, and gables adding to the scattering architectural skyline of the College. The vertically stacked, protruding window frames rising story by story to culminate in a flush lucarne or dormer in the roof once again echoed in brick similar features found on the Renaissance chateaux of the Loire. As at Music, the treatment of the external walls placed classical details on a picturesque body, an approach to design called at the time "Free Classic."

The walls of Stone formed fit companions to those of College Hall. There Billings had borrowed some features of Ware and Van Brunt's paneled brick style; here Ware and Van Brunt devised their treatment of Stone's polygonal apse by varying that of their own Memorial Hall at Harvard. In addition to the lively articulation of its walls, however, Stone Hall featured a number of Ware and Van Brunt's signature curvilinear corbie-stepped gables, a detail they had been using at least since Weld Hall at Harvard, and one they derived from the bold silhouettes of Dutch and Flemish Renaissance buildings. Stone Hall appeared as eclectic as anything built in the period. Alas, like College Hall in 1914, it burned and was demolished in 1927. Stone–Davis Hall now occupies the site.

By the time of his death in October 1881, Henry Durant had created a college campus consisting mainly of three bristling red-brick blocks situated along the north shore of Lake Waban and well removed from the outside world. Each varied a coherent instructional and architectural theme that followed the vision he had shared with Louise Hodgkins of a landscape dotted with educational buildings. But the embryonic unity of Durant's plan did not last. While the physical plant continued in the coming years to shatter into architectural fragments, those fragments took on a character different from the founder's vision. At his death Wellesley began to change. As Henry Durant's biographer wrote, while he "saw every rise of ground … crowned with the stately buildings of a university-to-be," Pauline Durant "beheld home-like cottages nestled in every glade." At his death his widow became secretary of the College, and Simpson Cottage, begun as Henry Durant lingered in his final illness, heralded the next generation of Wellesley's architectural development. That development resulted from a very different vision of the educational and social mission of the College. And it was to be led by a very different personality, the College's young new president, Alice E. Freeman.

CHAPTER THREE

THE ALICE FREEMAN YEARS

IN 1881 Alice E. Freeman became president of Wellesley College at the age of twenty-six. Six years later she resigned to marry Professor George Herbert Palmer of Harvard, but soon joined the Wellesley Board of Trustees and continued to exert her influence on the College until the presidency of Caroline Hazard. The years of her official leadership merged with those of her successors, Helen Shafer and Julia Irvine, who largely followed her reform program, to establish one continuous episode in the architectural as well as institutional history of the College. During these years changing policies toward educational and social values led to the building of residential cottages as well as an art building, a freestanding chapel, an observatory, and other structures of lesser importance, but the lack of a coherent vision for the Wellesley campus resulted in a state of architectural confusion that was not to be addressed for a number of years.

Abbot Thayer's portrait of Alice Freeman (1855–1902)—the best of the presidential portraits that today hang in the Clapp Library—presents her as small, young, attractive, and demure. In fact she was much more than the portrait suggests. A born leader whose experiences as a trailblazing female student at the University of Michigan and highly recommended professor of history at Wellesley joined with the diplomatic skills of a Madeleine Albright, Freeman led an internal reorganization of the College in curriculum, administration, and student life. She created the Academic Council, for example, and she saw to the appointment of secular leaders such as Horace Scudder, editor of *Atlantic Monthly*, to the Board of Trustees in place of the educators and men of the cloth who had dominated it in the Durant years. Not all she wanted was accomplished during her tenure as president, but her able if less inspirational successors carried on.

The interior of Rotch and Tilden's Farnsworth Art Building (1887-1889) contained galleries articulated in freely interpreted classical style. In this arched wooden frame between the galleries, for example, fluted pilasters topped by bulging Ionic capitals supported a Doric frieze of thin triglyphs and paneled metopies. In the far distance stood a Palladian motif in which Doric piers framed doubled Ionic columns. Although Arthur Rotch presented the building as Greek in style, his interior was a highly original mix of ancient forms.

Abbot Thayer's portrait of President Alice E. Freeman in the Clapp Library depicts a young and demure woman, but she was also a born leader who directed the second phase of Wellesley's institutional and architectural development.

With Alice Freeman's appointment as president the direction of Wellesley College passed to a new generation. For all he added to his models, Henry Fowle Durant had conceived of his institution in terms of Mount Holyoke and Vassar. Although he called it a college he ruled his students' health, morals, and spirituality as if he were headmaster of a seminary. Under Alice Freeman these religious and social bonds began to loosen, and, in the words of historian Patricia Ann Palmieri, the students became "collegiate women" rather than "boarding school girls." And the architecture of the college they inhabited became gradually decentralized.

Although his late vision of a campus of dispersed buildings suggests that he had begun to recognize that it was an ideal whose time had passed, Henry Durant had originally followed Mount Holyoke and Vassar in herding all the students and faculty within one architectural corral far removed from public life. The model of the asylum upon which Wellesley and its antecedents had been designed had gone out of fashion at about the time College Hall accepted its first class. The new women's collegiate pattern was set at Smith, which opened its own doors in 1875. Those doors were in buildings located in the town of Northampton, Massachusetts, and they let students into not only a main building housing the administrative and teaching spaces, but also individual, domestically scaled residential quarters separate from the classroom building. This accessible, atomized campus plan created a new relationship between the student and the community, one in which the individual began to take charge of her own life, and it dramatically altered the architectural development of women's colleges in general and Wellesley in particular. Somewhat ironically, this change returned the students, architecturally at least, to the ambience of the "cult of domesticity" that they as "new women" had sought to escape.

During Alice Freeman's years of leadership and influence architecture continued to play its role as reflector and shaper of the institution and its image. The personal patronage of Durant gave way to that of the Board of Trustees, but its leading voice, even after her retirement from the presidency, continued to be Alice Freeman Palmer's. In November 1884, recognizing the trend away from the housing of students in what the landscape architect Frederick Law Olmsted, Jr. later called "great barracks" like College Hall, the trustees appointed a Committee on Cottages and began to build smaller residential units. This was in part to change the College's image beyond the limits of the campus. Late in 1887 Freeman proposed to the executive

committee of the trustees that photographs of the cottages be published in order to bring them "more before the public." Historian Helen Lefkowitz Horowitz further sees Alice Freeman's adaptation of the cottage system of residential planning, popular on women's colleges in the late 1800s, as an instrument of her secularization and domestication of the school. Architecture, as always, was enlisted to make apparent a program, in this case a movement to reform the seminary into a college. Wellesley felt the need for expansion too, for by 1880 College Hall was woefully overcrowded.

One of the first of the series of cottages that form an important aspect of Freeman's architectural program she inherited from the Durants. These were "cottages" in the nineteenth-century sense, larger than what we now think of as a cottage, but built of informal materials such as wood shingles. In 1881 Pauline Durant turned over Waban Cottage to Wellesley as a student residence, while the first cottage to be erected by the College itself rose during Henry Durant's last year, if not necessarily from his last wishes. In late May 1880 the College announced receipt of a gift of $15,000 from Michael H. Simpson for a dormitory in memory of his wife, a trustee. The program called for "a small family house for the accommodation of girls whose physical condition renders the congregate plan [i.e., life in College Hall] too severe a strain upon their nervous systems." We can imagine Durant's opinion of that as a man who believed the shrinking-violet image of nineteenth-century womanhood could be erased by vigorous work in mind and body! In any event, when it was finished by the Giddings firm of builders in 1881 (the year of Henry Durant's death) Simpson Cottage formed the Wellesley prototype for several more domestic dormitories that, as they were erected, slowly dispersed part of the student body across the College campus. Although

Norumbega Hill viewed from the south, with the wooden Norumbega Cottage to the left and the lithic Farnsworth Art Building to the right. Farnsworth introduced a jarring contrast to the prevailing architecture of the early campus. Its appearance set up a stylistic debate between the irregularly picturesque and the smoothly neo-classical that was to last until the arrival at Wellesley of Ralph Adams Cram in the next century. Both buildings fell victim to the erection of the Jewett Arts Center in the 1950s.

The construction of Simpson Cottage began the residential decentralization of Wellesley College. In the Durants' original scheme all students and faculty lived and worked in College Hall. After the 1875 opening of Smith College, which was laid out with a series of small residential "houses," Wellesley entered a period of cottage building that lasted into the 1890s. Tudor Simpson, the last of Wellesley's cottages to survive, was designed in 1881 by Van Brunt and Howe to provide an intimate, homey atmosphere for those students who found it difficult to live in College Hall.

altered and extended with an incompatible brick wing added sixty years later, Simpson remains the only one standing. It is the last vestige of the cottage system that dominated architectural thinking about residential accommodations on campus through the 1880s and into the early 1890s.

Simpson sits hidden on its wooded knoll some distance from the lake front. The design came from Henry Van Brunt's firm, now called Van Brunt and Howe with the departure of William R. Ware for New York, and the elevation to partnership of Frank Howe, formerly a draftsman. About twenty students were to find residence there. The first-floor plan loosely grouped "chambers," a parlor, and a dining room around a central stairhall reached by a short corridor from the entrance porch. The architects placed the kitchen in the basement. The plan of the second floor distributed more chambers around the central stair. Although there was central hot-air heating, every room had its own fireplace. As it became less important as a source of warmth during the nineteenth century, the fireplace grew increasingly conspicuous as a nostalgic symbol of "hearth-and-home" coziness. The student who lived in Simpson had a very different relationship to the community as a whole than did she who was still housed on the fourth floor of College Hall. A resident of Simpson became part of a nuclear family within an extended family.

The cottage exterior is as fittingly domestic in character, as that character was conceived in the early 1880s. It is Tudor in style, with irregular massing composed of a red-brick ground story that gives way to a faux half-timbered second story beneath a tall slate roof punctuated with slender brick chimneys.

Simpson Cottage was Henry Van Brunt's last work at Wellesley, although he seems to have expected to be named the architect of the art building, but it was not the last of the College cottages. Norumbega, erected during the summer of 1885 with funds gathered from a variety of sources including Trustee Eben Horsford, was the first to be erected by the Committee on Cottages. An obscure local architect named Frank Hurd designed it. Situated on the western brow of a hill (soon to be named Norumbega Hill) between College and Stone Halls and, like Simpson, well back from Lake Waban, it was the first structure on the site of what came to be called the Academic Quad. Norumbega was enlarged in 1902 according to a design by architect Julius A. Schweinfurth, and pulled down in 1956 to make way for the Jewett Arts Center.

Prosaically named Decennial Cottage at ground-breaking, Norumbega received its poetic redesignation to honor Horsford and recall his belief that Norsemen settled a city of that name on the banks of the nearby Charles River in the sixteenth century. The new cottage was intended in part to ease the pressure of overcrowding in College Hall, and, according to Horsford's letter soliciting funds for its erection, would be inhabited by "the more sensitive among our ladies as a dwelling of relative quiet, without the range of activities which necessarily prevail where large numbers not only recite and attend lectures, but receive friends and study, eat and sleep under the same roof." Clearly the residential aspect of Durant's academical-village-under-the-mansards had fallen into disfavor less than a half decade after his death.

Hurd's plan for Norumbega cannot be found, but we know that the cottage originally contained accommodations for some thirty-four students, some faculty quarters, and a presidential suite. As at Simpson a broad entry led to the central stairhall from which one could reach the president's rooms, reception room, and dining room on the first floor. Reflecting the development in residential planning that had occurred in the United States in recent years, the design, according to one reporter, exemplified "modern ideas of open interiors with simple furnishings." Among the latter were wicker chairs. The library and parlor of the presidential suite, first occupied by Alice Freeman, could be thrown together through wide doors, while here, as throughout the cottage, picture moldings and chair rails drew horizontal lines through all the rooms. The president's bedroom, according to our source, exhibited a "Clarence Cook" ideal. Cook was a leading critic of furniture and decoration whose *The House Beautiful* of 1878 championed "simplicity" as "a good part of beauty."

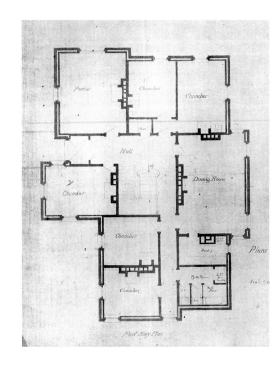

The plan Van Brunt and Howe laid out for Simpson Cottage in 1881 grouped parlor, dining room, and students' bedrooms around a central stairhall. The chambers were free of closets but each contained a fireplace, the ancient symbol of hearth and home. Here a few students could escape the hubbub of congregate life in the "great barracks" of College Hall, which put "too severe a strain upon their nervous systems." With the building of the cottages Durant's highly centralized college began to deconstruct.

Norumbega Cottage was built in 1885 from the design of Frank Hurd, extended in 1902 by Julius Schweinfurth, and pulled down in 1956 to make way for the Jewett Arts Center. The first of a series of residential units put up in the 1880s by the Committee on Cottages, it contained students' rooms, faculty quarters, and a presidential suite. A rambling irregular pile of clapboards, shingles, and brick, spindles, turned posts, and carved ornament, Norumbega brought to campus the Shingle Style, the currently fashionable residential architecture of seaside and suburb.

Like its open plan, the exterior of Norumbega reflected the latest architectural fashion. It rose from the hill as a three-and-one-half-story asymmetrical gabled mass of clapboard and shingle walls and brick chimneys. Although the Committee on Cottages originally envisioned a "plain cottage of wood," Hurd specified particularly fine detailing, with porte-cochère and covered entry framed by spindle transoms above turned posts, each story on the principal elevations marked by overhangs, ornamental shingle patterns, carved wooden decorative panels in the pediment over the entry and elsewhere, and geometric-patterned art-glass windows in the dining room. The whole treatment had the energetic surfaces of a work in transition from the Queen Anne to the Shingle Style, echoing this period's general trend in suburban American residential design.

Pressure continued through these years for more housing on campus for students (many were unsatisfactorily lodged in Wellesley village), so Pauline Durant came forward in 1887 with funds to erect a second cottage on what was now called Norumbega Hill. Named Freeman Cottage to honor the recently retired and now Mrs. Palmer, it opened in 1888 and fell victim in 1934 to the construction of Pendleton Hall. Frank Hurd is credited with the design for Freeman Cottage too, in an early newspaper account, but he is not named in the trustees' minutes, and it was a work inferior to Norumbega in the quality of its detail. We should probably question the attribution until documentary evidence comes to hand.

The plan of Freeman Cottage is also lost. Intended for about forty-five students plus some faculty, as with its sisters it contained parlors off the entrance and hall leading to the central stair and a first-floor dining room. The exterior formed a rambling, awkwardly massed, gambrel-roofed pile of shingles, clapboards, and brick chimneys that appeared about to tumble over the edge of the hill. It sported a broad entrance piazza with turned posts, but its detailing lacked the verve of Norumbega's, and the decorative accents seem mere tokens.

Wood Cottage followed on the heels of Freeman. Begun in 1888 and opened in 1889, it too vanished in the 1930s. Caroline A. Wood, a trustee, left $50,000 to the general fund of the College, and the Board of Trustees elected to build a third cottage in her honor. Whether Hurd's work at Norumbega, and possibly Freeman, had left them dissatisfied we do not know, but the trustees selected the Boston firm of Allen and Kenway to design the new building (although Hurd did more work for the College in the next decade).

The new building continued the trend toward larger cottages established by Norumbega and Freeman as the program called for some fifty students plus faculty, and Allen and Kenway created a close variant of those earlier houses. An entry off a corner piazza led to a stairhall from which one either found the reception room and parlor or proceeded into the living quarters stacked on three floors along a double-loaded corridor. The kitchen and dining room were in the basement. The structure was of wood, and partially of fire-resistant mill construction (fear of fire in these cottages was constant in the minds of the trustees). Clapboards covered the asymmetrically gabled exterior, those at the top floor set into an exposed frame.

Wood was the last residential cottage designed for Wellesley College. The 1890s saw the gradual reversal of the ideal of the 1880s, a trend away from smaller residential units that had characterized the presidencies of Freeman, Shafer, and Irvine toward larger buildings, as the College again sought to reshape its image. By the turn of the century the old Committee on Cottages had become the Committee on Dormitories; in 1900 the College erected Wilder Hall, a large brick neo-classical block that rose in jarring contrast to its neighbors on Norumbega Hill, and by 1902 the trustees had

Alice Freeman first occupied the presidential suite in Norumbega Cottage. When it was new, according to one reporter, it exemplified "modern ideas of open interiors with simple furnishings" espoused by critic Clarence Cook's book on furniture and decoration called The House Beautiful *(1878). Rooms flowed together; picture moldings and chair rails visually tied room to room; delicately ornamented fireplace frames focused the spaces; and wicker furniture lightened up the heaviness of the mid-Victorian interior.*

Wood Cottage Wellesley College Mass.

Wood Cottage came from the drafting room of the Boston architectural firm of Allen and Kenway in 1888. It was the last of the timber residential buildings erected on what had come to be called Norumbega Hill (and is now known as the Academic Quad). Fear of fire danced attendance on these cottages. Here the structure was partially of mill or slow-burning construction. The exterior followed the lead of Norumbega and Freeman: it was a picturesque pile of clapboards and half-timbering.

decreed that future residences were to accommodate no fewer than one hundred students. By then leadership on campus had passed to Caroline Hazard, and the mission of the College had taken off in a new direction.

At the end of this period, however, as if to perpetuate the cottage scale of student life abandoned with the creation of the Committee on Dormitories, the campus saw a rash of Greek and special interest "society houses" erected across the landscape. These became intimate gathering places for selected groups of students. The Phi Sigma Kappa house designed by Charles A. Cummings, Zeta Alpha house by Ralph E. Sawyer, and Tau Zeta Epsilon house and Elizabethan Hall for the Shakespeare Society, the last two by Warren, Smith & Biscoe of Boston, were all built between 1898 and 1903. "Shakespeare" as it has come to be called appropriately assumed a picturesque English Tudor look with exterior faux half-timber walls, while the others presented to the campus the frigidity of frail neo-classical temples. Within, however, most of the houses contained cozy living rooms with exposed dark woodwork, fireplaces of brick, and Mission and revival furnishings. This stylistic dialectic between exterior and interior paralleled that of more monumental work of this era. Archival photographs of these houses and the parlors of the Hazard dormitories demonstrate that Wellesley College in the early twentieth century housed fine interiors in keeping with the Boston Arts and Crafts movement, and it is a tragedy that so little survives.

If the cottage system adopted in the 1880s effectively altered Henry Durant's original conception of an all-purpose, one-building residential college, other structures erected during this period in fact carried on his vision of monumental, hill-crowning and valley-gracing edifices housing various departments of the institution. Chief among these architectural additions were the Farnsworth Art Building, the Houghton Memorial Chapel, and the Whitin Observatory. (The Chemistry Building erected from Frank Hurd's design to the north of Norumbega Hill in 1894 was a flat-roofed, clapboarded, utilitarian box.) Not only did Farnsworth, Houghton, and Whitin continue the addition of new buildings foreseen by founder Henry Durant, they also precipitated a debate about the future style of campus architecture at Wellesley. And that debate added new voices to those of the Durants and trustees in the shaping of Wellesley College.

In January 1886 Henry Van Brunt wrote to Eben Horsford that he had learned the College had received a "liberal fund" for the erection of an art building. The architect had had several conversations with Henry Durant about such a building, he wrote, "and it was our understanding that, when it came to fruition, we were to be employed as his professional advisors." He added, "I know Mr. Durant's views on the subject." Durant's vision of

In the years around 1900 special interest groups on campus began to erect "society houses," Elizabethan Hall (now called Shakespeare) and Tau Zeta Epsilon among them. Both were the work of the firm of Warren, Smith & Biscoe of Boston. The original TZE house, which stood at the foot of the hill now crowned by Green Hall, was neo-classical without and neo-medieval within. This Arts and Crafts ensemble, with its exposed heavy wooden trusses, massive fireplace, oriental throws, and especially its ponderous Mission-style furniture, was once characteristic of many interiors on campus.

FARNSWORTH ART MUSEUM

Wellesley's future did begin with an art school on a hill, and in early 1886 his boyhood friend Isaac Danforth Farnsworth made the realization of that wish possible when he bequeathed to the College $100,000 for a building for the fine arts. Whether or not the trustees were upset by problems at Stone Hall, Van Brunt lost the commission, although his former partner did gain a hand in the project. In June 1887 the trustees accepted the design of Arthur Rotch of the Boston firm of Rotch and Tilden. Perhaps because the firm was relatively untried in monumental work, the trustees also hired Professor William R. Ware, now of Columbia University, as consultant. The College dedicated the building in September 1889 and pulled it down in 1958 to make room for the terrace in front of the Jewett Arts Center.

Rotch and Tilden was a relatively new firm when it received the commission for the Farnsworth Art Building, but it had already designed gothic churches and classical libraries. George Thomas Tilden apprenticed with Ware and Van Brunt, then studied at the Ecole des Beaux-Arts in Paris. Arthur Rotch, the dominant designer during their partnership, graduated from Harvard and represented the new generation of architects, one trained in the classical language at both M.I.T and the Ecole, and equally at home in the artist's studio and the drafting room. Born to wealth, Rotch lingered in Europe during the 1870s, studying and sketching the history of architecture, and as a result, was well-grounded in precedent. In the mid-1880s, when he undertook the Wellesley commission, he appeared as a slender, aristocratic figure with sharp features behind a luxuriant handlebar moustache. At his untimely death less than a decade later friends remembered him as both kindly and conscientious.

The plan and exterior massing of Rotch's design for Farnsworth reflected the building program, which called for three major divisions: galleries, lecture hall, and instructional spaces. The architect was assisted in establishing this organization by Elizabeth H. Denio, who had studied with famed *Kunstgeschichter* Anton Springer in Leipzig and visited many of the art galleries of Europe before beginning to teach the history of art at Wellesley in 1885. Rotch's I-shaped plan placed the main entrance and galleries in the south wing, the large lecture space in the narrower central block, and the library, studios, and art history classrooms and laboratories in the north wing.

The recessed entry passage on the south, flanked by small rooms to right and left, gave access to Farnsworth's central hall. The lecture room and instructional spaces up ahead were closed from view, while to right and left extended two-story skylighted galleries. Paneled arches flanked by curiously wrought Ionic columns upholding a Doric frieze surrounded the doorways from the hall into the galleries. Palladian motifs, in which fluted Ionic columns framed by Doric piers embraced the central opening, outlined alcoves at the ends of the galleries. Such details were blatantly uncanonical, and as a whole more Roman Renaissance in style than Greek.

Arthur Rotch's address to the assembled College at the dedication of Farnsworth went beyond an explanation of the design of the building itself to suggest something about its educational mission. He had, he said, provided a room in the building which, "with malice aforethought," he hoped would be used for the teaching of architecture. Practicing female architects were rare

Henry Durant's expanded vision of Wellesley College began with an art school on a hill. The bequest of his friend Isaac Danforth Farnsworth made this building possible. Designed in 1887 to 1889 by the Boston firm of Rotch and Tilden in consultation with Elizabeth Denio, the college's professor of art history, the Farnsworth Art Building contained classrooms, galleries, and studios within a neo-classical shell to which the architect Rotch attempted to give "the simplicity, the severity, the plain masses and concentration of Greek architecture."

through the next several generations, and Rotch's wish had to wait nearly a century for complete fulfillment. Wellesley did, however, in 1907 appoint Eliza J. Newkirk '00 (later Rogers) to the faculty, an architect trained at M.I.T and in Philadelphia who designed many houses and other buildings in the Wellesley area. In the decades since her appointment architectural history has taken pride of place at the College, and in the 1980s architecture finally became a major in full partnership with history and studio in the Department of Art.

The exterior of a building, Rotch said at the dedication, should reveal its plan. It was an idea he had picked up at the Ecole des Beaux-Arts. In Farnsworth the "museum-like character is indicated by the high, unbroken wall surface of the exhibition galleries, while behind them, above the low corridors [flanking the central lecture room], a frieze of windows announces a large hall.… [In the north wing] numerous windows indicate subdivisions within, of a less public nature."

There exist in College Archives studies for two of the building's elevations made after the plan had been established. They are unsigned but presumably executed by Rotch, who was a gifted watercolorist. That of the south elevation shows the final *parti* in all but some minor details: a central entrance recessed behind two fluted Ionic columns with geometrically patterned balustrade above, and squeezed between towers square in plan and two-stories high beneath crisp triangular pediments. From this central salient windowless wings reached right and left. Seen from the valley south of its site on a wooded section of Norumbega Hill, Farnsworth reached out more than 140 feet of grey neo-classical stonework.

Slated hipped roofs capped the building. Rotch and Tilden rusticated the Berea sandstone exterior everywhere except the towers, which were dressed stone above a rusticated base. The unfenestrated gallery walls were ornamented by a frieze of roundels and squat pilasters. The roundels remain today, embedded in the terrace that now occupies the site. They are memorials to Farnsworth and the cottages destroyed in the mid-twentieth-century transformation of Norumbega Hill into the Academic Quad.

The second watercolor shows the east elevation. This study envisioned an articulation of colossal Doric pilasters on the exterior of the rear wing, with a suggestion of figured panels between first and second floors. Classrooms and library occupied the lower floor, while the north-lighted studios were located upstairs. In the event economy prevailed: the two-story side walls of the rear remained without classical armature or decorative panels. Contemporary accounts say that the project came in under budget.

Arthur Rotch's explanation of his design at the dedication drew heavily on nineteenth-century associationism. He took pains to justify the building's siting and its style. "[T]he temple of art should sit on a hill, so suggestive ... in its beauty of classic groves and mounts of the muses, [and] should be built from inspiration at the purest source," he said. He went on: "[W]e have tried to keep in view the simplicity, the severity, the plain masses and concentration of Greek architecture ... because of the traditions which so closely connect it with all European art schools and museums." (He made no allusion to the freely rendered Roman Renaissance details inside the building.)

Rotch was probably eager to defend his design for Farnsworth because its monochrome classicism radically departed from its picturesque neighbors on Norumbega Hill as well as the rest of the College's red-brick visually energetic architecture. His design promulgated an architectural law unto itself. Although the building seemed more fashionably eclectic than scholarly Greek, in Farnsworth neo-classicism first arrived at Wellesley. It would not quickly disappear.

The classicism of Farnsworth stood in stark contrast to the rest of the campus. Its formalism confronted the informality of Durant's buildings and its neighbors on the hill. From its dedication until the middle of the second decade of the twentieth century, the architecture of Wellesley exhibited what has been called the great debate. As always the College's dilemma reflected national trends. The question was: should the prevailing style of new buildings be formal and classical or informal and medieval? The history of the design of the Houghton Memorial Chapel in the second half of the 1890s exemplifies this issue and more.

"[A]nd just there in the center a new stone Chapel": thus Henry Durant had ended his vision of the future Wellesley College campus. During the 1880s, at just the moment the College was attempting to define itself in relaxed religious terms, a movement among students began to agitate for a chapel removed—like so much else during these years—from the precincts of College Hall. Although they collected a small amount of money, nothing of the idea materialized for a decade. But the fact that it was the students, not the Board of Trustees, who initiated the project is significant. The results of teaching women to think for themselves would now become apparent on the campus itself. The new collegiate woman was beginning to make herself heard at Wellesley.

Student fund-raising became unnecessary when the children of the late William S. Houghton, a trustee, gave the College $100,000 for the erection of a chapel named for their father and dedicated to religious and academic assembly, but student voices continued to be heard throughout the ensuing problem of selecting the site. When complete, the Houghton Memorial Chapel, designed in 1896–1897 and dedicated in 1899, formed a quasi-Gothic counterpoint to classical Farnsworth, and the two set the polarities of early twentieth-century discussions about the stylistic future of the College.

A number of possible sites for the chapel filtered through the trustees' meetings. One proposal placed it next to the Farnsworth Art Building up on Norumbega Hill, but the board preferred a "broad, level" location, south of the hill, between the lake and Rhododendron Hollow. The announcement of this decision "called forth a vigorous protest from alumnae and others who deprecated any injury to the rare silvan beauty" of the proposed location, according to Julia Irvine's annual president's report of 1897. In fact the petition from alumnae, faculty, and students read at the trustees meeting of April 17, 1897 asked that the building not be located in the woods near Longfellow Pond because it would "change the entire rural aspect in a way to destroy its reposeful influence, beauty, and usefulness." This constituent challenge to the authority of the trustees had its short-term effect: they ultimately situated the chapel on a "broad elevation" between Stone Hall on the east and the music building to the west. A decade later, however, following the advice of Frederick Law Olmsted, Jr., the College plunked the College library (now Clapp Library) down upon the silvan site the protest briefly spared, and in the extension of the library in the 1970s Longfellow Pond became a concrete basin.

The trustees in that meeting of April 1897 also accepted the definitive design of the chapel submitted by the New York architectural firm of Heins & La Farge. It was a commission the firm had barely won in a limited competition conducted by the College in the previous year, its first but not its last architectural competition. Asked by the building committee his opinion about competitions and possible competitors in June 1896, the architectural educator A. D. F. Hamlin of Columbia University, after consulting his colleague William R. Ware, prescribed a paid, limited contest with professional judges. He also recommended to the building committee four Boston firms "competent to produce a creditable and artistic Renaissance [i.e., classical] church": Peabody & Stearns, Clarence H. Blackall, A. W. Longfellow, Jr. and Andrews, Jaques and Rantoul. It remains unclear whether Hamlin got the idea that the chapel would be modeled after Renaissance work from the trustees' committee, or merely preferred that style himself.

For whatever reason the final list of competitors contained only two names from Hamlin's recommendations. Letters went out in June 1896 from committee head Horace Scudder to four architectural firms inviting them to compete for the chapel commission: Shaw & Hunnewell, a local partnership that had designed Wellesley's town hall in the early 1880s; A. W. Longfellow, Jr. and Peabody & Stearns, both major Boston offices; and Heins & La Farge. (Scudder rejected an offer from Edward B. Chestresmith of New York, an architect and husband of an alumna but otherwise little remembered, to design the building free of charge.)

The letter of invitation outlined the program: $100,000 budget including memorial windows and organ, seating for 1,300 in chairs (not pews), and acoustic properties suitable to women's voices. It also requested that the proposed design be of a building "academic in character, and especially adapted to worship, though not limited to an ecclesiastical order." Broad directions indeed! Obviously the committee at this point had no predetermined opinion about style despite Hamlin's mention of the Renaissance.

The letter also called for entries to include a plan, sections, elevations, and a perspective all rendered in monotone. Competitors would receive $300 for their submissions. But the statement that the "designs were to be the property of the college" called forth protests from professionals who thought they provided ideas not drawings, and that provision was ultimately set aside. In the end the requested drawings did not contain enough information, for after the entries were submitted in September 1896, the cautious building committee called for letters explaining materials and heating and ventilation. It also asked for an estimate of the cost of the finished product, including grading, and whether or not that estimate had been obtained from contractors. These the competitors unanimously and wisely declined to provide.

The trustees notified Heins & La Farge in October 1896 that they had won the commission, but their proposal underwent revisions over the next several months and, as we have seen, not until April of the following year did a definitive design receive approval. Only two of the four competition entries are known in detail, that of Peabody & Stearns based upon a surviving perspective, and that of Heins & La Farge based upon the existing building, although we also have a brief glimpse of Shaw & Hunnewell's entry. The letter sent by that firm to explain its design mentions "grey limestone columns, cornices, etc." and walls of grey brick. In the interior, the letter said, the architects wanted to avoid the look of the "modern upholstered church" with its black walnut furniture and red carpets. Columns and cornices suggest a classical design, but without the drawings we can never be certain of the style of building they proposed.

Of the two designs we do have, one envisioned a building based upon Hamlin's Renaissance precedent; the other borrows Gothic details. Here the debate is fully joined: would the College develop as a Gothic revival campus, or would the neo-classic direction initiated at Farnsworth prevail? The trustees in 1896–1897 chose the former over the latter, although the building they selected in fact represented something of a compromise.

Robert Swain Peabody studied at the Ecole des Beaux-Arts in Paris, and was a gifted artist and draftsman. He took the lead in Peabody & Stearns's design. The unsigned grisaille perspective of the partners' entry shows a chapel based upon a Latin cross inscribed within a rectangle that rises to a shallow conical roof resting on a low drum and surmounted by a tholos-lantern. The twin-towered main façade stands behind a tetrastyle portico of fluted Corinthian columns supporting a triangular pediment. The chief ornamental features other than the columns, towers, and lantern were the pronounced cornices and round-arched arcades.

In the letter sent to explain the design, Peabody & Stearns said they thought stone for the exterior would break the budget and specified instead light-colored brick and light terra cotta, the prevailing chromatic of the emerging Renaissance Revival, although they also thought concrete walls and terra cotta would do as well. The latter is an astonishingly early proposal for the architectural use of concrete, a material that came into its own only in the early twentieth century. The interior would be plastered. The inspiration here was the "domed and short-armed" centralized church of Northern Italy, as they wrote, "in the time of Bramante," although the influence of Palladio's chapel at Maser is more apparent on the exterior. The proffered design justified Hamlin's recommendation of the firm, and if realized would have been a splendid advocate for the classical side of the great debate.

But the project of Peabody & Stearns did not come close to winning. Despite the Houghtons' preference for A. W. Longfellow's now-lost proposal, the original Heins & La Farge scheme narrowly bested it by a trustee vote of eight to six (the board ignored Professor Hamlin's recommendation that the choice be made by professionals). With this decision the trustees for the first time opted for other than a local architectural firm to design a major building at Wellesley. Their choice included principals George Lewis Heins and C. Grant La Farge, both graduates of M.I.T. The pair formed one of the up-and-coming practices, and their projects included such prestigious work as the Episcopal Cathedral Church of St. John the Divine in New York, a plum of an architectural commission they, as young and inexperienced architects, had won in competition in 1889. The prestige associated with that achievement certainly stood them in good stead with the trustees. (Grant La Farge's being the son of John La Farge, famed artist and decorator of H. H. Richardson's Trinity Church on Copley Square, Boston, did not hurt either.) Of the two, George Heins became the contact man for Wellesley's chapel.

The Heins & La Farge competition drawings for the chapel are no longer available, but we do have a description of and something of a justification for their design. They took a position midway between the extremes of the great debate. They proposed a stone exterior and a red slate roof, they wrote, because "we wish to harmonize in general effect with the music hall and the art building, the chapel forming as it were a mean term between its next nearest neighbors, being in color similar to the art building and in general composition similar to the music hall." This is an early if flawed (and perhaps deceptive) example of an architect thinking about the relationship of his building to the rest of campus. The roof and lantern of the chapel do echo the color and forms of Music Hall, but Farnsworth up on wooded Norumbega Hill was hardly a proximate neighbor. We have no way of knowing whether this sophistry got Heins & La Farge the commission, but we do know that a few years later, in a 1902 letter to Wellesley President Caroline Hazard, the firm flatly stated that at the time of the design of the chapel, Music Hall "could properly be neglected so far as it would affect the style and treatment of the Chapel." Although the original Heins & La Farge proposal won the competition, it did not satisfy everyone on the building committee, and it required major and minor revisions.

The fraught history of the construction of the Houghton Memorial Chapel, which included the first builder "throwing up" the contract, therefore requiring his replacement in midstream and the intervention of lawyers, is well documented in College Archives but need not detain us here. From the exterior the building as erected displays a fully articulated Latin cross surmounted by flared red-slate roofs and crowned by a crossing lantern square in plan and spiky in silhouette. The apse is polygonal; the other arms are square-ended and contain entrances surrounded by elaborate frames of piers, niches, and carved cornices. The flat-arched windows enclose decorative patterns of Gothic bar tracery. This tracery joins with token buttresses, Tudor arches, the combination of pointed windows and high gables in the apse, and the pointed tower to proclaim the building's Gothic leanings.

The serene interior rises to higher architectural achievement. The narthex turns the Latin cross of the exterior into an interior Greek cross. It is a broad open space, the central crossing a breathtaking span uncluttered by columns that was achieved by steel structural trusses supporting the roof. These are hidden beneath the decorative oak overhead arches and hanging bosses that seem to dance and leap above the vast room. Light enters through the central skylight beneath the lantern, and through broad openings largely filled with stained glass. Walls of exposed buff Roman brickwork rise above paneled wooden wainscotting. The decorative details deserve attention: the stained glass by John La Farge, William Comfort Tiffany, and others; the Alice Freeman Palmer Memorial by Daniel Chester French; the glazed iron-work lamps; and the furnishings, including sedilia, pulpit, rush-seated and

straight-backed chairs, and lectern, all made by Irving and Casson in the spirit of the emerging Boston Arts and Crafts Movement.

The existing chapel—especially the even-armed interior—looks as if it were a centralized church of the Renaissance finished in Gothic details. We need merely glance at any of the contemporary Gothic churches of Ralph Adams Cram to confirm Heins & La Farge's compromise. Just as Ware and Van Brunt used classical details on a picturesque body at Stone Hall, producing there a Free Classic design, so Heins & La Farge used Gothic details on a fundamentally classical body at Houghton. "Free Gothic"? Whereas Gothic is skeletal, Houghton Memorial Chapel is mural. Whereas Gothic churches seem to rise effortlessly from the ground, the chapel sits heavily on a knoll above Billings Hall with dressed Amherst stone walls resting on a contrasting Milford granite base. Peabody & Stearns's proposed chapel was an uncluttered

The Houghton Memorial Chapel is the work of Heins & La Farge of New York. Wishing, as they wrote early on, to harmonize with both picturesque Music and neo-classical Farnsworth, they designed a heavy-walled and Tudor-detailed compromise between the two. The site too was a compromise, as faculty, students, and alumnae objected to the original trustees' proposal to locate it near Longfellow Pond (the present site of Clapp Library). The chapel was dedicated in 1899.

Latin cross, and so was Heins & La Farge's, but Peabody chose the round arch and Heins & La Farge the pointed. Therein lay the principal difference. Neo-Gothic—even nominal Gothic—for the moment had triumphed over classical design.

If the competition for the Houghton Memorial Chapel exemplifies the stirring of a debate about the proper style of campus buildings, the history of the Whitin Observatory adds detail to the story. The College was open scarcely a year when it identified a need for an observatory. When Trustee Sarah Elizabeth Whitin, widow of a textile machinery manufacturer in the Blackstone Valley of Massachusetts, donated the facility in 1898, she did so because of her long interest in astronomy and her friendship with Sarah Whiting of the physics department. As Whiting noted in the draft of a letter to Whitin, they both recognized the educational value of beautiful buildings. Whitin's ultimate outlay was $30,000.

The project began to take shape when David P. Todd, director of the observatory at Amherst College, at Mrs. Whitin's request sketched out a preliminary scheme. Todd's main focus—like those of all the professionals concerned—was on the quality of the instruments to be contained within the building rather than the beauty of the architecture. He proposed a rather utilitarian structure hidden by vegetation. But he might also have had the older campus buildings in mind (excepting Farnsworth) when he suggested that the observatory walls be "of common brick laid in red mortar covered with ivy thickly."

The donor assumed a major role in the design and execution of the building. Todd jotted down his ideas in her Whitinsville parlor, she selected the architect and criticized his design, and she prescribed the principal building material. She wanted marble, not brick. Although her friend Professor Whiting, sensing that the new material would add to the architectural cacophony of the College, "objected to marble as alien to the general public building material of the grounds," Sarah Whitin had her way. As the architect wrote to Professor Whiting (no doubt giving her the benefit of longer experience dealing with willful clients), "the merits of a brick structure were so fully stated to Mrs. Whitin, [but] she so much preferred a marble building ... that I question the policy of pressing the subject further." And he went on to cite the marble beauties of the Corcoran Gallery in Washington, D.C. and the State House in Providence, Rhode Island, although he also hoped that a marble observatory would "not recall the [tomb of the] great King Mausolus."

The open interior of the Houghton Memorial Chapel results from the use of hidden steel arches above the arching woodwork of the ceiling. A letter asked competing architects to design a building of "academic character" although not necessarily of an "ecclesiastical order." That meant different things to different competitors, but in the end the building committee selected Heins & La Farge's design.

All this makes it sound as if style rather than cost was uppermost in Whitin's mind, but the truth may lie elsewhere. In an intraoffice memo of September 1900, John C. Olmsted (brother of Frederick Law Olmsted, Jr.) of the landscape design firm that was consulted about the grounds, wrote that the building was originally to be of brick, but Norcross Brothers, the builders, wanted to use marble from their quarry in Georgia, and offered to supply it at their own expense. The switch may have been accounted for because, as he wrote about the landscape plan itself, "Mrs. Whitin was close and didn't want to pay much." In the end neither the donor's determination nor the builder's generosity paid off. As the distinguished architectural critic Montgomery Schuyler wrote in 1912, "the exquisite marble, exquisitely wrought, serves neither its practical nor its picturesque purpose any better than rough brick would have done."

The architect of Whitin Observatory was Henry Ayling Phillips. The first graduate of the new school of architecture at M.I.T., Phillips accompanied Arthur Rotch to the Ecole des Beaux-Arts in Paris. He had an office in Boston and a home in the Blackstone Valley and probably knew Mrs. Whitin before she selected him to design her observatory. Except for a later project for the Hazard Quad, the rest of his career remains clouded in obscurity. Mrs. Whitin's letters mention Phillips frequently. His surviving correspondence was addressed to Professor Whiting who acted as the client. Although she kept the Board of Trustees informed of the progress of the work, her voice, a faculty voice, joined the donor's in directing the execution of this building.

In September 1898 Sarah Whitin sent a formal request to Pauline Durant, then secretary of the College, for permission to build at her expense a small observatory. The College accepted Henry Phillips's design soon thereafter, and, following the intervening winter, let contracts in April 1899 to Norcross Brothers of Worcester, and dedicated the building in October 1900. Norcross was then the leading contractor in the nation (the firm had, however, been rejected as the builder of the Houghton Memorial Chapel). In 1906 the observatory received a sympathetic addition and the nearby neo-classical residence from the designs of Frank Angell of the firm of Angell & Swift of Providence.

Phillips's design, preserved on a tracing-paper drawing showing plan, section, and elevations, followed closely the schema established by David P. Todd of Amherst. The circular Equatorial Room surmounted by a high dome ultimately built by Warner & Swasey of Cleveland sits in the middle of the

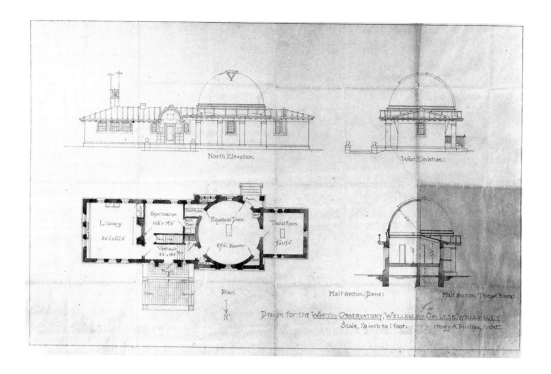

Design for the WHITIN OBSERVATORY, WELLESLEY COLLEGE, WELLESLEY.
Scale, 1/8 inch to 1 foot. Henry A Phillips, Archt.

long rectangle. The running mechanism of the finished dome was designed for "young ladies." The Transit Room extended to the east, and to the west sat the Spectroscope and a comfortable library complete with brick fireplace and sturdy furnishings.

The observatory rose on the highest unoccupied hill on campus in order to achieve a clear view of the sky. It needed to face true north, because the transit telescope had to follow the meridian, and that explains why the building was sited without regard for the rest of the campus. It refers not to earth but to the heavens. The placement of the hooded main entry on the north, an entry that turns away from the main approach from the campus, has over the years caused it to become nothing more than an elaborate back door.

As critic Montgomery Schuyler noted, Mrs. Whitin's insistence on marble produced a rather unhappy result. The exterior appearance of the small building is one of low squat walls and flat gables crushed beneath the arched mass of the dome. The Georgia marble laid up in flat bands of alternating width is an overly monumental material for the size of the building. Phillips's comparative examples were inappropriate: the Corcoran Gallery and the Rhode Island State House are massive in size as well as material. Phillips specified standing-seam copper for the roof of the observatory (the architect's "artistic soul," the donor wrote at one point, "rebels at anything that has to be painted"), and would turn over in his grave if he knew of the white paint that now covers the metal roof. Its copper decorative acroteria and other embellishments derive from Greek architecture. The Whitin Observatory proved to be a major new facility for the educational program of the College, but it was an odd duck architecturally, and scarcely a distinguished addition to the campus. It made more apparent than ever the need to end ad hoc decision making by donors, trustees, and faculty members and establish guiding principles embodied in a master plan for the campus.

Red brick or marble, picturesque or formal, medieval or classical: these characterized the competing sides of the great debate we find running through the histories of the Houghton Memorial Chapel and the Whitin Observatory. Gothic faced Greek, picturesque confronted formal, and no two buildings were sited in any meaningful relationship to one another. "Individual benefactors and individualistic architects," wrote Montgomery Schuyler, "have imposed their individual notions, to the detriment, or rather to the nullification, of anything like a general architectural scheme" for the campus. But change was afoot. When the College dedicated the observatory in 1900 the ceremonies were led by Caroline Hazard, Wellesley's new president. Although the realization of a comprehensive campus plan had to wait until after she left that office, and after the fire that destroyed College Hall in 1914, it was President Hazard who first confronted the issue of a coherent development of Wellesley College's architecture.

Henry Phillips gave the Whitin Observatory a comfortable interior, with beamed ceiling, brick fireplace, low bookcases, cane-seated chairs and sturdy tables, oriental rugs, and astronomical models. By 1900 the electric light was standard technology. Notice the beautifully wrought andirons and tools: such crafted appointments were usual in campus buildings at the turn of the century.

*The College sited the Whitin
Observatory on its highest unoccupied
hill for an unobstructed view of the sky.
Its location and orientation isolated it
from the rest of the campus.*

CHAPTER FOUR

THE IMPACT OF CAROLINE HAZARD

THE DEDICATION in June 1899 of the Houghton Memorial Chapel marked the first public appearance of Wellesley's newly named president. Caroline Hazard's appointment in May represented a break with the past that carried over from her qualifications to her architectural impact on the campus. Although she had something of a literary reputation, Hazard lacked an earned academic degree and had never taught, facts that separated her from her predecessors in office. She was a vigorous and cultivated member of the Rhode Island establishment, however, and she was wealthy.

Hazard's charge was not only or perhaps even primarily an academic one. At her appointment she found Wellesley financially strapped and under pressure to expand. When Alice Freeman Palmer approached her about the position, Palmer said she offered her the opportunity to play a major philanthropic role in higher education. But not only her own status and wealth attracted Wellesley to Caroline Hazard. Add the hope that through her contacts with other members of what used to be called the "ruling class" she could lure their financial support in the coming years. By the end of her decade Hazard had done just that, with architectural donations from John D. Rockefeller, Andrew Carnegie, and a host of slightly more hidden lights. "Under her leadership," wrote the Board of Trustees at her retirement in 1910, "large sums of money were raised, first to remove the debt and then to provide added endowment and new buildings." And Caroline Hazard herself proved to be as generous a friend of the College as she was an able administrator. She paid for her own contributions to Wellesley's growing collection of buildings, and she had an impact on their appearance as well. Nor did her interest in Wellesley and its surroundings wane after she left office, for she chaired the College's Grounds Committee as late as the 1920s.

The main reading room at the center of Shepley Rutan and Coolidge's original library (now Margaret Clapp Library) was furnished with sturdy chairs and massive Renaissance-style tables designed by the firm. Portraits of past presidents (including Abbot Thayer's Alice Freeman in the distant left) line the walls beneath the plastered segmentally vaulted ceiling. Fireplaces in libraries were common into this period, although an open flame would seem to be the last thing one would want in a building filled with books.

Caroline Hazard's impact on Wellesley College extended well beyond her tenure as president. She was the first to try to bring order into the campus layout, and she added many new buildings. As late as the 1920s she chaired the Grounds Commitee.

Caroline Hazard (1856–1945) was forty-two when she joined Wellesley. Photographs show her as a robust figure of medium height with a look of firm determination in her eyes. She was a woman of the world, not an inmate of the ivory tower. She had honed her administrative skills doing social work in her family town of Peace Dale, Rhode Island. During her presidency Wellesley continued to emerge from its reclusive beginnings to embrace society as a whole. "The day of cloistered learning has gone by," she said, "knowledge for service is what we seek." The impact of this fresh breeze upon the educational and social life of the College has been discussed elsewhere, but as usual programmatic change created architectural impact.

President Hazard's building program drew upon many sources. Not least among them was her drive to increase the population of the College. To run an institution with a minimal fiscal endowment, Wellesley needed to increase the number of its tuition receipts. In her first five years at the helm enrollment climbed from 688 to 1,051 students, and by the end of her tenure it had nearly doubled. More students required more buildings. During the years of Hazard's leadership the College complex expanded by five dormitories, a power plant, a gymnasium, a library, the president's house, and other structures, and the administration finally began to think of the campus as a potentially coherent entity. The location of some of the most imposing of these new buildings at the public edge of the campus along Central Street and the Boston & Albany railroad tracks indicated that Wellesley College stood ready to meet the world, and to face it with some impressive architectural credentials.

Early in her career at Wellesley President Hazard employed hometown architects for work on campus. The Billings addition to the old Music building, additions to Whitin Observatory, and the president's house, eventually to be named "Oakwoods," were all designed by the Rhode Island firm of Frank W. Angell and Frank H. Swift. Angell, the leader of the partnership, had trained with Providence architect William R. Walker. A distant cousin of Wellesley's president, he had worked for the Hazard family at Peace Dale in the 1880s.

Where Wellesley presidents before Caroline Hazard had lived among the students, she separated herself from the student body. Where Alice Freeman had been content to live in Norumbega Cottage, for example, Hazard required more imposing quarters. She paid for and lived in Oakwoods, which became College property at her resignation. Angell & Swift gave her a house characteristic of the suburban domestic architecture of the era: Shingle Style with Colonial Revival details and a few Asiatic touches.

In 1901 the Rhode Island architect Frank Angell designed "Oakwoods" for his cousin, Caroline Hazard, who paid for the house and donated it to the College at the end of her presidency. It survives as a typical example of the suburban Shingle Style popular at the end of the nineteenth century.

The trustees' minutes call it a "building worthy to be the home of the President, with provision for proper entertainment of our many guests." The architect designed the house in 1901 and the president occupied it in 1902.

Hazard and Angell sited Oakwoods (without much regard for how it fit into the existing campus) on a wooded knoll near Stone Hall, with views south and west over the Natick road, the Natick hills, and Lake Waban. On a ninety-foot-wide rubble stone base, faceted shingled walls rise two stories in the central mass to a shingled gambrel roof and one story in the asymmetrical east and west wings. Inside the dining room, dark green walls rose above mahogany wainscotting, while the twenty-by-thirty-foot reception room in

WILDER HALL, WELLESLEY COLLEGE, WELLESLEY, MASS.

Wilder Hall was Julius Schweinfurth's first work for the College. It opened in 1900 and vanished with the erection of Green Hall in the 1930s. It differed from the other residences on Norumbega Hill not only in name—it was a hall, they were cottages—but in external materials and architectural style as well. Wilder took the form of a neo-classical, pedimented pavilion of red brick with white trim. Its blind arcade and Palladian motif echoed other neo-Bulfinchian work designed by Boston architects at the turn of the century. Frederick Law Olmsted, Jr. thought it added "to the existing confusion" of campus buildings.

the west wing had walls of green Japanese paper and Oriental hangings. Carved into the mantle of the fireplace in the study was a line from a poem by Sir Walter Raleigh: "Scallop Shell of Quiet." Hazard placed this heraldic shell on many a College building.

Not only the new president required quarters. Increasing enrollment of students meant increasing pressure to house them. One of the first of the new dormitories erected during Hazard's tenure was Wilder Hall, the fourth residence located on Norumbega Hill and the first built in a decade. It appeared, however, markedly different from its shingled sisters. It took the form of a "hall" not a "cottage," and that distinction signalled the new architectural countenance of the College. Situated in the center of the campus, but on the western edge of Norumbega rise, it looked down the main road toward the entrance to the campus and was thus one of the first collegiate buildings a visitor would see as she travelled the road from this direction. Wilder Hall suggested change. Wellesley faced the new century in formal attire.

Wilder Hall came to Wellesley through the gift of Charles Wilder, a town resident, in 1899. It differed from the other residences not only in name; it broke architecturally with all the existing buildings on campus. The homey ambience of the 1880s cottages became a thing of the past. Initially intended to house fifty students, but designed to be easily expandable, Wilder sat on a broadly rectangular plan with central entrance and stairhall and rooms off a double-loaded corridor. It rose three and a half stories of red brick and white wooden trim to one coherent hipped roof. The architect divided the axially balanced long façades horizontally into a base of blind round-arched windows surmounted by two stories of rectangular openings punched through the brickwork. He centered each of these elevations with a pedimented pavilion whose colossal pilasters rested on the base and supported a high triangular pediment. The middle bay rose from the frontispiece to a Palladian motif and echoing window embraced by the pilasters, and then to a bull's-eye cartouche in the pediment. The flat neo-classical *parti*, the relative thinness of the detailing, as well as specific features such as the blind arcade and the Palladian window, matched much of the neo-Bulfinchian or Federal Revival work of many Boston architects at the turn of the twentieth century.

Wilder was one of several buildings designed for the College by Julius Adolphe Schweinfurth. One of three sons of an immigrant German engineer, all of whom achieved architectural prominence, Schweinfurth travelled and sketched extensively in Europe in the mid-1880s, before and after which he drafted in the office of Peabody & Stearns. A slight, cigar-smoking, rather dapper-looking figure with clipped hair and moustache, Julius Schweinfurth was a gifted draftsman, watercolorist, and designer in the revival modes of his time. In 1895 he formed his own firm and gradually built a national practice. By the time Wellesley called him to design Wilder, Schweinfurth had executed a number of picturesque cottages and neo-classical houses. Wilder marks the beginning of his heyday, a decade during which he provided Wellesley with several major additions and designed many significant works elsewhere.

Although red brick Wilder Hall shared its classicism with its neighbor, the grey-stone Farnsworth Art Building, the two were very distant cousins, and neither meshed with other buildings on campus. As architectural critic Montgomery Schuyler asked in 1912, "what has the mild Colonial [sic] of Wilder Hall … to do with the strict classic of the Farnsworth Art Building or with the … pure white marble [sic] of the College library?" As the landscape architect Frederick Law Olmsted, Jr. said in a letter to Caroline Hazard in 1902, the new dormitory "introduced … still another distinct type of architecture to add to the existing confusion." While it did nothing to create a more unified campus plan, Wilder did much to make one seem more desirable. It pointed the way toward a more formal campus architecture than had existed before.

Hazard's career at Wellesley coincided with college and university expansion across the nation. It also coincided with the maturation of comprehensive planning in the United States. This was a movement called the "City Beautiful," which made an attempt to subject the ragtag nineteenth-century city to controlling overall design in the neo-classical style of the coeval Renaissance Revival. The guiding model was the Court of Honor at the World's Columbian Exposition held in Chicago in 1893 (although Thomas Jefferson's University of Virginia was the ultimate source), with its axial layout and conforming classical buildings. The City Beautiful movement's most conspicuous Boston-area monument is the original Cambridge campus of M.I.T. The actual achievements of the movement proved spotty in the long run, but in the early years of the twentieth century the ideal drove planning schemes from whole cities to college campuses. Wellesley under President Hazard felt its impact.

The ideal site for a City Beautiful layout was a flat, open, and well-defined plain. The campus that Hazard inherited was a large rolling landscape of alternating woods and meadows. It was dotted with buildings built over the recent quarter century with little regard for architectural coherence. Recognizing the need for some kind of prescription for controlling the direction

In 1902 President Hazard paid out of pocket for several outstanding architects and planners to propose schemes for the placement of new campus buildings. C. Howard Walker's plot plan concentrated on three areas: a science building to balance College Hall, a group centered on the axis of Music Hall with a new library to echo Houghton Memorial Chapel, and a U-shaped arrangement of six new dormitories and Wilder Hall balanced along the axis of Farnsworth. As did all the proposals, Walker's envisioned the demolition of the cottages on Norumbega Hill. As with all the proposals, nothing came of his scheme.

of the architectural expansion she had in mind, Hazard in 1902 out of her own pocket paid for a number of designers to come up with proposals for a master plan. She chose most distinguished professionals. They were C. Howard Walker of Boston, architect-in-chief of the Omaha Exposition of 1898 and soon to hold the same position for the St. Louis World's Fair of 1904, Heins & La Farge, architects of Houghton Memorial Chapel, and Frederick Law Olmsted, Jr., now head of the Brookline landscape design firm founded by his illustrious father, and member of the McMillan Commission, which was preparing plans for the restoration of Pierre L'Enfant's neo-classical layout of Washington, D.C. Collaborating with Olmsted was the Boston office of Warren, Smith & Biscoe headed by English-born Herbert Langford Warren, Jr., who presided over the School of Architecture at Harvard. Hazard requested Olmsted to look over the Wellesley campus with the view "of giving *me* [emphasis added] some idea of placing future buildings." When the time came to pay Olmsted's bill, she sent her personal check.

The three proposals had many similarities. The Olmsted report took the form of a letter written in March 1902. Of interest here are his remarks about buildings; the next chapter will discuss his impact on the landscape. Future development should concentrate buildings so as to alter that landscape as little as possible, he wrote. Build on the plateaus where the buildings should be sited to emphasize the division between the flat tops and the escarpments. Thus, new structures on Norumbega Hill (some to replace what Olmsted considered the "temporary" cottages) should follow the edge of the escarpment and ought to be continuous, thereby reducing "the deplorable tendency to scattering [sic] buildings through the grounds." Such an arrangement, he explained, would make "an architectural composition in perfect conformity with the topographic conditions." Other recommendations included placing a building, perhaps the library, to the west of the Houghton Memorial Chapel and the Music Hall (the juxtaposition of those two existing buildings seemed to Olmsted to produce a "lame and quarrelsome chorus"); eventually building dormitories on the rise north and west of Norumbega Hill; siting a new gymnasium west of that; and preparing a comprehensive block plan to guide future decisions about the placement of buildings.

President Hazard accepted Olmsted's recommendation that Warren's firm prepare the block plan, and by November 1902 a plan and preliminary report from Warren, Smith & Biscoe were in her hands. Since the immediate need was for additional dormitories, the report concentrated on Norumbega Hill. The existing cottages, it said, sit athwart the edge of the hill and "interrupt

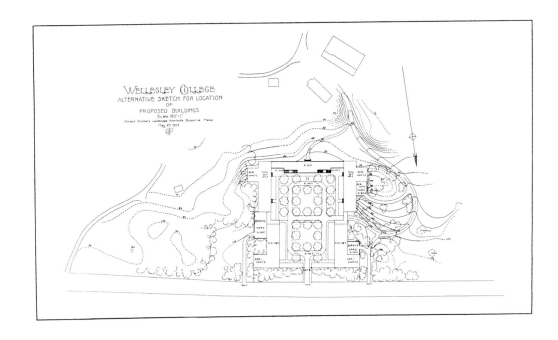

Although Frederick Law Olmsted, Jr. disapproved of the site, his office did prepare preliminary schemes for the layout of what came to be the Hazard Quad at the request of Caroline Hazard herself. In this 1903 schematic the Brookline firm shows four L-shaped dormitories grouped around an axial courtyard perpendicular to the perimeter road and the Boston & Albany train tracks. This was to prove highly influential on the ultimate layout of the Quad.

and contradict it." In Warren's vivid simile: "They are a little like independent and self centered students seated glumly facing hither and yon in a reading room, instead of a party of friends gathered about the hearth or the table." Warren like Olmsted assumed that these insubstantial and inflammable cottages would give way to more permanent structures, so his proposal called for an arrangement of new buildings balanced around the axis established by the long dimension of Farnsworth. The style of the new works should harmonize with the natural surroundings and with the existing buildings, Warren advised. Additions should be domestic in scale and detail, and follow the variety of outline and the free classical components of the older buildings. This, the report said, seemed to call for works echoing those of the "early Renaissance in England," the Elizabethan or Jacobian styles in which classical detail joined broken and picturesque masses.

Olmsted and Warren continued in the next year to press for new residential development on Norumbega Hill, but the trustees were understandably reluctant to spend money they did not have to tear down cottages to build expensive new dormitories. Olmsted had himself foreseen the eventual development of additional residential buildings north and west of Norumbega on Central Street, and, with Hazard's prodding, he and Warren roughed out alternative proposals for that site. In March 1903 Hazard wrote to Warren asking for a general scheme for a quadrangle there, including the style of architecture. Could the buildings "be quite plain with some relief of Elizabethan gables," she prompted. In response Olmsted's office reluctantly sketched a series of alternate arrangements for a quadrangular development of the Central Street site. When the decision was finally made to build there rather than reshape Norumbega Hill, that scheme proved prescient, but by then Olmsted had washed his hands of the whole affair.

The letter written by Heins & La Farge to accompany their block plan, both prepared in November 1902, begins by criticizing Olmsted's focus on landscape as the starting point for development, but in the end the firm's ideas seem largely to conform to the landscape architect's prescriptions. Since this plan would have impacted on the landscape too, it will reappear in the following chapter. Architectural considerations are the focus here. "This is a problem of architecture," they wrote, "with landscape treatment as accessory and subordinate, rather than a problem of landscape architecture with buildings subordinated." They continued, "We may regret the potential obliteration of natural features," but they seemed to think that that was the broken eggs required to make a smooth architectural omelet. Nonetheless, Heins & La Farge followed many of Olmsted's suggestions, and their block plan looks like an illustration to his letter. Both proposals recommend a flexible approach to style combining classical detail with irregular massing. The Heins & La Farge proposal focused on three groups of buildings: one on Norumbega Hill, one on College Hall Hill, and one completing the chapel–Music Hall pairing. In the latter two cases they proposed balanced axial groupings of new and old buildings; in the former case they planned to complete the development of the hill to create a "formal, but unsymmetrical" whole.

In general these ideas follow Olmsted and Warren's lead, although Heins & La Farge wrote adamantly that buildings on hills should overflow the edge of the escarpment with projections that would reach a lower level. "This would produce a certain picturesqueness and interest, and would … unite the buildings with the hill." Precedents for such charming massing can be found in both medieval and classical architecture. "This is a consideration … which is independent of the style of architecture." This interlocking of site and massing characterized the Day & Klauder-designed buildings erected after 1916, especially Founders, Green, and Pendleton Halls.

Architect C. Howard Walker's proposal for the development of the "Buildings and Grounds" differed from the others in that he provided for areas of outdoor activity: athletic fields between Norumbega Hill and the observatory and a skating pond as part of his redesign of the area in front of Music. He also envisioned a botanical garden west of Norumbega Hill. His architectural development, however, like that of Heins & La Farge, concentrated on three spots: a science building north of College Hall intended to balance it around an east-west axis, a group centered on the north-south axis of Music, with a new library to answer the chapel and other buildings to form a court (the buildings shaped by the overall scheme rather than by internal

One of President Hazard's final requests of the trustees was for still another master plan to guide the addition of College buildings. The trustees empowered her successor, Ellen Fitz Pendleton, to order the Boston firm of Shepley Rutan and Coolidge to prepare such a plan as early as 1912. Two new groups of buildings were envisioned: a science center on Simpson—or Great—Meadow, and new dormitories on the site of the orchard near Homestead. The Shepley firm shaped each as three sides of a quadrangle facing the lake. Nothing came of this proposal either.

necessity), and Norumbega Hill. For the chief focus Walker suggested a U-shaped arrangement of six new dormitories (and Wilder Hall) balanced around the long axis of Farnsworth to form "Norumbega Court." The bare back end of Farnsworth would be gussied up with a portico to face the courtyard. In Walker's arrangement too the existing cottages would have to go.

The earlier ad hoc placement of individual buildings bedeviled these attempts to bring order to the campus. In the Warren, Heins & La Farge, and Walker plans axes dictate various groupings but there is no overall coherence. With the creation of the Hazard Quad after 1903, as we shall see, another detached symmetrical pod was added to the campus conglomerate.

Nor did the completion of the Hazard Quad lay to rest the ongoing demands for more dormitory space for the expanding College, demands that run like a river in flood through the trustees' minutes during these years. Apparently unimpressed with the proposals of 1902, among her last requests of the Board of Trustees as College president (although not as a continuing

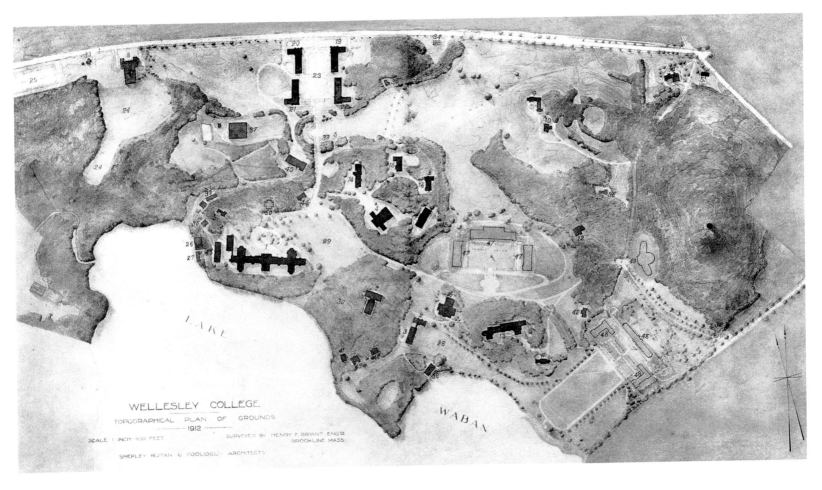

WELLESLEY COLLEGE
TOPOGRAPHICAL PLAN OF GROUNDS
1912
SCALE 1 INCH = 100 FEET   SURVEYED BY HENRY F. BRYANT ENG'R
BROOKLINE MASS.
SHEPLEY RUTAN & COOLIDGE ARCHITECTS

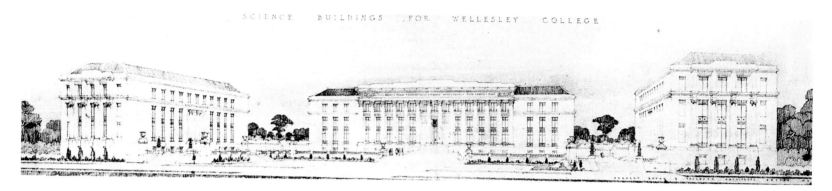

influence on the College), Hazard asked for a survey of the Wellesley grounds that would (again) provide information about where to locate future dormitories, and "in fact, in regard to the site of all future buildings." The board empowered her successor, Ellen Fitz Pendleton, to request the Boston architectural firm of Shepley Rutan and Coolidge (architects of the library) to prepare a developmental plan early in 1912.

The trustees had in mind specifically the siting of two new groups of buildings: more dormitories and a new science complex. The Shepley proposal for the science center looked like a smaller version of the buildings of M.I.T. in Cambridge, but actually predated that layout. It located axially balanced, neo-classical science buildings on three sides of a terraced courtyard on Simpson—or Great—Meadow, buildings as at M.I.T. with Corinthian colonnades and the names of great scientists inscribed in the frieze. The proposal for new dormitories placed them on a site in the orchard (northwest of Homestead). They too would form three sides of a court facing southwest, with a long, tree-lined lawn stretching to the lake. Had this scheme reached fruition, the campus would have achieved two more isolated if internally coherent groupings of neo-classical blocks.

It did not. The fire that destroyed College Hall in 1914 created a break with the past, and the discussions about the campus plan that followed were conducted in a very different atmosphere. After a proposal for a drastic neo-classical makeover by the Shepley firm, as we shall see, the commanding presence of Ralph Adams Cram, Day & Klauder, Frederick Law Olmsted, Jr., and Arthur Shurtleff, working for a committee eventually chaired by Caroline Hazard, brought the great debate to resolution.

Although Hazard's attempts to shape an architecturally coherent campus during her presidency resulted in nothing tangible, the projects she commissioned of Olmsted and his rivals did initiate thinking about the relationship

The proposed science center of 1912 envisioned by Shepley Rutan and Coolidge conformed to the expectations of the national Renaissance Revival that fostered Welles Bosworth's original design of the Cambridge campus of M.I.T. as well. Both complexes assume an axial alignment of long horizontal buildings articulated with classical colonnades and the names of great scientists inscribed in the frieze. Such a layout is better suited for a flat site, and Wellesley College is fortunate that nothing came of this proposal to reshape the rolling terrain of the Durants' park.

between buildings and buildings and between buildings and landscape that would continue to underlie the architectural history of Wellesley College. And if the president's campus planning projects came to nothing above ground during her tenure, she did manage to create a comprehensive and centralized campus system of underground heating tunnels radiating out from a power plant. Drawings by A. D. Houghton of New York dated July 1902 show a gabled, rubble-stone plant that was never built. In the same year John D. Rockefeller granted the College $150,000 for the tunnel system, and in the next his gift paid for a utilitarian brick power plant designed and built by Rockefeller engineers west of Norumbega Hill (and added to several times subsequently). The power plant's chief architectural feature remains the tall octagonal and tapered brick smokestack rising above the plantings intended to hide the raw building itself. Rockefeller engineers had no interest in landscape design, and Olmsted was sore pressed to get them to route the heating tunnels in such a way as not to deface the existing terrain.

Like the other 1902 plans, Olmsted proposed that new structures be grouped rather than scattered, that they exhibit some design uniformity rather than be discrete entities spotted across the landscape, but he alone of this planning generation proceeded from the character of the landscape to the distribution of future buildings. He preferred small residential units rather than the "great barracks" of College Hall, but thought the cottages on Norumbega Hill should be replaced with buildings that better conformed to the classicism of Wilder. In the future the College might locate dormitories on the site of what came to be called the Hazard Quadrangle at the entrance to the campus opposite the commuter railroad out from Boston. Although Olmsted wrote that the resulting "exposure to the outside world" was one disadvantage of the site (and thereby revealed his lack of understanding of— or opposition to—the direction in which Hazard was taking the College), the trustees had just that exposure in mind. The quadrangle became one of the major and most public architectural features of the campus, and it is rightly named after the mover and shaker in the president's office at the turn of the twentieth century.

The need for new living space for the increasing student population still existed after Wilder opened. The immediate impetus for beginning the construction of the four large and ornate dormitories that make up the Hazard Quad was the $60,000 bequest of Martha Pomeroy, sister-in-law of the donor of the Whitin Observatory. Both women assumed hands-on attitudes toward their buildings. Sarah Whitin demanded marble walls and that suggested a classical design; Pomeroy's will directed the College to erect a stone dormitory "in the Elizabethan Gothic style of architecture" and thus established the look of the entire layout of the quadrangle.

Not that the College needed to be forced to build in Elizabethan style. In these anglophile years Wellesley—like many another American college—began to think of itself as an intellectual descendent of the late medieval colleges of England. Hazard herself greatly admired the Lady Margaret Beaufort (1443–1509), the grandmother of Henry VIII who contributed much to Christ's College, Cambridge, an educational foundation housed in Tudor-Elizabethan-Jacobean residential quadrangles. H. L. Warren's report of November 1902 mentioned works of this era as suitable models for additions to the campus, and in March 1903 President Hazard herself asked pointedly about "Elizabethan gables" on this site. The architecture of the new dormitories that rose from Martha Pomeroy's impetus would make manifest the connection between the "Oxbridge" colleges and Wellesley, just as it would enhance Wellesley's public image.

This is not to say that Wellesley held a monopoly on the Elizabethan Revival style in the early twentieth century. Far from it. The year 1902 saw the completion of Cope & Stewardson's dormitory quadrangle at the University of Pennsylvania in Philadelphia, for example, in red-brick and white stone Elizabethan forms, while the same firm's winning design of 1899 for the new campus of Washington University in St. Louis placed a Tudor gateway motif on the administrative building at the center of a plan organized by quadrangles. In the choice of Elizabethan style for the Hazard Quad as well as, later, Tower Court, Wellesley joined a widespread contemporary movement to link academic America with the schools and great houses of late medieval-early Renaissance England.

Sarah Whitin sat in on the Board of Trustee meetings when the discussion turned to the new dormitory funded by her sister-in-law, and she could thus assure that Pomeroy's will would be honored. In fact, early in 1901, when the Pomeroy bequest was known but not yet received by the College, Whitin had "her" architect, Henry Ayling Phillips, draw up a design for a dormitory to be built with her sister-in-law's money. "Mrs. Whitin has a set of very beautiful plans,—far too beautiful, I am afraid," wrote Caroline Hazard to Horace Scudder in February of 1901. "They are done by the same man who built her charming little observatory, and are in every way most delightful, —a dining hall running up two stories with a gallery at one end of it, spacious and beautiful reception rooms, and altogether it would be an Elizabethan building unexcelled for beauty in this country. But we haven't anything like the money ... to build it. Taking this as a starting point, we may be able to cut down." In fact it became the point of departure for a four-fold scaling-up.

Phillips's drawings are unlocated. Although his design clearly influenced the final dormitories, he did not get the commission. With Pomeroy's bequest in hand by 1902, the trustees called for another limited competition to determine the design of the new residential project. In this case the competitors included Coolidge & Carlson, A. W. Longfellow, Jr., and Julius Schweinfurth, all major Boston firms. Rates had gone down since the chapel competition, for each of these entrants received just $250 although planning a larger work. The ever-expanding needs of the College, and more optimistic assessments of the monies available or procurable, were reflected in the fact that the original program envisioned not one but two dormitories to be built immediately, with two more to be added in the near future.

Henry C. Holt of the Boston firm of Wales & Holt, who occasionally taught architectural history at the College, drafted the terms of the competition. His program called for conformity to Olmsted's proposals about siting new dormitories in a quadrangle, and it clearly dictated the style of the buildings: "The design shall be an adaption to American conditions of materials, climate and convenience, of the historical style technically known as Elizabethan, [for] the definition of which [the contestant] is referred to Blomfield's 'History of Renaissance Architecture in England.'" In directing competitors to consult Reginald Blomfield's standard work of 1897, Holt was merely following the dictates of his era, an era in which the academic study of architecture resulted in buildings rich in scholarly references.

The trustees in consultation with Henry Holt awarded the commission to Julius Schweinfurth in September 1903. We do not know Coolidge & Carlson's or A. W. Longfellow's competitive projects, but Schweinfurth wisely chose a layout that closely followed Olmsted's proposal of May 27, 1903. In that "alternative sketch" four roughly L-planned buildings form a courtyard that contains formal planting and widens as it recedes from the road. The sketch envisioned entry through a gate centered between the two buildings on the road and a terrace facing the rest of the campus to the south. The schema reserved the short strokes of the Ls for servants' quarters. The demography of

DORMITORIES·WELLESLEY·COLLEGE·

the College had shifted during Caroline Hazard's presidency, from Durant's self-sufficient "calico girls" to young ladies who required domestic help.

Olmsted's proposal well describes Schweinfurth's winning layout. At each of the corners of his proposed quadrangle rises a five-story Elizabethan tower square in plan with corner turrets. These house a dining room on the first level and a reception room above. The long stroke of the L contains four stories of roughly eighty student rooms, while the short three-story stroke was originally intended for servants. The southern pair of dormitories (eventually Beebe and Shafer Halls) are set wider apart than the front pair (Pomeroy and Cazenove Halls). One would enter the formally planted courtyard through a gateway in a fence along the road; the courtyard terminated at a terrace on the south. (The gateway and fence eventually became the link between Pomeroy and Cazenove and was erected in 1919 from Schweinfurth's 1916 design.)

The winning architect also closely followed the donor's prescription about style and Henry Holt's direction as to its source. The walls of dark red brick set in white mortar are enriched by lintels, copings, parapets, quoins, and beltcourses of Indiana limestone. Green slate covers the roofs, except for

Julius Schweinfurth won the competition for the design of the Hazard Quad by following the layout suggested by Frederick Law Olmsted, Jr., using the Elizabethan style prescribed by the terms of the contest, and turning the aerial perspective of his 1903 entry over to David A. Gregg, the presumed draftsman. At this point only two dormitories were to be built, with two more to follow. This view from the north, with highway and railroad at the bottom, clearly demonstrates Wellesley under Hazard reaching out to the world beyond the campus.

95

the oxidized copper ogees of the turrets. Oriels and bays of mullioned windows animate the walls while the skyline breaks into ogee roofs and ranks of Flemish gables along the tops of the main wings. These are defining elements of Elizabethan style as found, say, at St. John's College, Cambridge, and other examples in Blomfield's and other studies available at the time of the competition.

Among the reasons why Schweinfurth won the competition might be the fact that, although an accomplished draftsman himself, he chose a brilliant delineator to present his proposal. The aerial perspective of his entry dated September 1903 was probably the work of the master perspectivist David A. Gregg of M.I.T., who drew for any number of local firms. (In his 1916 obituary of Gregg, Schweinfurth wrote that the artist "had revolutionized architectural rendering in this country, and may, in fact, be said to be the father of architectural rendering.") The terms of the Wellesley competition called for plans and elevations, and a bird's-eye perspective taken from the railroad side (Holt was well aware of the public face of this proposed complex). This perspective might have "light indications of color and shadows, without accessories." When the contestants asked Holt if they might show "roads, paths, trees, grass, and sky," he replied that such embellishment was "both necessary and desirable provided it is not overdone." Gregg's delicately colored version of Schweinfurth's design evokes simultaneously both grandeur and charm, and that the trustees and Holt found irresistible.

There is another drawing of the proposed buildings that is equally impressive. This envisions Pomeroy and what became Shafer as seen from the northwest in a roughly four-foot-wide watercolor and gouache perspective.

Since it is brightly colored it must post-date the competition, and since Schweinfurth was an accomplished watercolorist it may well be from his hand. Like the aerial perspective this view shows diaper patterning on the walls of the towers, as well as a fountain in the middle of the courtyard and other ornamental features. The handling of color emphasizes Pomeroy, as Shafer remained merely a dream at this date.

The College erected the dormitories in the Hazard Quad in sequence. Ground broke for Pomeroy and Cazenove at the end of 1903. Pomeroy opened in 1904 (with President Hazard lighting hearth fires in the hall and dining room) and Cazenove in 1905; Beebe followed in 1908 and Shafer in

Julius Schweinfurth's link between Pomeroy and Cazenove was designed in 1916 and finished in 1919. It effectively closed off the Hazard Quad from the highway and the B&A railway tracks on the north side of the campus. Above the central arch of the ground-level arcade, books and swags flank the head of Minerva, Roman goddess of intellectual and manual skills.

Each of the dormitories in the Hazard Quad had its own dining room. Pomeroy's reflects the elegance of the new Wellesley under Hazard. White starched table cloths sparkle in the rectilinear ambience. Flatware and rolled napkins in metal rings are set at every place. All is prepared for hungry students and the help to wait on them. Note the tile fireplace surround, the candelabra on the mantel, the stiff wooden chairs, and the bare incandescent bulbs spaced along the bottoms of the main girders.

1909. Not everything originally envisioned by Hazard and Schweinfurth came to pass, however. Perhaps the most unfortunate loss was the Tea House discussed by client and architect in 1905 (and apparently sketched, although no drawing is now known).

Although built and furnished over a period of years the interiors of the Quad dormitories varied one decorative approach. The main rooms, the nineteen-foot-high parlors, and the lower dining rooms below all showed exposed wooden trusses or beams, dark woodwork, tiled fireplaces with wooden surrounds, and wicker or Mission furnishings. All were characteristic of the turn-of-the-century Arts and Crafts aesthetic.

The Hazard Quadrangle architecturally raised Wellesley's visibility to the outside world. It redirected the College away from its introvert origins toward a more extrovert future. President Alice Freeman had begun the process of change, but her domestic cottages remained as remote from the world as College Hall. That outside world could now recognize something new at Wellesley. Noticing this complex in 1910 the *Boston Evening Transcript* said that "railway travelers [on the Boston & Albany line] have a glimpse of the most important buildings" of the College. The quadrangle dormitories opposite the commuter railroad themselves became a symbolic gateway to the College, and a welcoming one, unlike Hammatt Billings's barriers at East and West Lodges. The towers of Cazenove and Pomeroy flanked a triumphal passageway into a major female educational institution that now laid claim to being part of the larger society.

The buildings of the Hazard Quad are composed of red brick set in white mortar, with lintels, copings, parapets, quoins, and beltcourses of limestone. The roofs are green slate except for the copper agees topping the turrets. Oriels and mullioned window bays enrich the walls while rows of dormers animate the roofs. All this is characteristic of Elizabethan Revival design.

Despite the proposals solicited in 1902 Wellesley adopted no master plan under Caroline Hazard. Other major buildings constructed during her tenure, such as the gymnasium and the library, were said to take their cues from neighboring buildings, but in fact differed in style and, although sited according to Olmsted's recommendations, spread upon the land largely without reference to other buildings.

The construction of the gymnasium followed the move of the Boston Normal School of Gymnastics to the Wellesley campus. The school had been largely supported by its founder, philanthropist Mary Hemenway (who died in 1894), who wished to put it on a permanent basis. With her trust expiring in 1909, the trustees proposed in 1907 to give the College $100,000 for a building on condition that another $200,000 be raised to support the program. This proved difficult until Hazard herself made up some of the shortfall; nonetheless, Julius Schweinfurth's original design had to be modified to meet a reduced budget that reached $120,000, and the envisioned swimming pool did not materialize until much later. Construction of the building went forward between 1908 and 1909 on a site west of the Hazard Quad and facing Central Street. It came down in the 1980s during the transformation of the complex into the Keohane Sports Center.

The new Mary Hemenway Gymnasium at Wellesley housed the Department of Hygiene and Physical Education. For all its awkwardness as architectural composition and its isolation from the rest of the campus, it was an innovative structure in the realm of buildings devoted to exercise. One feature particularly drew the attention of the press: sixty students, under the watchful eye of a monitor, could bathe in shifts in the area beneath the large gym. Between uses the baths could be sterilized with steam.

The building took second place to no other collegiate gym of its day in the facilities it contained, but as an addition to Wellesley College architecture it left much to be desired. A "head house" containing east and west entries, a small exercise room, lecture rooms, library, and offices faced outward toward the Boston & Albany train tracks, and the gymnasium proper tailed behind it to the south. The modified Elizabethan front section sat on a plan in the shape of an angular C. Three-story walls of red brick with Indiana limestone trim rose to a top story of diapered brick patterns and a flat coping varied by roundels and crenels. On the elevations Schweinfurth framed boldly projecting segmental arches on the ground floor and tall pointed windows above between blocky piers. The critic Montgomery Schuyler had trouble

identifying the historical sources for Schweinfurth's treatment here, but in the end he thought that it would be difficult "to name any example of collegiate architecture in this country which has … more 'life' than this."

His assessment might have been different had he considered the building as a whole. The demands of the program caused Schweinfurth's design to fall into architecturally diverse shapes and scales, within two ill-matched parts. The shape and scale of the gymnasium proper answered to the need for a large open exercise space through the use of seventy-foot steel trusses. Its high pointed slate roof with ridge monitor sat above low brick walls divided by piers marking bays of a different width from those of the front building. The overall form suggested the collision of two different building types, as indeed was the case.

The building that rose coeval with the gymnasium created a different sort of confrontation. Hammatt Billings's library in College Hall overflowed with books by the late 1890s. In 1897 L. B. Godfrey, the College librarian, published the fact in the *Wellesley Magazine* (and published it again to a wider audience in an 1899 issue of the *Library Journal*), and he also proposed the erection of a new library on campus. To aid in raising funds from alumnae and others he had the well-established Boston architectural firm of Hartwell, Richardson & Driver develop a library plan, which he also published. (In the absence of any other documentation we may assume that the Hartwell office drew the plan in hopes of eventually landing the commission. Less likely, Godfrey paid their fee.) The drawing showed a symmetrical layout focused on a reading room in the shape of a forty-eight-foot-high (presumably domed and skylighted) rotunda on the model of the British Museum, the Library of Congress, and other favored precedents. Godfrey and his architects suggested yellow brick with light Cleveland sandstone trim both inside and out, fire-proof stacks, slow-burning construction for the rest of the building, and other features to the estimated cost of $200,000. Such a sum reached well beyond anything spent on buildings at the College to this date and for a while to come.

The plan and materials of the Godfrey–Hartwell proposal suggest neo-classicism, and it was a neo-classical library that Wellesley eventually erected. In 1905 the College applied for and received from Andrew Carnegie $125,000 toward the erection of the library. Carnegie, the innovative Pittsburgh steel magnate and philanthropist who believed that "A man who dies rich dies disgraced," during his lifetime dispensed what was then a staggering $350 million in gifts including $4 million for college libraries. One condition for acquiring Carnegie funds was that the College had to add an equal amount to its permanent endowment, a wise condition ensuring that the institution would continue to be financially healthy. Not until 1907 could Caroline Hazard announce the completion of that task, and in late 1908 the trustees accepted the design of the Boston architectural firm of Shepley, Rutan and Coolidge. Construction began in April 1909 and the library opened the following summer. As we shall see, it has been added to several times by the successive Shepley firms and others.

Shepley Rutan and Coolidge was founded on the deathbed of famed architect H. H. Richardson to carry on the many projects his early demise had left unfinished. The firm operated on a national scale and included, among other buildings to its credit, the plan of Stanford University (1890), the Art Institute and the Public Library in Chicago (1892), the library at Brown University (1903), and the Harvard Medical School (1903–1907). Most were built in neo-classical style. The firm exists today under the name Shepley Bulfinch Richardson and Abbott.

By the time of the firm's work at Wellesley, George Shepley was himself dead, and the most active members were George C. Shattuck and Charles Allerton Coolidge, who were both trained at M.I.T. As the most visible member of the team, Coolidge was much honored and internationally respected at the time of his death.

The library stands on a site that had been spared by the opposition of faculty, students, and alumnae when it was proposed to place the Houghton

Memorial Chapel there in the previous decade. By 1902, when Frederick Law Olmsted, Jr. recommended that the library be put near its present location, that struggle had been forgotten, and Heins & La Farge and C. Howard Walker had also placed the library there in their developmental plans. Finally, the distinguished architect and landscape designer Charles A. Platt established this as the definitive site (although that seems a small task for such an important designer).

The program called for a library to house 110,000 volumes. Shepley Rutan and Coolidge's plan formed a T with the cross arm facing north overlooking Rhododendron Hollow and housing entrance hall, offices, and English Room to the right, and five tiers of stacks to the left. On the original drawings there is an area in the basement designated as a "Draughting Room," complete with drafting tables. Arthur Rotch's idea for such a room in Farnsworth seemed to have migrated to the library, where Professor Eliza Newkirk seems to have instructed her students of architectural history in the basics of drafting. The reading room beneath a segmentally vaulted molded ceiling was in the stem of the T. The architects designed the massive Renaissance reading tables. The room remains, buried in the center of a building several times extended in recent years.

The building's structure is steel frame on load-bearing walls. When the College accepted the design in 1908 the Shepley firm estimated equal costs for either exterior limestone or brick and stone. In the end they chose limestone, they said, to harmonize with the chapel and the Farnsworth Art Building. We have heard that one before. A simple squarish shape with flat roof and flat walls except around the salient in the center of the main façade, the building's style, like that of so many buildings of the era, follows the Italian Renaissance version of classicism. The main façade rises a story and a half between a low base and a high parapet. Around the entrance in the center of a three-bay salient there occurs an armature of engaged three-quarter Ionic columns and pilasters, with bands of Greek ornament and copper details to contribute refinement. The bronze doors installed in 1911 and bearing allegories of *Sapienta* and *Caritas* (ironically, respectively a man and a woman and child) are the work of the sculptor Evelyn B. Longman (later Batchelder). The classical bronze figures flanking the entry are copies of the *Lemnian Athena* and the *Hesta Giustiniani*. The new library turned out to be the Parthenon of the Wellesley College campus, easily out-classicizing the Farnsworth Art Building and the Whitin Observatory. It was also classicism's swan song on campus.

The original section of what is now the Clapp Library (here to the left), the central block facing Rhododendron Hollow, was paid for by industrialist and philanthropist Andrew Carnegie, commissioned by President Hazard (her scallop shell graces the cornerstone), and designed by Shepley Rutan and Coolidge. It opened in 1910, the last of the important stone neo-classical buildings on campus. Copies of antique figures, the Lemnian Athena and the Hesta Giustiniani, flank the main entrance. The bronze doors installed in 1911 bear low-relief allegories of Sapienta and Caritas (ironically, a bearded man and a woman and child) by sculptor Evelyn Longman.

The Shepley firm was to design other buildings at Wellesley into the post-World War II era, but one other commission from these earlier years deserves notice here. Shepley Rutan and Coolidge designed what is now known as Lake House, a building awkwardly notched into the slope west of College Hall and built in 1912–1913 as the "Servants' Dormitory Building" to house the help who worked in its big neighbor. When the hall burned the next year the new building became a student residence.

Lake House is a long narrow block capped by a flared hip roof bristling with gabled dormers. The elevations are of dark red Flemish brickwork. The building's proportions follow the foundations of a power plant dismantled in 1903. The architect divided the long three-story-high walls into fifteen bays. The lowest windows of the principle or western façade are set in round-arched openings, those of the floor above in segmentally arched openings, those of the top floor in rectangular openings. Students enter through a fan-lighted doorway framed by a Georgianesque Federal frontispiece in the center of the façade facing the end of Lake Waban. To the left of the entry on the first floor is a grand living room warmed by a fireplace. The upper floors are bisected longitudinally by double-loaded corridors. At least half the roughly seventy-five rooms enjoy views of the forested landscape beyond the water.

Lake House, well hidden today by the Tower Court–Claflin complex and little known to all but its residents, represents a simple, handsomely detailed and finely proportioned example of that neo-Bulfinchian style that characterized Wilder Hall and many another Boston building designed in the early twentieth century. It rose after Caroline Hazard's tenure in office, but continued her expansionist policy. Her own architectural achievements, marked by her signature scallop shell, although not without some failures, make her presidency a pivotal age in the history of the campus. She brought Wellesley College into the twentieth century. Her program of expansion (including enrollment, endowment, and buildings) greatly enhanced the College's presence in the academic world and on the landscape. She scattered architectural monuments such as the Hazard Quad and the College library, but she also left unrealized her desire to create a uniform campus plan. It took a fire at College Hall to focus attention on that unfinished business. Although that fire seemed a major disaster at the time, College Hall had in fact outlived its usefulness, and its destruction made possible a comprehensive reorganization of the campus during the tenure of President Hazard's successor, Ellen Fitz Pendleton.

CHAPTER FIVE

A SECOND LANDSCAPE IMPULSE

A view across the Alexandra Botanic Garden toward Norumbega Hill, 1949

THE PROGRESSIVE EXPANSION of the College in the early decades of its history compromised the campus landscape. As seen in the preceding chapter, the siting of new buildings, changes in circulation, expanding use, and increasing student numbers threatened the landscape of the founders Henry Fowle Durant and Pauline Durant. Further pressure came from the introduction of team sports and thus for playing fields. The College's early classes had made do with a regime of indoor gym activities or outdoor walking or rowing; team sports required flat areas of grass constructed on a topography where none existed and the first fields were installed in 1896.

The changes to the landscape drew protests. In 1894 students, alumnae, and faculty formed a "Committee to Protect the Aesthetic Beauty of the College Grounds and Buildings" and lamented the erosion of the original "wild beauty of the park." The re-routing of College roads also attracted criticism for much the same reason. Two years later the committee objected to the site proposed for the new chapel on the wooded rise between Longfellow Pond and the recently constructed Music Hall (where Clapp Library now sits), an area filled with rhododendrons like the hollow to the north.

A new president, Caroline Hazard (1899–1910), promptly addressed the problems posed by the College's development. Within a few months of taking office in 1899 she ordered demolition of the large boathouse erected six years earlier on the edge of Green Beach (below Severance Green, then called College Hall Green) declaring that "the lake shore is our most beautiful possession and no building which would endanger its beauty can be placed upon it." Despite this action, Hazard was acutely aware of the College's perilous

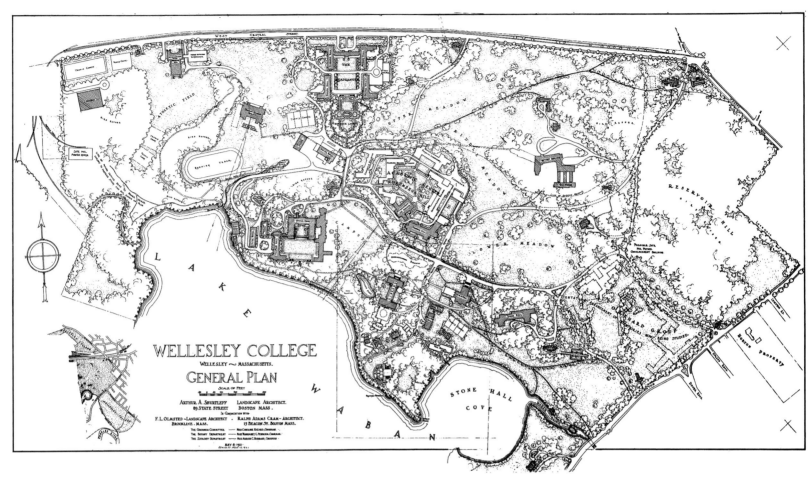

1921 Master Plan of the Wellesley campus. The forested areas are labeled "bird refuges" and are left as bare areas with trees indicated only around the circumference. For the paths and roads, by contrast, the plan provides precise detail of flanking trees. Note the ring of meadows around Norumbega Hill, in the center of the plan, and of the restriction of the name "campus" to the area known today as Severance Green.

financial position. One means of raising money was to double student enrollment. But more students meant more buildings. Unlike her predecessors, Hazard was the first to realize the necessity of an orderly planning process.

As Chapter 4 discusses, focusing on architectural implications, to provide her with ideas for expansion Hazard contacted early in 1902 three leading firms with landscape practices: Heins & La Farge of New York, C. Howard Walker of Boston, and the Olmsted Brothers of Brookline. Their ideas resulted in different outcomes for the buildings and the landscape. For the buildings, as discussed in the previous chapter, a new dormitory complex for 600 students was started in 1903 on the hill to the northwest of Norumbega, later to be named for Hazard. For the landscape the outcome was no less decisive, but it was deferred and in some respects indirect. This came about because the most influential ideas were presented primarily as a written document. It was the work of Frederick Law Olmsted, Jr. (who had assumed leadership of the firm from his ailing father in 1894) and took the form of a nineteen-page letter, dated March 24, 1902 and addressed to President Hazard. Its importance for the Wellesley landscape cannot be exaggerated. For the next fifty years the letter assumed the status of a reference document and was subjected to repeated readings and interpretations.

That Olmsted chose the written word over the drawn design may be explained by the difficulty of describing the qualities of the College landscape let alone representing them. The Durants had left no written explanation of their landscape. Although generic characterizations abounded, like the "wild beauty of the park" quoted above, these lacked analytical clarity and thus offered little guidance to the trustees when they faced decisions on the siting of new buildings or the parts of the landscape they should protect. The placement of the Chemistry Building in the Upper Meadow (now Munger Meadow) was a case in point (see page 18). To some its location in the landscape was appropriate, to others not. On what basis was one to decide? The truth was that the landscape was complex and irregular. As such it was hard to define. Yet without an understanding of its component parts discussion veered wildly. It was this absence of a guiding set of principles that Olmsted's letter filled.

His letter to President Hazard opens with a series of brilliant observations about the landscape's unique qualities. The campus comprised an "immensely significant expression of geological history" composed of an "exceedingly intricate and complex topography." This endowed the landscape with a "beauty which often attaches to the type of glaciated topography [when it is] fortunately accentuated by the distribution of trees." Three kinds of shape constituted its essence: "irregular plateaus of slightly undulating surface rounding over rapidly into steep sloping sides; second, rounded ridges and hummocks usually less high than the plateaus and showing no flat space on top; third, the mostly flat meadows between these hills." Together these features composed "a landscape not merely beautiful, but with a marked individual character not represented so far as I know on the grounds of any other college in the country."

Turning to his brief from President Hazard, Olmsted advocated the placement of buildings in harmony with the campus's existing topography. Buildings should be sited on the hilltops but in such a manner as to accentuate their topographical character. It was essential to recognize that "the plateaus are larger and are made up of two fairly distinct parts, the upper flat and the escarpment, so that a dividing line of construction which follows the edge of the flat simply recognizes a natural division and emphasizes it." Escarpment-

The northeast side of Norumbega Hill looking across the Middle Meadow (in front of the Science Center) toward Simpson Cottage (in the center of the image). Photo c. 1912

edge placement for buildings, Olmsted argued, would mean that they would follow "its curve with their length by various angles and breaks ... forming an almost continuous line with [it]." The meadows were to be left untouched.

Toward the end of his letter Olmsted addressed circulation and the grounds. For circulation he proposed a new entry to the College at the terminus of the town of Wellesley by Fiske House (a relocated domestic residence used initially as a dormitory, which was placed at the northwest tip of the Durant lands). From there the road would run by Simpson Cottage (now the infirmary), down across the Middle Meadow towards Wilder Hall (where Green Hall now sits) with a connection to the former road system at Rhododendron Hollow. For the grounds, Olmsted confined his recommendations to three practical needs: better drainage of surface water, placement of electric and telephone wires underground, and the substitution of permanent concrete footpaths with a pebble top for the wooden duckboard walks.

Olmsted's geological references and his characterization of land form touched a particular New England nerve. From the 1830s forwards, both academic and popular opinion embraced a fascination with geology and the narrative history of the land its study produced. This fascination influenced disciplines as diverse as biblical scholarship and landscape painting. Sensitivity to geology's regional character had been a prominent feature of the work of Olmsted's father, who made special efforts to incorporate geology into his park systems.

Hazard responded at first with enthusiasm to Olmsted's ideas. She sent a copy of his letter to the other two firms submitting proposals. The response of one, Heins & La Farge, survives and their reaction throws light on the originality of Olmsted's letter and the difficulties conventional landscape architects (for Heins & La Farge worked both as architects and landscape architects) had in understanding it. Directly contradicting Olmsted's naturalistic approach, Heins & La Farge recommended a campus composed of a series of axially linked rectangular quadrangles with the centers filled with formal gardens. An unambiguous priority should be given to architecture *over* landscape and they urged that Wellesley should be "devoted to the purpose of a great college and not be solely a public park." Such bluntly phrased contrary views derived, as already noted, from the City Beautiful movement prompted by the 1893 World's Columbian Exposition in Chicago. With sufficent will, and money, they could be imposed regardless of the intrinsic qualities of the site. To Heins & La Farge the "genius of the place" counted for little; their design, imposed regardless of site, would give Wellesley the formal "look" that they deemed appropriate to a college.

When Hazard subseqently approved construction at the Quad that would later take her name, Olmsted withdrew his services; he had become disaffected by the scale of the undertaking and to some extent by the site (even though his firm had reluctantly endorsed it). His withdrawal did little to affect the ultimate influence of his letter, however. Like prophecy its value lay at a distance. Within fifteen years, after the great fire of 1914, Olmsted's letter was to chart the decisions that have given Wellesley its particular form into the present day. Even before the fire, Olmsted's letter was by no means filed away and forgotten. It was shown to architects called in by the College for different projects and references to it, or repetitions of its language, surface in their reports and recommendations.

The massive rebuilding following the great fire that consumed College Hall in March 1914 resulted in a new vision of both architecture and landscape at Wellesley, as Helen Lefkowitz Horowitz explains in *Alma Mater*. It culminated in the construction of the College's new Academic Center, today called the Academic Quad, on Norumbega Hill. The hill had been used for dormitories since the 1880s and had been seen by everyone, including Olmsted, as continuing that function. Although Olmsted's views on this and on other matters to do with architecture were not taken up, when it came to the development of Norumbega Hill his recommendations ultimately prevailed. His 1902 letter to Caroline Hazard had argued that architecture should adjust to the landscape, be restricted to the hills, and be positioned in broken irregular forms on the rim of the escarpments. All these recommendations were followed by the trustees. Similarly, Olmsted's concepts determined the reordering of the landscape around the proposed Academic Center that now became the heart of the College. The new center was to be land-surrounded, unlike College Hall, which had overlooked Lake Waban with distant prospects seen over the flat expanse of water. Irregular grass-covered valleys were to frame the new buildings, which were to perch on the escarpment of the Norumbega hilltop whose sides were tree-shrouded.

The decision to relocate the College's academic buildings on Norumbega Hill emerged hesitantly. The two leading architectural firms employed by the Board of Trustees to advise on the new complex—Coolidge

& Carlson of Boston and Day & Klauder of Philadelphia—began by recommending construction in the meadows. Coolidge & Carlson favored the Middle Meadow (in front of the present-day Science Center; see page 144), Day & Klauder the Upper Meadow (now Munger Meadow). Each showed schemes containing eight and more buildings (a mix of science buildings, dormitories, administrative, and alumnae buildings), all previously under one roof in College Hall, to be arranged in Beaux-Arts symmetry with straight linked pathways, tree-lined allées, and aligned views.

The trustees weighed both proposals seriously. Their uncertainty had the effect of uniting the opposition of two powerful groups at the College, the alumnae and the faculty. Both emerged in the post-fire period as vocal advocates for Olmsted's views on the organization of the campus. Faculty memoranda to the Board of Trustees voiced three axiomatic principles. The grounds should present a unified landscape-architectural scheme under one supervising mind; they should dominate the architecture "which should be made to fit the land as if it grew out of it"; and the woodlands, which constituted a particular character of the grounds, should be divided into three categories. For the last these were described as one "to be set apart as permanent wild woods," a second "as cultivated wooded park," and a third "as in time to be cut down and built upon." Alumnae views supported the faculty. The October 1916 *Wellesley Alumnae Quarterly* urged protection of the shape of the hills, the texture and extent of the woodlands, and invoked the responsibility to perpetuate "the same regard for the trees, the hills, and the natural beauties of Wellesley which characterized Mr. and Mrs. Durant." Using these criteria the magazine rejected Day & Klauder's proposal because "it would not conform to the natural slopes of the grounds. On the contrary they seem to crash the hills and slopes into an urban dead level."

Resolution of the impasse between the faculty and alumnae on the one side, and the design consultants and trustees on the other, came from the appointment early in 1916 of a supervising architect, Ralph Adams Cram. Although Cram is usually thought of in reference to architecture, his influence on the Wellesley landscape was just as important as his role in guiding its architectural development. Cram grasped immediately, even intuitively, the qualities of land form enunciated by Olmsted. His first report to the trustees written a matter of days after his appointment spoke of "the natural beauty of the entire tract" and urged "the most conservative policy in the matter of changing grades, removing trees, and altering the already fixed nature of the landscape." He continued: "The essence of the territory is extreme and picturesque irregularity, with beautiful woods, groves and isolated trees. This quality should be preserved; nothing should be done towards attaining an artificial irregularity either in grades or forestrying.... [T]he terrain should largely determine the placing and alignment of buildings, wherever the orientation shall permit, regardless of academic regularity, while every care should be taken to preserve good groves, clumps of trees, and even single trees when these are notably fine."

Cram urged the trustees to establish the principle "that the unique topographical and landscape qualities of the grounds must determine not only the general design but the disposition, alignment, and composition of the buildings; that formalized arrangements at the expense of the topography should scrupulously be avoided; and that the buildings and groups should grow out of their sites and environment, not impose themselves on them; and that the great and beautiful features of hills, valleys, meadows, groves, and winding roads should be preserved inviolate, and as a setting for architecture akin to them, not rebellious against them."

Cram's arrival at the College voided the prospect of a formalized Beaux-Arts campus. Instead, Wellesley found in Cram the guiding hand to shape development in a manner explicitly connected to a past identified with its founders, the Durants. By defining the qualities of the landscape, first Olmsted and then Cram steered Wellesley to an understanding of the interrelation of topography and landscape and, in turn, to their synthesis with architecture.

To structure the decisions on the landscape the trustees established a separate committee to oversee the design and maintenance of the College grounds. To chair it they turned to former President Caroline Hazard. It was she who had commissioned Olmsted to provide her with planning ideas that resulted in his 1902 letter. With characteristic style and energy Hazard took charge of the process; she selected the landscape architect, directed planning matters, and undertook on-site decisions.

For the landscape architect, Hazard looked to Arthur Shurtleff, one of the leading members of the profession who had begun his career in Olmsted's office. Work started on a master plan in December 1919, drawing upon a wide constituency consisting of several committees and departments at the College. At a meeting on December 2, 1919, Arthur Shurtleff could refer to "the many

WELLESLEY COLLEGE

WELLESLEY ~ MASSACHUSETTS.

GENERAL PLAN

SCALE OF FEET

50 0   50   100   200   300   400

ARTHUR A. SHURTLEFF   LANDSCAPE ARCHITECT.
89 STATE STREET   BOSTON MASS.

IN CONSULTATION WITH

F. L. OLMSTED ~ LANDSCAPE ARCHITECT · RALPH ADAMS CRAM ~ ARCHITECT.
BROOKLINE · MASS.   15 BEACON ST. BOSTON MASS.

THE GROUNDS COMMITTEE —— MISS CAROLINE HAZARD, CHAIRMAN.
THE BOTANY DEPARTMENT —— MISS MARGARET C. FERGUSON, CHAIRMAN.
THE ZOOLOGY DEPARTMENT —— MISS MARIAN C. HUBBARD, CHAIRMAN ·

MAY · 2 · 1921 ·
REVISED TO NOV. 15, 1921.

The title plate for the 1921 Master Plan. Shurtleff and Olmsted were the two leading landscape architects in the country, Cram the pre-eminent Collegiate Gothic designer and planner. A further mark of the importance accorded the landscape at this period is the chair of the Grounds Committee, Caroline Hazard, the former president of the College who returned from retirement to undertake this responsibility.

points made by President Pendleton, Treasurer Morse, Mssrs. Cram, Klauder, Olmsted, Day, Coolidge and Carlson, Woods and Austin, together with Misses Kingsbury, Sherwin, Hazard, Stockwell, Conant, and Farlow." The last group were trustees and toward the end of the same document Shurtleff emphasized Hazard's role in the formation of the ideas. In addition, it is clear that Hazard reveled not only in taking broad policy decisions but in making on-site decisions. A paragraph in the correspondence of Shurtleff to Olmsted dated December 16, 1920, records the circumstances governing the "irregular planting" of twelve oaks between Longfellow Pond and Lake Waban and notes that their location was "determined on the ground by Miss Pendleton, Miss Hazard, and myself." That the two most powerful women at Wellesley and the leading landscape architect in the nation should undertake this responsibility says volumes about the supreme regard for the landscape at the top levels of the College at this time.

The resulting master plan took the committee three years to complete. Submitted in May 1921 (and revised in November of the same year), it is signed by Arthur Shurtleff "Landscape Architect," Frederick Law Olmsted, Jr. "Landscape Architect," and Ralph Adams Cram "Architect." Working relations between all three were close, with oversight Cram's responsibility. Also listed on the title block were Miss Caroline Hazard, Miss Margaret C. Ferguson (botany department), and Miss Marian C. Hubbard (zoology department). Drawn with considerable detail (it even included a number of

The Class of 1916 gates of the Fiske Gateway were constructed 1922–1923 and designed by Putnam & Chandler. The gateway surmounted by American eagles formed the new main entrance to the College for forty years, and was displaced only in the early 1960s when the entrance was moved to the west of the Hazard Quad.

individual trees), the plan depicted contours; specified footpaths, streams, and ponds; and gave explicit form to woodlands, which were labeled "bird refuges." It also provided ideas on the sites of future buildings.

One immediate need concerned a new entrance and road system for the College, an idea advocated by Olmsted in 1902. The East Lodge entrance had been chosen in 1868 because it seemed as if Route 16 would develop into the town's main thoroughfare. The popularity of the Boston & Albany railway line and the tramway that ran parallel to it along Route 135, the Natick Road, led to its becoming the axis of commerce and development. In fact, the new Hazard Quadrangle had been oriented towards this roadway. Reflecting the reality of growth, it was now proposed that the College's entry and circulation system commence at the end of the town at the Fiske Gateway. From there the College road was to pass by Simpson Cottage, and then cut across the Middle Meadow to approach Green Hall from the east, which was planned to provide a suitable entry façade. This new roadway was built in 1923 and served the College until 1961.

To accent the new town-gown boundary, a monumental gateway was conceived displacing the former East Lodge with its park-guardian character. Symbolic as much as serviceable, the Fiske Gateway also matched academic fashion of the era. Between 1905 and 1920 many colleges and universities were constructing impressive gateways to their campuses (Bowdoin, Harvard, Smith, Mount Holyoke, Vassar, and Williams, for example), which they often

Middle Meadow (now the Science Center meadow) in 1919. Old Stone dormitory is visible on the left (it burned down in 1927), and the Houghton Memorial Chapel. Duckboard walks were still in use, as were overhead utilities; work to phase out both had begun toward the end of Caroline Hazard's presidency.

The original roadway of the College can still be seen; it ran in front of the chapel with the meadow extending to its full intended width. For today's appearance compare with a similar view shown on page 271.

Arthur Shurtleff's garden scheme, never built, was intended to complete the south side of the Hazard Quadrangle. Completely out of step with the landscape of the College, the garden's elaborate parterres, balustraded terracing and walkways, and fountains would have provided a setting for genteel strolling and interaction in tune with the lifestyle of the Hazard Quad dormitories, with their built-in servants' quarters.

fenced in as well. If gateway and fence expressed seclusion and withdrawal from urban involvement, they also affirmed status. Wellesley's gateway, provided by the Class of 1916, displayed a classicizing design by the Boston firm of Putman & Chandler. Built of sandstone, a material unused at the College before (or since), it featured a motor entrance framed by eagle-topped pylons with flanking pedestrian gateways. Gates were intended, and the architects envisioned a magnificent baroque pair in iron at the center, which the Class of 1916 could not afford.

More significant was the 1921 Master Plan's formalization of an arc of three meadows on the east, north, and west sides of Norumbega Hill. These were preexisting, but the plan sanctified them as the distinctive structuring device of the new campus. They provided a critical framework for the new Norumbega Hill-centered College. Equally important, they affirmed the variety and irregularity critical to the landscape, thereby projecting a unique character at the heart of the campus that was different in kind from that of men's colleges. From Wellesley College's beginning the meadows had signified biodiversity and recalled a grasslands imagery. Now they also evoked an unformalized freedom, a quality of particular significance in a period epitomized by the empowerment of women (the suffrage movement had finally secured women's right to the vote in 1920).

Not everything the plan proposed got done. One feature of startling incongruence was an elaborate formal garden intended to complete the south, or open, side of the Hazard Quad. This bizarre component was Shurtleff's particular project, a holdover from an earlier scheme that can be seen first on Day & Klauder's 1916 West Meadow plan, where Shurtleff is listed as "landscape architect" on the title block. The later version of this garden is known through a signed, powerful forty-inch-high rendering. Notations indicate the scheme (to be located where Munger Meadow stands today) went through six stages in the late summer of 1920 and suggest patrons intent on imminent implementation, most likely the Severances, who had earlier paid for flower beds in the Quad itself as a memorial to their daughter, Alexandra.

Keyed to the architecture of the Quad, the garden was set out as a series of terraces and linked to the formal arrangement envisaged for the Quad itself by its architect, Julius Schweinfurth (whose drawings show a central fountain with symmetrical allées of ornamental fruit trees running the length of the north and south sides). Shurtleff's design relates to garden schemes originating in France and Italy, and popularized in the United States in the estate work of Charles Platt. Intended as a garden for strolling and social interaction, it complemented the students' residential life eased by servants. Different from anything else at the College, Shurtleff's scheme would have been financially ruinous to maintain. It reflected his predisposition for bold geometric compositions (he constructed similar schemes in Franklin Park in the mid-1920s and at Colonial Williamsburg, where he held responsibility for the landscape) as well as his preconceptions about Wellesley and student life.

The support of the Severances had earlier been gained by the botany department; Coolidge & Carlson's East Meadow plan of 1914 (page 141) shows a botanic garden on a diagonal in the northwest of their plan. After a further courtship of seven years, the botanists persuaded Mrs. Severance to fund a twenty-two-acre botanic garden on a land parcel running north from the Quad to the Fiske Gate (labeled on the 1921 Master Plan as the Upper Meadow).

The development should be seen as part of larger plans for this area of the campus. Cram had urged development of the hillside opposite Norumbega (where the Science Center now stands) as the site for the botanic garden. As a first step in 1922 new greenhouses had been constructed behind what is now Sage; Mrs. Durant's greenhouse on the east side of the College (see page 7) had deteriorated to unsafeness.

The traditional arrangement for a botanic garden was formal, and as such ideal for the comparison of related species, but Wellesley's was modeled on a picturesque scheme like that planted with success by Olmsted senior and Francis Sargent at Harvard's Arnold Arboretum (part of the Emerald Necklace, Olmsted's seven-mile-long park system extending from the Boston Public Garden to Franklin Park). Early designs for the Alexandra Botanic Garden include one by Shurtleff. He proposed a unifying axis running from the town to the base of Munger with a central circular pool, formal flower beds, and informally massed shrubs. Like his Hazard Quad scheme, this design was quietly shelved. In the end Professor Helen Davis '12, a member of the botany department, set out the garden. A botany major, Davis had been a student of Henry Saxton Adams, who had joined the department in 1903 and supplemented a decade of teaching with the design of campus plantings. Davis had gone on to do graduate work in landscape architecture, following in the footsteps of other women pioneers in landscape design such as Ellen Shipman, Beatrix Farrand, or somewhat later, Margaret Winters '28.

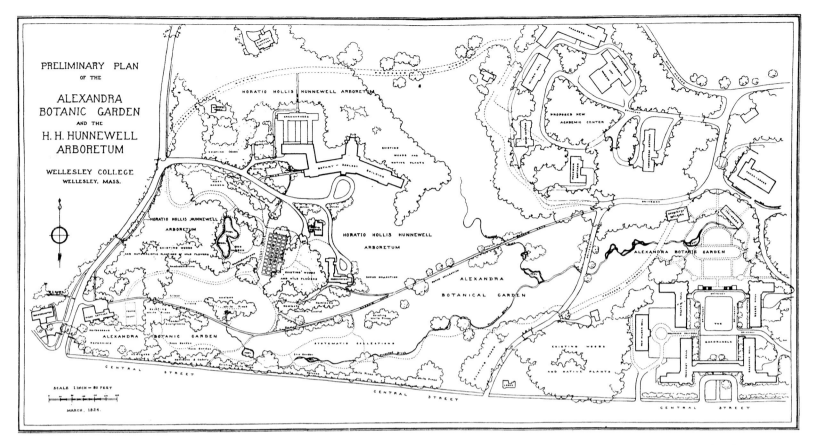

In place of Shurtleff's geometry, Davis produced an irregular naturalistic design. It was held together by a 900-foot serpentine brook winding more or less east to west. Characterized as the "Silver Thread," the diminutive stream originated in an electric-pumped miniature waterfall on the north slope of the arboretum, was crossed by small bridges, widened at intervals into settling pools, wound its way westward edged by water-loving plants, and terminated in a pond (Paramecium Pond) planted with waterlilies and featuring a central island with weeping willows and silver birch. The entire scheme was wildly unsuited to the sand and gravel topography of the site. Following a number of failures, resort was made by the builders to a concrete bed for the brook, pools, and pond.

Added to the Alexandra Botanic Garden in 1923 was an adjacent ten-acre tract designated as the Hunnewell Arboretum, the gift of Isabella Hunnewell Shaw. It was developed in a similiar style as the botanic garden with woodland glades for a rhododendron and azalea collection, a concrete-bottomed pond, and a rock garden complete with a grotto moistened by pipes to suggest sweating rocks. In keeping with their academic character, both the Alexandra Botanic Garden and Hunnewell Arboretum were placed under the control of the Department of Botany with a separate grounds crew.

The Helen Davis '12 plan for the Alexandra Botanic Garden substituted a picturesque design for the more formal plan drawn by Shurtleff. The Silver Thread stream rises against the bank on the lower left; it terminates in a smaller Paramecian Pond than the one constructed and was planned to extend across Munger Meadow. Shurtleff's proposed formal garden for the Hazard Quad is shown in dotted outline.

The Alexandra Botanic Garden and the Hunnewell Arboretum do not appear on the 1921 Master Plan. They were add-ons and drew heavily on the English picturesque. The grotto, miniature waterfall, serpentine stream and crossing bridges, the settling pools and terminating pond with island and waterlilies, and the irregular plantings all quote eighteenth-century models. These were known by travel to Miss Davis. Just as plausibly they reflect the influence of the leading scholar of this landscape type, Elizabeth Manwaring '02, professor of English at Wellesley, and a frequent lecturer on the romantic garden for the botany department. Manwaring's *The Italian Landscape in Eighteenth Century England* (1925) remained the standard treatment of the subject for nearly fifty years.

The concept of the Alexandra Botanic Garden and the form given it were without precedent at the College. Turning nature into a classroom, like Davis's historicizing design, stamped a character on this area unlike any other on the campus. The impact of these ideas is easily grasped through a comparison of the area in 1904 (see page 18), before work on the garden had been imagined, with the same area forty years later.

Although Wellesley College overlooked Shurtleff in the design of the botanic garden, he served as Wellesley's supervising landscape architect for twenty years. In his autobiography he claimed credit for the siting of the Student–Alumnae Building (1923), the design of the Hay Outdoor Theater (1936), the stone bridge constructed over the eastern outlet of Lake Waban (given by alumnae to allow President Pendleton to walk more expeditiously to chapel each morning), and planting schemes at the College involving "literally hundreds of minor matters scattered throughout decades."

The 1921 Master Plan served the College until after World War II, determining building placement when expansion demanded, controlling circulation, and maintaining the balance more or less between wooded hillside and pastoral meadow. Tensions surfaced nonetheless, some the consequence of technology. Management of the meadows and grass-covered areas became easier with the appearance of the motorized mower (invented in 1919 in Detroit). Its implementation at the College had unforeseen consequences: the smooth shearing of the mower with its aesthetic of evenness blurred the distinction between meadow and lawn, which led to the homogenization and standardization of the grounds. Alumnae were quick to spot the change. They decried the loss of variety, lamented the vanishing wildflowers, and criticized the

The Silver Thread stream of the Alexandra Botanic Garden runs east to west along a concrete-bottomed serpentine channel into Paramecian Pond.

Paramecian Pond was originally
constructed as the largest of the settling
pools connected to the "Silver Thread"
and was intended to continue down to
the lake (see plan on page 123) before
the new road causeway sealed what is
now Munger Meadow. The pond's
form and surrounds conjure a strongly
impressionistic garden sense different in
character from the rest of the campus.

disappearance of the generally "rougher character" of the landscape that they remembered. To them the landscape was becoming progressively suburbanized, a frequent criticism that appears in the alumnae magazine beginning in the late 1920s and '30s.

Looking backward to the 1921 Master Plan it is easy to take its accomplishments for granted. Our familiarity with the College landscape can lull us into believing it has always been thus. The plan promoted the principles governing the relation of architecture to landscape, a synthesis of built form and land form equalled only in the early development of the United States Military Academy at West Point, likewise orchestrated by Cram and Olmsted. For the landscape as such, the plan's great contribution to Wellesley lay not simply in the articulation of the Durants' vision as voiced by Olmsted and embraced by Cram. It gave form as well to a new land-oriented campus centered on Norumbega Hill, thereby providing at the heart of the campus a profoundly different image than that of the old lake-facing College Hall. Born out of the desire to preserve the land's topographical complexity and diversity, the plan's conceptualization of the meadows as the major structuring device at the heart of Wellesley created an image of nature and the institution that asserted the College's unique character.

CHAPTER SIX

THE GREAT FIRE AND AFTERMATH

A temporary administration and classroom building was constructed of plywood in fifteen days after the fire that destroyed College Hall. Used from 1914 until 1932, when Green Hall was finished, it was nicknamed the Hen Coop. The old Stone Hall dormitory that burned in 1927 is seen to the left of the Houghton Memorial Chapel. This photo was taken on May Day 1926; President Pendleton is standing on the steps of Founders on the right.

IN THE EARLY HOURS of March 17, 1914, a fire broke out in College Hall. Fuelled by the building's cavernous open corridors and flue-like centers, it burned uncontrollably for four hours. By dawn Henry and Pauline Durant's huge and expensively detailed building lay a smoldering wreck. Thanks to the College practice of fire drills the 280 resident students and 12 faculty evacuated the giant structure without a single injury. Rapidly joined by other students and townspeople, they stood on the College Hall Green to witness the ferocious crackle of the flames and the muffled roar of collapsing floors.

The challenges posed to Wellesley by the fire were unprecedented. Studies made in the days following the blaze showed the scale of the problem facing the Board of Trustees. To accommodate the functions lost in College Hall seven large buildings would be required: three dormitories, two science buildings (for "laboratories, collections and museums"), a liberal arts building (for classrooms, "recitation rooms" and offices), and an administration building. Estimates for the work totaled $2 million (close to $100 million in today's values reckoning a cost of $14 million per building), more than the total endowment of the College. As an interim solution to allow for classes to function, a large plywood administration and classroom building was erected in fifteen working days on Chapel Green, and quickly nicknamed the Hen Coop. The resulting shortfall in dormitory space is revealed in a survey taken in the late summer of 1914; of the 1,452 students at the College, 53 were living with their parents in Wellesley or adjoining towns, 773 resided on campus, and 626 in the Wellesley village.

The College's response to the catastrophe represented by the fire falls into two distinct phases. The first phase extending from 1914 to 1916, and the subject of this chapter, was marked by the construction of three new dormitories to provide accommodations for the students whose rooms the fire had destroyed and by strong argument over the location and style of the other four buildings. The latter posed by far the bigger problem. The two science buildings, liberal arts building, and administration building were to form, in effect, a new center for the College. Within a few months the trustees found themselves in conflict not only with one another but with their faculty and the alumnae of the College. The powerful women who formed the latter groups and who now ran Wellesley and who were to serve as client and to a large extent as patron of the new work asserted the need for a new style and type of building that embodied an institutional image different in kind from that conceived by the Durants. An earlier history of the alliance of faculty and alumnae may be recalled; in the 1890s the same group had united to oppose the siting of the Houghton Memorial Chapel.

The argument mounted by the faculty and alumnae focused on the appointment of architects and particularly of a supervising architect to monitor the new work. It carried widespread implications. With only a changed vote or two on the part of the Board of Trustees and a different process, the rebuilt Wellesley might easily have resembled M.I.T. Developed just a year before Wellesley's great fire, M.I.T. had been laid out according to principles of the Ecole des Beaux-Arts. Symmetrically grouped buildings constructed of an off-white limestone were arrayed along controlled axes to focus on a central building crowned by a dome. That Wellesley avoided this, or similar models like McKim, Mead and White's Columbia University or those adopted at many other institutions, reveals much about the College. Unlike most colleges where executive power was jealously tied to the top levels of the institution, Wellesley had evolved a distinctive decision-making process that digested dissent as well as allowed new ideas to percolate from the bottom up.

Credit for the decisions on the buildings and landscape is owing in good part to the prodigious skills of Ellen Fitz Pendleton 1886, president of the College from 1910 to 1936. One of the most unsung of Wellesley's presidents in the present day, her twenty-six years in office (which she relinquished at the age of seventy-two after the longest service of any of the College's presidents) saw two devastating fires (College Hall 1914, Stone Hall 1927), the construction of twelve major buildings, the reorganization of the landscape, numerous smaller building undertakings, the implementation of a new circulation and entrance system, significant improvement of the College's finances, and curriculum innovation. Pendleton had entered Wellesley as a first-year student in 1882, and following graduation returned in 1887 to join the mathematics department, teaching as well some Latin and Greek. Granted a special leave of absence "to pursue advanced mathematical studies" at Newnham College, Cambridge, she returned two years later and rose steadily within the College leadership. In 1901 President Caroline Hazard appointed Pendleton assistant to the secretary to the Board of Trustees (the position held by Pauline Durant) and later that same year elevated her to dean of the College. During Hazard's illness in 1905–1906 Pendleton served as interim president, and when Hazard retired in 1910 she assumed the presidency, the first alumna to hold the position.

Even before the fire, the need for more dormitory accommodation and enlarged science buildings was recognized, as too was the unsuitability of College Hall to provide for them. In 1912 the architects of the recently finished College Library—Shepley Rutan and Coolidge—were asked to submit a design for a large new dormitory complex for 600 students. Known as the Orchard group, the dormitories would have repeated on the east side of the campus the large-scale quadrangular design just used for the Hazard Quad on the west. Although the trustees turned to Shepley immediately following the fire for the temporary administration building, thereafter the firm fell out of favor. By May 1914 another Boston firm, Coolidge & Carlson (the Coolidge in the firm's name was no relation to the Coolidge in Shepley's), replaced them.

The destruction of College Hall provided the trustees with convincing proof of the disadvantages of housing so many of Wellesley's needs in a single building. Aside from this practical reason, however, there was a shift in the image of the College that the rebuilding gave shape to, as Helen Lefkowitz Horowitz was the first to recognize. The Durants' mammoth building expressed a monolithic, centralized control of education in all its many aspects. Within a few years of College Hall's opening the process of deconstructing this ideal had started. The fire's aftermath offered a new model of organization, more federal in character, of separate if not quite equal parts. Administration facilities, classrooms, and science buildings were to be developed separately from dormitories. Only the last would be rebuilt on the College Hall site.

Within twelve weeks of the fire the College received a gift of $250,000 toward the dormitory reconstruction with another $200,000 promised to complete it. The donor who at first insisted on anonymity turned out to be Ellen James, the wife of a New York businessman and philanthropist with no

President Ellen Fitz Pendleton 1886 in 1912, two years into her twenty-six-year tenure

Viewed from the south with Claflin dormitory on the left, Tower Court was constructed 1914–1915 by Coolidge & Carlson.

connection to the College, who had read of the fire and whose interest had been courted by a powerful trustee, Louise McCoy North '79. Mrs. James's gift came with several strings attached. The new building was to be fireproof, restricted to seniors, and "Gothic in style," and was to take a U-shaped form opening to Lake Waban (instead of the linear composition of College Hall). Its interior was to resemble College Hall by providing rooms for distinguished guests and visiting professors, and space for "formal and dignified social events and celebrations." Last but not least, Mrs. James indicated the wish for Coolidge & Carlson to serve as architects.

That firm's design took shape over the summer of 1914. It showed a complex of three dormitories: a central U-shaped building (Tower Court), and two somewhat smaller buildings, the west dormitory (later named Claflin) and east dormitory (Severance), each shown as parallel to Tower Court's side wings. For Tower Court the architects proposed a stocky, south-facing building, six stories high in the center and four on the sides projecting toward the lake. Placed about one hundred feet to the north of Old College Hall, Tower Court sits squarely on the center of the hill. Some of the building's heavy massing is moderated by stone gables and dormers, with courses of limestone (increasing in frequency as the building rises) enlivening the upper walls of brick. Windows are outlined in an artificial aggregate limestone and the roofline is punctuated by ventilating turrets, small towers, and tracery cresting.

The entrance of Tower Court lay on the north, like College Hall, but since the building was sited farther back than its predecessor, on the hill's downward slope, what is the basement story on the Quad side (and therefore invisible) appears as a full independent story to the entering student. To alleviate the formidable massing posed by this arrangement, the façade was broken into three parts, the center tower-like block pulled forward and faced in masonry with late Gothic relief carving, and the side wings lower in height and of plain brick. The centrally positioned dining room provides the base for the Great Hall, which in turn carries four floors of dormitory rooms. This organization meant dual entries, one on either side of the tower for each dormitory. Neither was given much prominence, a feature deemed problematic three years later when to correct this flaw a small-scaled porte-cochère was constructed for the west entrance only, topped by an apartment for distinguished visitors. To lessen the asymmetry of this arrangement, the porte-cochère was swung somewhat oddly to the west.

The imposing south façade of Tower Court is the one always photographed and provides a clear reading of the building with its high-rising center and lower wings. They enclose a stone-paved courtyard, screened on the sides with balustrades and with a central staircase leading to a spacious rectangular lawn running the full width of the building. Both courtyard and lawn are framed by neighboring buildings bordered by straight sidewalks while the south, or lake side, is screened by trees except for a panoramic vista over the lake opening on axis. The space conveys a distinctly proprietorial feeling, one of reserve and separation from the rest of the campus. Like Schweinfurth's Hazard Quad and in much the same spirit, Tower Court gives its residents a smoothed, regular, lawn-dominated, sunlit, enclosed space. As such it differed in character from the landscape enjoyed by the residents of Norumbega, Stone, or Simpson Cottages, which was marked by irregular porous boundaries, a canopy formed by trees, curving walks, and assymmetrically planted trees. The ambience of Tower Court evokes the social world of estates; appropriately, its landscape was finished some thirty years later by Fletcher Steele, the most accomplished and creative landscape architect and estate designer in the period 1930 to 1950. Steele provided a central focus, the spring flowering ornamental cherry trees, and skillfully emphasized the southern boundaries with graded plantings.

Dominating Tower's Court's interior, at its center, lay the Great Hall, an imposing, formal two-storied space, flat-ceilinged, and lit by high English Perpendicular windows toward the south and north. A vast fireplace with a carved and painted inscription in the form of a fifteenth-century manuscript page records the donor's gift. The space is entered from either side under overhanging carved-timber galleries and approached up flights of stairs, giving it a stage-like, formal, walk-through character. These qualities skillfully referred back to the great "Centre" at the heart of College Hall (described in Chapter 2). The Great Hall of Tower Court was likewise intended to provide "a suitable space for the more formal and dignified social events and celebrations connected with the College," in the word of the James gift. Smaller lounges on either side of the Great Hall served the students' everyday use, and as reception areas for gentleman callers. To complete the scheme Mrs. James contributed an extra $20,000 for furnishings, a special interest of hers. Magnificent Boston Arts and Crafts oak settles, refectory tables, and carved chairs were supplied by the William Ross Company of Cambridge, many hand-crafted by Johannes Kirschmeyer, a German emigré greatly in demand

*Completed in the 1950s by Fletcher
Steele, the Tower Court garden with
its open lawns and emphatic central
focus is memorable for its scale
and sense of privacy.*

Interior of the Great Hall in Tower Court c. 1920 (furniture by Johannes Kirschmeyer). The inscription over the fireplace that records the donor's gift was added two years after the building opened, replacing the carved seal of the College planned by the architects. It reads: With honor and gratitude, Wellesley College cherishes the name of Ellen Stebbins James whose sympathy with the ideals of the Founders of the College and generous interest in the high tasks of scholarship are expressed in enduring form in the gift of this building for the service of learning and the greater glory of God.

for ecclesiastical commissions. The andirons, standing lamps, and sconces were rendered in wrought iron, and the elevator doors for the side dormitories beautifully decorated with hammered bronze ornament.

The ambition of Great Hall was never fully realized. It had been conceived out of nostalgia for what had disappeared in the fire. Deprived of its intended public character when the hill was designated for dormitory use only, with other functions removed elsewhere, the space attempts to recall the grandeur of College Hall while expressing the social ambitions of the so-called gilded age. Notwithstanding its continuing use on occasion for College social functions, Great Hall retains a formal character not quite fitting into either dormitory or institutional life.

For the buildings replacing the lost classroom and administration spaces, Coolidge & Carlson proposed a site in the Middle Meadow to the east of Norumbega Hill (in front of the present Science Center). It was to be more or less equidistant from Tower Court, the Hazard Quadrangle, and the proposed Orchard dormitory group. The plan of what was to become Wellesley's new "Academic Center" (today's Academic Quad) is organized in keeping with Beaux-Arts principles. Buildings for science, administration, and the humanities are aligned along geometric axes, the main one running north-south, with side buildings disposed symmetrically along a formal grass-covered and tree-lined center. An alternate scheme was also considered that ran east to west with much the same disposition of buildings. In both schemes Coolidge & Carlson showed a botanic garden at the northwest corner, developed at a diagonal and taking the form of a stretched oval. The title plate on both plans identifies this feature as the work of the landscape architect, Arthur Shurtleff.

The Middle Meadow scheme remained under discussion in the fall of 1914. Dissent soon surfaced. The first stirrings focused on the placement of the Academic Center: a memo on October 27 from the Department of Art to the Board of Trustees addressed this issue. Conceding that the meadow offered a central location (in view of the proposed Orchard group), it nonetheless identified an alternative site as superior. This was Norumbega Hill. It is easy to see why it had not been considered before. With four dormitories (three clapboard cottages and the recently constructed Federal brick Wilder Hall) and the limestone Farnsworth Art Building, Norumbega seemed not merely built over but clearly typed as a residential area. It had been accepted as such by consulting architects, as well as landscape architect

Frederick Law Olmsted, Jr., for the preceding twenty years. Furthermore, the prospect of tearing down these buildings, some just a decade old and all functioning well, struck many as a gratuitous magnification of the College's fire-ravaged woes. Despite this, the art department championed the site as "unsurpassed in any college in the country" on account of its "natural beauty of contour and slope" and the "magnificence" its summit offered the proposed buildings. Furthermore, Norumbega's adjacency to College Hall Hill provided for the continuation of "a combined social and intellectual center which would still call faculty, students, alumnae and visitors to this traditional site." To further enhance this, the art department suggested terracing the western slope of College Hall Hill below Lake House to provide for an outdoor theater and with the terracing continued along the northern side "around to Shakespeare House."

As a means of deciding the issues involved in these proposals, the Department of Art urged the trustees in its memo to appoint a supervising architect. He should be a "man of vision," a "specialist in collegiate work," skilled in working with other firms of architects and landscape architects who would execute the work itself. The memo pointed out that this procedure had been adopted at "Princeton and other universities in this country with signal success." It ended by asserting that "the best man in the field would welcome the chance" to assume this role. No names were given, although everyone must have known that they referred to the controversial Ralph Adams Cram, whose charisma, outspoken views on social issues, and radical espousal of Gothic taste made him a figure of suspicion to some trustees. The Department of Art further outlined the principles that should govern the new work, arguing for a unified landscape-architectural scheme under one supervising hand, and declaring that "the Wellesley grounds ought to dominate the architecture which should be made to fit the land as if it grew out of it."

The last point was a barely veiled criticism of Coolidge & Carlson's Tower Court on which preliminary site work was about to begin. Such contrary views about the new building placed the trustees in an awkward position with regard to the donor, Ellen James. Her good will was as essential as it was tenuous. The College could not rely, as it usually did, on the claims of memory and association; Mrs. James had not been a student or even visited Wellesley. Furthermore, she showed herself to be no enthusiast for Wellesley's consensus process (protests over the proposed restriction of the dormitory to seniors had already exasperated her) and she now viewed the art department's observa-

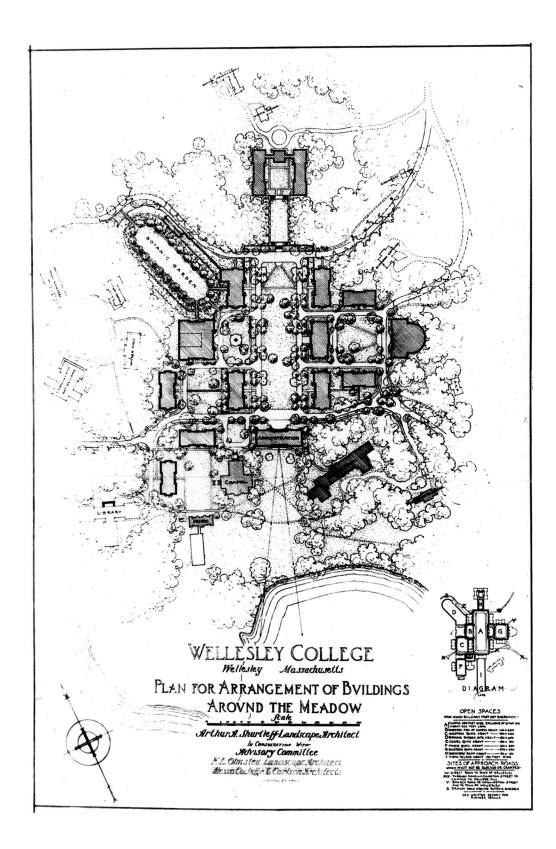

WELLESLEY COLLEGE
Wellesley   Massachusetts
PLAN FOR ARRANGEMENT OF BVILDINGS
AROVND THE MEADOW
Scale

Arthur A. Shurtleff Landscape Architect
In Consultation With
Advisory Committee
F. L. Olmsted Landscape Architect
Messrs Coolidge & Carlson Architects

DIAGRAM

OPEN SPACES

Coolidge & Carlson's 1914 plan for the
Academic Center, which they proposed
for the Middle Meadow (the area in front
of the Science Center today). The library
lies in the lower left of the drawing and the
chapel to the right of it. The landscaping
was designed by Arthur Shurtleff, whose
diagram of the "Open Spaces" appears
in the lower right.

Eliza J. Newkirk '00 emerged after the great fire of 1914 as the most articulate faculty advocate for the Norumbega Hill (now Academic Quad) development, and the appointment of Day & Klauder as its architects and Ralph Adams Cram as supervising architect. This luminous photograph was taken in 1910.

tions as an uninvited intrusion into what she considered an essentially private matter between the donor and the trustees. To make sure her views were understood, she threatened to discontinue her gift. In mid-November the criticisms had reached the point where, after a meeting with the art department committee, the trustees decided to postpone plans for the future Claflin dormitory.

Among those signing the art department memo was Eliza J. Newkirk '00, who was to play a major role in the changes that lay ahead. In Newkirk the faculty of Wellesley and its alumnae found not only an informed professional architect who had credentials and contacts with the major firms, but also an articulate advocate of a distinct point of view. Newkirk had graduated from the College in 1900 with a joint major in art and mathematics (in the latter she was therefore known to President Pendleton). After two years of teaching at the Walnut Hill School for Girls in Boston, she won a three-year fellowship for architectural study, two of which were spent at M.I.T., the third in Italy. In 1905 she joined the art department at Mount Holyoke College and two years later received her master of arts degree from Wellesley. Immediately hired by the College she began teaching in the fall of 1907, offering courses in architectural history. Further trips to Europe continued her study of domestic housing, a subject on which she published a number of distinguished professional papers beginning in 1910. At the same time Newkirk started architectural practice, working in both Boston and Philadelphia. In 1913 she opened her own independent office in Boston, becoming one of the first professional women architects in the United States. Her 1915 class letter reported her absorption with the design of small houses (twenty-seven still stand in the town of Wellesley), renovation work, and a gymnasium and administration building for the Walnut Hill School. She was later to design two large faculty housing buildings at the College: Shepard and Hallowell. Newkirk had also served as an architectural consultant to Frank Miles Day, the principal of the Philadelphia firm of Day & Klauder, one of the largest firms working in what was known as the "Collegiate Gothic" style.

On Jan 15, 1915, the cornerstone of Tower Court was laid. Two weeks later discussions began on the issue of a supervising architect, the art department committee now being amalgamated into the new Faculty and Alumnae Committee. When the trustees discussed the matter they considered three names: "R. A. Cram of Boston, Charles Platt the landscape architect of New York, Mr. Frank Miles Day of Philadelphia." The minutes record that the name of Charles Platt was "at once dismissed because his work has lain almost entirely with country houses and landscape work." Faced with the choice of Day or Cram, the Faculty and Alumnae Committee clearly favored Cram. In a long memo to the trustees dated February 6, 1915, the committee stated that it saw in Cram's work gifts in "great architectural compositions" aided by an imagination that had "an heroic quality." These would enable him "to suggest visibly something of the splendid character of Wellesley as we see it—its faithfulness to duty, its justice, steadfastness and patience, its unselfishness in service, its aspiration...." The committee drew an important distinction between residential buildings where architectural effects could be "charming and intimate" and academic buildings where the observer should be "raised to a higher plane of thought and emotion, as one is moved at West Point and Princeton."

The views of the faculty and alumnae were not well received by the trustees. Communication between the committee and President Pendleton revealed that the trustees were leary of Cram's "temperament and extravagance." One articulate opponent was the College treasurer, Lewis Kennedy Morse. While he was willing to concede the opinion of the Board of Trustees' chairman, Bishop Lawrence (the Episcopal bishop of Massachusetts), that Cram was "a genius" on account of his work at the Cathedral of St. John the Divine in New York, Morse distinguished between the needs of a cathedral and those of Wellesley College. "A Cathedral demands architectural effects and does not have to consider an income on the investment"; it can therefore "take the large risks which the poverty of a Woman's College does not allow." Wellesley needed creative genius less than practicality, Morse believed. The architect should be someone with a "sense of economy," and the capacity to adapt to contemporary needs. Morse even disapproved of the rising mass of the half-completed Tower Court, fearing that it would establish expectations too high for the future.

When the time came for the trustees to put the two names to a vote, there was no contest. Frank Miles Day emerged as the clear winner by a majority of eleven to five. In defining the powers of the supervising architect the trustees decided that his approval was needed for any new building, that all plans for such were to be subject to his "criticisms and revisions," and that the same applied to any renovation. Similar broad powers were extended to the landscape and also for decisions on "all memorials from donors in the shape of statues, bas-reliefs, and medallions" (these powers were transferred in 1933 to the consulting landscape architect). With the new procedures in place the trustees agreed to approve the start of design work in May on the second dormitory on College Hall Hill, the future Claflin, on which progress had been halted following criticism the previous November. Although architects Coolidge & Carlson were retained, their plans would be developed in "accordance with suggestions by Day & Klauder."

The drift of these suggestions can be readily seen in the resulting building. Developed as a wing to Tower Court, Claflin was linked to it by an entry in a more clearly defined style. It took the form of a medieval gatehouse with an arched passageway divided into triple bays with elegantly cut rib vaults. Above, a limestone story featured a bay window with tracery, cornices adorned with shields and heraldic devices, and bas-reliefs. Such explicit medievalisms had been absent in Tower Court, except in some final details such as the tracery cresting the roof or the decoration of the interior of the Great Hall (in both of which Day & Klauder's influence may be suspected). The new Claflin dormitory was a three-story block, with polychrome walls of brick and limestone although features like the main doorway, windows, and gables showed a tangible increase in Gothic motifs. At the southern end, turned at right angles to suggest an enclosing side to the quadrangle, the architects placed the communal living room. This featured a high-ceilinged, single-story gabled hall with a pitched roof, a Gothic fireplace, and a minstrels' gallery above the entrance door. Such references to medieval great halls again contrasted with Tower Court's flat ceilinged, squared-off, "staged" Great Hall, which had turned out more Tudor than Gothic despite Mrs. James's preference.

By June 1915 criticism was gathering around the work of Coolidge & Carlson, even with the Gothicizing embellishments attributable to Day & Klauder. This led the College to change architects for the third time in just over a year. On June 28 the trustees now turned to their recently appointed supervising architects, Day & Klauder. The choice made much sense. The Philadelphia firm enjoyed an important practice in university work with projects underway at Princeton, Yale, Johns Hopkins, Cornell, Pennsylvania State University, New York University, and elsewhere. In order to familiarize the Wellesley community with their work—and to rally support, doubtless—the Farnsworth Art Museum organized an exhibition of Day & Klauder's university designs. It is worth stressing that all three firms used in this brief period by the College represented the cream of the profession: Shepley Rutan and Coolidge had designed the new campus at Stanford, and Coolidge & Carlson were working at the University of Chicago.

The trustees requested plans from Day & Klauder for a new dormitory group, preferably to be located in the old orchard (more or less where the New Dorms are), the same site proposed by both of their predecessors; and for ideas for the administration building and classrooms. Designs for both survive. For the Academic Center, Day & Klauder proposed in October 1915 a scheme remarkably similar to Coolidge & Carlson's. Day & Klauder also wanted the center to rise up in the Great Meadow and to take a Beaux-Arts form, the main difference being that they favored a location to the north of Norumbega Hill (approximately where Paramecium Pond lies) rather than to the east, as advocated by Coolidge & Carlson.

Opposition to the Day & Klauder meadow scheme was swift. One critic was Frederick Law Olmsted, Jr. At the urging of Treasurer Morse he had been present at a meeting early in the firm's relationship with the College, and his 1902 letter remained the guiding document for the relation of architecture to landscape at Wellesley. Opinion now shifted to support the Norumbega Hill proposal, not only for the administration building but also for the liberal arts building and the two science buildings to house the Departments of Chemistry and Physics and Psychology. Day & Klauder readied designs for the Norumbega location, which were discussed and adjusted at a flurry of faculty and trustee meetings.

On November 12, 1915, the Board of Trustees formally accepted the idea of developing Norumbega as the site of the "Academic Center of the College." What had begun eighteen months earlier as a suggestion of the Department of Art now received the full backing of the faculty and trustees. Day & Klauder were instructed to prepare publicity to show to Wellesley alumnae clubs across the country.

The firm's ideas for the new center developed rapidly. By November they had produced no fewer than nineteen schemes. Their latest version— Scheme 19—showed development of the hill in two parts. On the east slope the plan showed three buildings: a liberal arts building facing south (the future Founders Hall), an administration building facing east where Wilder stood (Green Hall), and science buildings facing north (the two proposed buildings became one, Pendleton Hall) shown as linked by a gateway to Green Hall. For the administration functions Day & Klauder proposed a central building with symmetrical wings oriented toward the meadow. The importance of this side was underlined by the adoption of a new road system designed to bring visitors and students directly into the center of the College

Day & Klauder's Scheme 19 of 1915 for the so-called "Linked Hills" concept for the science buildings and a student–alumnae building. It shows the western slope of Norumbega on the right side (where Jewett Arts Center now stands) and the eastern slope of College Hall Hill on the left (where Shakespeare sits under the lefthand label "Lab"). The handwritten notations are by President Caroline Hazard and they remain the sole source to identify the intended buildings. The Student–Alumnae Building forms the left boundary. Plans were made to move Shakespeare to join the other society houses.

after passing through a monumental gateway entrance at Fiske House near Central Street. From there the new road passed the base of Water Tower Hill, turned to run past Simpson Cottage, and then cut across the meadow at an angle to confront the new administration building.

Scheme 19 was called a block plan and the projected buildings appear as simple shaded blocks. What style they were to be constructed in remained undetermined. Two surviving elevations reveal polarized positions. An early version portrayed the buildings in Collegiate Gothic style (see Chapter 7). In early 1916, however, the Board of Trustees asked the firm to work up an alternative in the classical style. Presented by Frank Miles Day to the trustees on January 21, 1916, it was characterized as "Italian Renaissance and Free Classic." Composed in formal symmetry it consisted of a four-story central building flanked on either side by balanced towers and with a monumental entry resembling a Roman triumphal arch with triple portals and an attic story. The wings extend at right angles and are in turn fronted by lower pavilions with a triple-arched two-story center separated by pilasters. Consistent with this formality, the courtyard is shown descending to the meadow in three terraces complete with balustrades, curving stairs, and a fountain. Day's earlier version in Collegiate Gothic, it should be pointed out, was essentially similar in plan and even massing, if markedly different in detailing, and used identical landscaping.

The second part of Scheme 19 involved the south half of Norumbega Hill. It was based on the "Linked Hills" concept of architecturally linking Norumbega to College Hall Hill. This part of the scheme is known through a surviving plan and a dazzlingly drawn elevation. The latter, seen from

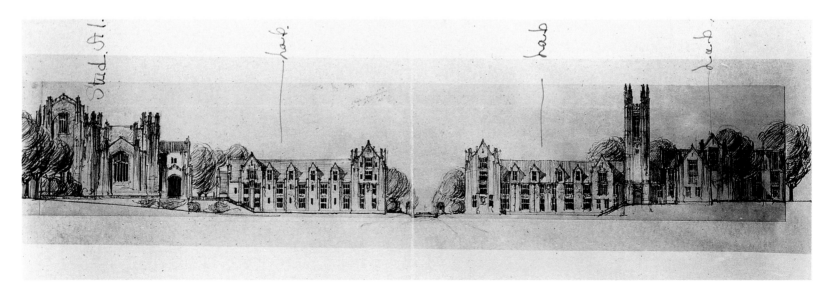

College Hall Green, shows buildings descending the western slope of Norumbega (where Jewett Arts Center now stands) and mounting the east slope of College Hall Hill behind Shakespeare. At the base of the hills, the two buildings for the sciences were to be set back and flanked by sentry-box pylons that framed a formal entrance axially aligned with the Hazard Quad lying to the north. Powerful massings marked each termination. Partway up the slope of College Hall Hill, notwithstanding the precipitous topography, a multi-gabled and richly pinnacled Student–Alumnae Building was projected to take the form of a large Gothic Hall lit by an imposing south-facing English Perpendicular window. On Norumbega a Gothic tower also in English Perpendicular was to mark the corner of Farnsworth (astutely omitted from the drawing to avoid the jarring collision of Gothic with neo-classical). Toward College Hall Green, terraces fronted with handsome balustrades and ranges of stairs descended the hillsides. Despite the basic symmetry of the overall organization, an impression of irregularity was achieved by varying the axes of some buildings and by cleverly juxtaposing the detailing. Day & Klauder show the surrounding landscaping with a similar classical vocabulary, like their proposals for the east side of Norumbega.

Day & Klauder's alternative schemes presented the trustees with a formidable dilemma. Which were they to select and how were they to decide? And what of the cost? On the last question estimates prepared by the firm showed that their classic version was ten percent cheaper than was their Gothic scheme. With Day & Klauder pliant on the matter, willing and able to turn their hand to either classic or Gothic, the choice fell fair and square on the Board of Trustees. And they were divided on the matter. During this period, marked by indecision and the tension resulting from divided views among the board members and between the board and the faculty and alumnae, the future of Wellesley's architecture and its landscape lay in the balance.

CHAPTER SEVEN

A NEW VISION: COLLEGIATE GOTHIC

IN THE EARLY MONTHS of 1916 the Board of Trustees faced a perplexing choice. Their architects, Day & Klauder of Philadelphia, the most widely respected campus designers in the country, had placed before them two alternatives for the construction of the new Academic Center (now the Academic Quad) on the Norumbega Hill site to replace College Hall, consumed by fire in March 1914. One alternative showed the buildings in the "Italian Renaissance and Free Classic" style, the other in the "Collegiate Gothic" style. Although eighteen months earlier the board had agreed to Gothic as a condition of the gift of the Tower Court dormitory, members now had second thoughts about using the style for Norumbega Hill. A sizeable faction favored classic. No such doubts divided the faculty and alumnae on the other hand; they had consistently championed Gothic. Had the choice between styles been merely a matter of formal preference, the controversy could be easily passed over as little more than an interesting but minor episode. The strong feelings revealed something different. Behind the choice lay a very visible statement about institutional identity—how Wellesley saw itself and how the world saw Wellesley.

A mechanism existed for solving this kind of debate, at least in theory. It had in fact been devised by the trustees themselves and involved the office of supervising architect. In addition to offering general advice, the supervising architect served to monitor and adjust the designs of the working architects. A year earlier the office had been filled after a contentious vote when Day & Klauder had won election over Ralph Adams Cram of Boston. Subsequently, the College had opted to use Day & Klauder as working architects, leaving the office of supervising architect vacant. For the board to appoint Cram

Severance Hall, interior corridor. Designed in 1926 by Day & Klauder, the building's placement on the ridge of the escarpment of Severance Hill entailed a composition that followed the slope of the hillside. As a result the interior has no fewer than twenty-one floor levels in a three-story building providing richly interlocking spaces.

Architect Ralph Adams Cram
c. 1930, photographed at his home
in Wayland, Massachusetts

would be to reverse the entrenched positions of a majority to whom Cram was simply unacceptable. Meanwhile the faculty and alumnae mounted another campaign for Cram's appointment, the latest in a sequence extending back nineteen months. The struggle between the board and the faculty and alumnae raises a number of important questions. Why did Cram engender such strong opinions pro and con? And why was his appointment deemed by many so necessary to the success of the new Academic Center?

Although barely known today by the public, the name of Ralph Adams Cram occupies an important place in the cultural history of the early decades of the century. A maverick in many ways, Cram defies conventional categorization. Tagged in his own day as the "American Goth," he managed to be a number of things, not all of them consistent. He was both a social activist and an arch conservative, an autodidact and a university professor (serving as chair of M.I.T.'s School of Architecture from 1914 to 1921 although he lacked a single academic degree), a progressive utopian and a revival medievalist. In addition, he was a prolific writer (thirty books and 400 papers), determined traveller, far-sighted city planner, devout churchman, tireless thespian, aggressive polemicist. And all these roles served as it were as backdrop to his primary calling as an architect. A formal list of Cram's work has yet to be compiled, but it is known that he designed over one hundred churches and cathedrals as well as numerous university commissions, including buildings for Yale, Princeton, Williams, West Point, Bryn Mawr, Rice, Sweetbriar, Wheaton, and Phillips Exeter Academy. Honors descended on him regularly; Harvard, Princeton, Yale, Williams, Notre Dame, and other institutions granted him honorary degrees. At his death in 1942 the *New York Times* referred to him as "one of the truly great men in America."

How the Board of Trustees resolved the deadlock on the issue of the buildings' style and on Cram's appointment has yet to be uncovered. The bare outlines can be retrieved from the trustees' minutes, although they reveal nothing of the way the argument went. In March 1916 the minutes record that "after much discussion it was voted to recommend that the Gothic Style be adopted." Doubtless the decision did much to placate opinion outside the board and for this group better news was shortly to follow. The April trustee minutes include mention that Cram joined the trustees in their deliberations, and the May minutes note his appointment as supervising architect. A clue to the resolution of the Cram appointment comes from the Day & Klauder files. It emerges that Cram visited the College with architect Frank Miles Day some days before the trustees met in March when they opted for Gothic. One suspects that it may well have been Frank Miles Day who swung opinion around. He was a longtime friend and professional colleague of Cram's and the board respected and warmly liked him.

The trustees' capitulation on Cram represented a resounding victory for the Faculty and Alumnae Committee. As the committee predicted, his presence brought immediate benefits. Most particularly, it entailed a better process; even his enemies acknowledged Cram's superb planning skills. It also brought reassurance. In 1916 Cram enjoyed rare prestige in academic circles. In part this came from his social and university contacts, including the support of Woodrow Wilson, his former patron at Princeton, who was then running for the office of president of the United States. Not the least important for raising confidence was Cram's unreserved espousal of Collegiate Gothic. He was not simply persuasive, he was evangelizing. For the waverers on the board, Cram's unwavering certainty swept away their uncertainty.

As already noted, the Faculty and Alumnae Committee had championed the architecture of Cram's firm—Cram, Goodhue and Ferguson—as a model for the College. It cited specifically their work at West Point (1903) and at Princeton (1907, where Cram continued as supervising architect until 1929). Both projects were developed in the Collegiate Gothic style. One important question, therefore, was why Collegiate Gothic seemed to the women of this generation as the style most appropriate for their image of Wellesley.

Collegiate Gothic refers to the style developed in America for university buildings and was based on the traditions at Oxford and Cambridge. It had appeared first in the 1890s, notably at Bryn Mawr in the work of the Philadelphia firm of Cope & Stewardson. By 1902, however, with both principals in that firm dead, leadership in the style had passed to another Philadelphia firm, Day & Klauder (Klauder had worked as a draftsman for Cope & Stewardson). What distinguished Collegiate Gothic from other medieval-influenced styles such as Ruskinian Gothic or Richardsonian Romanesque was its much freer use of plan and composition in combination with a greater accuracy of detailing. Liberated from historical imitation in the larger matters of architecture, Collegiate Gothic allowed for adaptation to modern functions and typologies.

To the Wellesley trustees, the attraction of Collegiate Gothic lay only partly in its association with academic status or fashion. Were these the deciding factors, the classic style of M.I.T. or Columbia University, or the Federal style of Harvard, could have qualified as well, and, as already seen, the classic was seriously considered by the trustees in January 1916. The choice of Collegiate Gothic and its appeal for the next twenty-five years involved a number of additional factors, however. From the start the style had been associated with England and recalled a model of education that contrasted to the German system. The difference was understood as the opposition between Anglo-Saxon undergraduate education based on the humanities and German research-oriented, science-based graduate education. Behind this opposition lay the concept of the residential college that Cram associated with Oxford and Cambridge and for which there was no counterpart in Germany. Cram articulated the distinction with characteristic bluntness when he delivered a lecture to the Royal Institute of British Architects in London in 1912 on the subject of American university architecture. Trumpeting the virtues of the Anglo-American residential college, he asserted that it led to the development of "personal honor, clean living ... good fellowship, obedience to law, reverence and the fear of God—all those elements that are implied in the word 'Character.'" These principles could be celebrated in the United States, according to Cram, following a lapse into "Germanic specialization" and "insane secularism," which he blamed on "the corruption of Germanic influences."

By 1916 this line of reasoning had taken on a much sharper tone in the context of the massive slaughter of World War I (1914–1918), which was depicted as a crusade of Anglo-French moral virtue confronting German barbarism. Just how keenly the Great War was felt at Wellesley can be glimpsed in the long Roll of Honor lists printed in the *Wellesley Alumnae Quarterly* throughout 1917 and 1918. These tabulate graduates, husbands, and brothers serving at the front in France; alumnae roles included ambulance drivers, signalers, nurses, and surgeons. Nor should it be overlooked that the Commander in Chief of America's Expeditionary Force, General Pershing, a wildly popular and trusted soldier, was married to an alumna.

A second factor in the appeal of Collegiate Gothic was the belief that its residential forms were inherently appropriate to higher education. Quadrangles, sunny lawns, gateways, towers, armorial devices, canopied niches, ivy-covered walls, traceried windows all provided an ambience redolent of lineage, study, liberal arts values, and reflection. To university clients Gothic made reference to a documented past and provided reassurance in a period of rapid social change. As Cram put it, Gothic gave buildings not simply the accents of history but the substance "of ancestry and connection." As such, Gothic transcended the limits of time and space; it also provided the antidote to democratic, mass education associated with the burgeoning state university systems.

A further factor was the rising tide of the women's movement. Most clearly manifest in the second decade of the century with the call for suffrage (the vote was finally granted to American women in 1920), feminism extended to higher education. Oxford and Cambridge had conceded to allowing entry to women students in the 1870s, at the same time as Wellesley's foundation. President Ellen Fitz Pendleton 1886 had attended Cambridge in the 1880s. An architecture that linked the idea of women as the rightful inheritors of a past previously denied them carried an obvious attraction.

And last was an element of the style that rendered its European origins adaptable to an American context. Collegiate Gothic's freer and more organic approach to architecture, its flexibility and irregularity, was contrasted to the formality, axial symmetry, and ordered regularity of classic design. Replying to Wellesley Treasurer Lewis Morse's request for guidance on the matter of style, Cram argued in a letter of June 22, 1916 that Gothic "was appropriate historically and theoretically for architectural expression of higher education while it is insistently demanded [at Wellesley] by the peculiar nature of the terrain and landscape." The Gothic he had in mind was that used at Oxford, which Cram praised as "supple, vital and beautiful," providing a model for the College that was "mobile and adaptable" and capable of translation into what he called "feminine Gothic."

Seen in this light, Gothic offered one further pragmatic benefit. It provided an architectural unity that could bind together distinctive building typologies (such as classrooms, dormitories, science buildings, and administration offices). Critics of the style such as writers Upton Sinclair and Thorstein Veblen pilloried the pursuit of modern university research behind what Jean Block has called "medieval dream façades." On the other hand, Gothic offered the benefits of a kind of visual uniform; to its period it was as distinctively "university" as academic regalia. Detached from its ecclesiastical antecedents in Europe, Gothic in America could be attached to secular structures to provide reassuring historical references. In this sense it was less a populist panache, in the mode of a Disney theme park for example, than a cultural blend with distinct forms and quotations, many carrying "class" connotations.

Within weeks of Cram's appointment his influence had changed Day & Klauder's design for the Academic Center. Their earlier ideas for

Norumbega (crystalized in Scheme 19) had proposed treating the hill as a roughly symmetrical courtyard oriented east to west. This Cram faulted as violating the spirit of the land. He objected to its "formality and mathematical regularity" and urged a design that complemented the "strikingly picturesque contours" of the hill. Five further schemes from Day & Klauder followed rapidly throughout the summer and early fall. By November 10, 1916, just a few days after Cram's long-time patron at Princeton, Woodrow Wilson, won election as president of the United States, the Board of Trustees approved Scheme 24. Much had occurred during the intervening months. Foremost, the "Linked Hills" scheme for the western slope of Norumbega had been abandoned, on account of cost as well as the disruption to the landscape resulting from the screen of buildings dividing the north from the south side of the campus.

All attention now focused on the eastern half of Norumbega Hill. Day & Klauder's proposal for the liberal arts building (the future Founders Hall) was retained, but Federal-style Wilder was to be torn down and replaced by Collegiate Gothic Green Hall (several schemes actually proposed jacking up Wilder and moving it in parts to the site of modern day Munger). Where the complex opened toward the meadow, the genteel terracing, curving stairs, and fountain were dropped and replaced by a formidable rampart that emphatically closed it off. Constructed of rusticated limestone and some twenty-five-feet high at the hill's base, it ran across both Green and the east side of Founders. As a motif the rampart wall emphasized the citadel character of the buildings. In keeping with this idea, a new entrance road was to run up the side of the rampart to pass through a twin-arched, barrel-vaulted gatehouse, hollowed out of the building overhead; the staggered arches spaced one behind the other suggested a portcullis while the blind panels on either side recalled medieval arrow slits. Once through the gatehouse, the visitor turned sharply left to pass through another deep archway, entering a grassed court-yard fronting a cloistered arcade and entrance lodge that screened the base of the main building.

Features like the ramped entrance, gatehouse, cloistered arcade, tower, and postern-like doorways recalled the architecture of the Middle Ages. They were not intended as literal copies of medieval forms, however, but rather as prompters, even metaphors. The distinction is easily grasped if the rampart wall on the east is followed around to the north where it runs for another 120 feet before terminating as a lithic flourish then disappearing into the hillside.

In keeping with a kind of generic medievalism, there was no firm agreement from the principals on the precise architectural source. When the Department of Art had championed Norumbega for the Academic Center in the previous year, their argument rested solely on the criterion of "beauty." Now more specific models were invoked. One recalled a walled Italian hill town. The image was President Hazard's, an avowed Italophile, and is first recorded in her 1906 annual report in which she proposed to the trustees a new dormitory between Farnsworth and Wilder "… built at an angle, with a stairway leading up the hill between its two wings and a clock tower crowning the whole. Norumbega is such a beautiful little hill that we could have a cluster of buildings there which would have the effect of an Italian citadel.…" A second source comes from Cram who in June 1916 congratulated the College on the adoption of Day & Klauder's scheme, which evoked for him "the same spirit which has made Mont St. Michel an architectural monument of all time." Yet a third image was presented in the *Wellesley Alumnae Quarterly* of July 1917 by the Faculty and Alumnae Committee, which declared the scheme "comparable on a smaller scale to the effect of the hill towns of Italy or of a great chateau like Amboise on its height overlooking the Loire valley."

On January 11, 1917, Day & Klauder's revised design for the Academic Center, Scheme 24, was formally approved by the Board of Trustees and working drawings ordered for Founders. These were agreed to on April 2, five days before the United States entered World War I. The same meeting voted to memorialize the donor to Tower Court, Ellen James, with an eight-foot-high carved inscription over the fireplace in the Great Hall. This was now rendered as a late-medieval manuscript page, its inscription starting with a five-foot-high foliate initial.

Gothic was spreading elsewhere. Two months later the College adopted a new seal "designed by William Aldrich with Mr. Cram's approval." The new design was, in fact, a medievalized coat of arms. The former seal, still retained by the Alumnae Association, inscribed the motto *non ministrari sed ministrare* around a Chi-Rho symbol (the first letters of *Khristos*, Christ's name in Greek). The coat of arms, like the Latin inscriptions carved elsewhere on the buildings, conjured a chivalric European past. The shield circumscribed by the College motto featured an open ancient book (the book of knowledge) with the words *incipit vita nova* (the poet Dante Alighieri's phrase quoted by Henry Fowle Durant in his address on "The Spirit of the College") surmounted by a "chief or a cross Crosslet in a field between two wells" (the cross

Green Hall east façade looking toward the "gateway" entrance supporting the President's office. The roadway was intended as the principal entrance to the complex. After the redesign of the College's road system in 1961, traffic was redirected and the roadway became an exit road. This decision robbed the approach to Green of its intended metaphorical meaning.

The seal of the College at its foundation. It remains the seal of the Alumnae Association.

The coat of arms adopted in 1917, designed by William Aldrich and approved by Ralph Adams Cram. This more medievalized emblem is widely used today.

Crosslet was from the Durant family arms, the wells an allusion to the maiden name of Horatio Hollis Hunnewell's wife, Isabella Pratt Welles, after whom in sequence their great house, the College, and the town were named). In a similar vein, when it came time to implement new road and path lighting, Cram proposed a design that combined a lantern and shepherd's staff, a subtle union of the College's pastoral responsibility with scriptural overtones (based on Psalm 119.105: "Thy word is a lamp unto my feet and a light unto my path").

Attention now turned to the formidable task of raising money for the four buildings of Scheme 24: the classroom and offices building (Founders), the administration building (Green), and the two buildings to house the Departments of Chemistry and Physics and Psychology (the two subsequently combined into a single building, Pendleton). To aid potential donors in the visualization of the scheme the trustees ordered a model of the Academic Center, which was placed on display in the Farnsworth Art Building. Some seven by six feet, elaborately detailed, complete with landscaping including several plaster automobiles, it cost the considerable sum of $1,000 (approximately $50,000 in today's money). The model is generally accurate at least as far as overall massing is concerned. For the elevations it proved most accurate for Founders, somewhat less so for Green, and hardly at all for Pendleton.

The College had sufficient funds only for the construction of Founders, and the trustees therefore resigned themselves to a process of sequential building. Green followed twelve years later, and nearly twenty years were to elapse before Pendleton was completed.

Despite the war, restriction on materials, and the fear of appearing unpatriotic on account of building (the last discussed at length by the trustees), the need for classrooms and offices was deemed so desperate that government permission was obtained for work to commence on Founders. The building was organized in two parts: toward the library it showed a symmetrical façade (accentuated until the late 1930s by an axial pathway that descended the hillside from the central doorway); toward the Middle Meadow it gathered scale as it descended the hillside (a feature cleverly concealed by broken forms terminated by stacked gables), and turned at an irregular angle to the north. For materials, brick predominated, although certain parts such as the side of Founders facing the Academic Quadrangle were clad heavily in limestone worked with blind tracery and enriched with heraldic shields.

The masterpiece of the Academic Center complex was the administration building. The program was formidable. The building was to include

offices of the president, dean, and registrar, a trustee room, bursary, faculty common room, offices for the "Christian Association" and other student organizations, a post office, bookstore, telephone exchange, and two large meeting halls. The flanking wings were to serve for classroom and recitation rooms as well as faculty and administration offices. Funded in large part by a $500,000 gift from the two children of the legendary Hetty Green just before the Great Crash on Wall Street, the building was named after their mother. Some irony attached to the choice because of her reputation as the "wicked witch of Wall Street"—a sobriquet earned in the 1890s when hard-fisted trading made her the richest woman in America.

Anchoring the entire complex was the imposing tower in the southeast corner, Galen Stone Tower (the gift of Galen L. Stone, a Boston banker and College trustee from 1915 to 1925). For its design Cram exercised his authority as supervising architect and raised Day & Klauder's proposed tower by a further thirty feet, drawing freehand on their design to provide more imposing pinnacles at its summit and a twenty-five-foot traceried window toward its top. Buttresses set diagonally at the corners begin in brick and break out in limestone as the tower gathers height; they narrow the face of each side and these in turn are divided by slim rising pilasters that eventually frame the traceried windows. Loosely based on English cathedral crossing tower models, the detailing and proportions contribute to a remarkably elegant and lightly profiled tower. The tower's purpose is manifestly aesthetic, although no less useful in consequence. It rises like a beacon in the dispersed landscape to signal the center of the campus, likening Wellesley to the prestigous

*Green Hall interior courtyard with
its Latin inscription visible at the base
of the Galen Stone Tower*

"Ivies," where a cult of towers and spires in the same years appears at Princeton, Yale, Harvard, Duke, Chicago, Michigan, Williams, and other campuses. Additionally, Galen Stone Tower endowed the Academic Center with a distinctly Oxford and Cambridge ambiance with ecclesiastical overtones, established at the tower's base with the carved Latin inscription from Psalm 127.1: *"Nisi Dominus aedificaverit domum in vanum laboraverunt qui aedificavant eum"* ("Except the Lord builds the house, those who build it labor in vain"; the same verse had been inscribed by Pauline Durant in the Bible she laid in the cornerstone of College Hall in 1871)—and at the tower's top with the thirty-bell carillon. Cram, it might be added, had forsaken Unitarianism for an avid Anglo-Catholicism, and the chairman of the Board of Trustees was Bishop Lawrence, the Episcopal bishop of Massachusetts.

One problem astutely solved by Day & Klauder involved the scale of the architecture needed to fulfill the Academic Center's program. To break up the expanse of roof over the building's side wings (and at Founders), they employed twin-storied dormers and a "parallel ridge type" roof over different height massings. The latter resulted from the placement of the building on the brow of the Norumbega hillside, a placement exploited by the doubled gables to give a play of lively irregularity. The architects explained this "parallel ridge" system in a paper in the *Architectural Review* (May 1921, vol. 12, no. 5) as a device originated for Wellesley to avoid "the bulk of this kind of building resulting from a single sloping roof with its inevitable thickness of gable." The internal plan showed a central corridor running longitudinally through the center of the building with offices at right angles. With the building ledged into the hillside, the architects explained, the parallel ridge meant that one roof spanned from an outside wall to the "more distant wall of the corridor" while "the span of the other ridge repeats on a higher level, on the opposite side of the building. The lower story below the edge of the hill extends only half way through the building. The next story which is level with the courtyard, on the top of the hill, extends entirely through the building. The third story, the second floor above the level of the courtyard, extends only half way through the building." The two ridges thus lie one above the other, and since the twin forms could be extended to unequal distances longitudinally, they formed unequal and interesting terminations. The same irregularity amounting to whimsy marked doorways and entries, a number of which were burrowed unpredictably through wall thicknesses to connect different levels or cause the visitor to exit unexpectedly into the landscape.

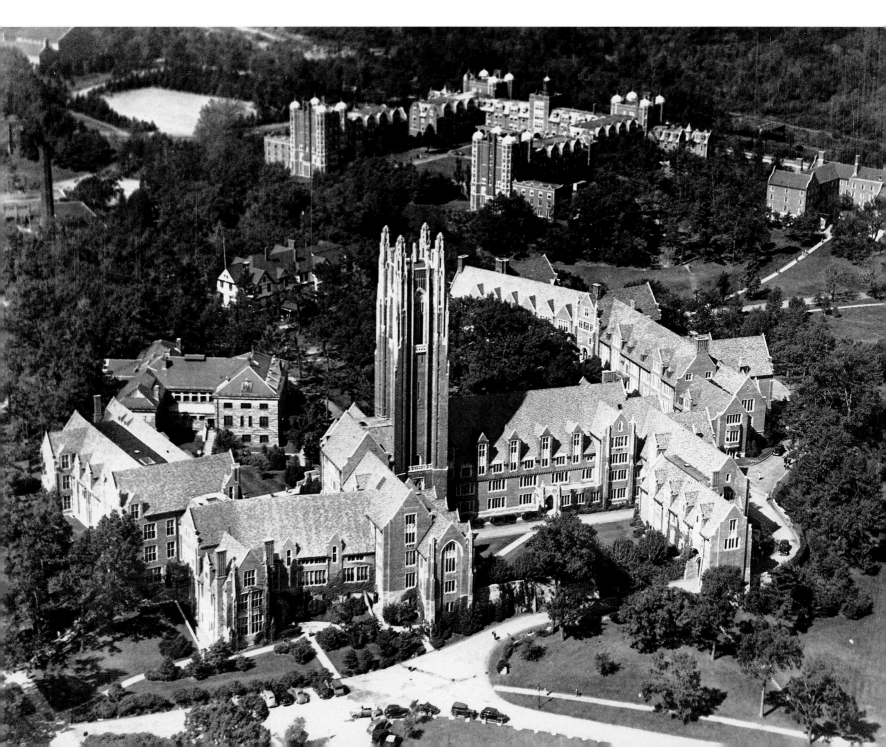

Aerial view of Founders, Green, and Pendleton Halls, probably taken in 1937. Behind Founders may be seen the Farnsworth Art Building and above it the timber Norumbega dormitory (where Jewett now stands).

Not everything proposed by Day & Klauder and Cram got built. One casualty of the decade that elapsed between the design and construction of Founders was the cloistral arcading on the building's entrance front. A rib-vaulted porch was substituted. On the interior, similarly, the two-storied Great Hall at ground level was abandoned. Originally the hall was "to accommodate student gatherings, large receptions and entertainments. Here the student leaders may address their classmates or the entire student body in winter from the screens overlooking the Great Hall, and in summer from the terrace on the arcade overlooking the enclosed court on the east." As a setting for these declamations, a drawing illustrates the interior which was spanned by a hammer-beam roof (based on Westminster Hall, recently restored in 1917) with an elaborately traceried screen at the north and tall Perpendicular windows facing west. A second hall on the top floor provided further meeting space, the "Faculty Assembly Hall," which the *Wellesley Alumnae Quarterly* in 1917 described as suggesting the great halls of Oxford and Cambridge. What got built, however, was an austere, barrel-vaulted space with plain walls.

For the science component of the Academic Center, another four years were to pass before suffcent funds were in hand to start work. The Day & Klauder model shows the chemistry and physics/psychology components as distinct buildings attached to Green Hall with a roadway passing under the connector; in effect they formed a counterpart to Founders but on the north side of Norumbega Hill. When time came for construction, however, the three departments were amalgamated into one building, Pendleton, which was detached from Green Hall and placed to form a freestanding wing defining the north side of the hill.

Pendleton took the form of a splayed L with a prominent central entrance located in the angle. Hinged around and gripping the rim of the escarpment, bending as it were to embrace the hillside, Pendleton's place-ment, like that of Founders and Green, involved an additional story on the descending face of the hill. In massing, Pendleton is for the most part symmetrical; a central entrance is flanked by substantial two-story blocks with north-projecting wings and with modest single-story terminals. Much of this symmetry is disguised by the irregular treatment given the west and east sides. Thus fenestration on the west side is regular, with gables over the upper windows breaking the roofline and a flat-roofed terminal; on the east side a freer window composition was favored, and the terminal was gabled. Detailing is much simpler than that of Green: a granite base with a single

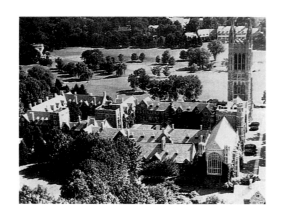

Princeton, Graduate Center, 1911, by
Cram, Goodhue and Ferguson, the most
compelling forerunner to Day & Klauder's
Scheme 24 of 1916. Apart from the flatness
of the Princeton site, important differences
are the enclosed quadrangles, the absence
of double-ridge roofs, and the ubiquitous
stone construction.

chamfer, plain walls with large rectangular-headed and mullioned windows, and drastically reduced ornament (at least from that shown on the model). These features were in part consistent with departmental identities and the need for laboratory space. Just as important, they coincided with contemporary architectural trends. The mid-1930s saw the widespread use of simpler Federal forms that had been used already at Wellesley for the construction of the new Munger dormitory in 1933. In addition, modernism with its anti-decoration, less-is-more aesthetic was beginning to appear in the larger cities and in small-scale housing.

The entire Academic Center—Founders, Green, and Pendleton—took nearly twenty years to build, from 1917 to 1936. If Green is the preeminent building of the group, the center stands in its general form and conception as one of the masterpieces of the Collegiate Gothic style in America rivalled only by Cram's United States Military Academy at West Point (1903) and Princeton's Graduate Center (1911). Both the West Point and Princeton buildings were stone throughout, however, and were given a much heavier appearance. At Wellesley the mixture of yellow-tinted Deer Island granite for the buildings' base, rose and dark brick for the walls, pale Indiana limestone trim for gable copings and window and entrance surrounds, and thick sheared-edge blue-grey slate for the roofs—all these provide an appealing colorism to complement the generally slender proportions and irregular forms. Day & Klauder referred to these refinements in gender terms as a "feminine" version of the style, a characterization used by Cram, as seen, and by the Faculty and Alumnae Committee who as early as 1914 advocated a version of Collegiate Gothic for Wellesley that would be a "lighter type not monastic or masculine." Similarly the double-ridge roof was developed specifically for Wellesley. Such stereotyping of style and materials along gender lines provides a wholly new slant on the College's preferences. They suggest rationales consistent with the emerging identities of women in the World War I years.

Despite the argument, time, money, and the accreted nature of construction needed to complete it, the Academic Center constitutes the most notable architectural achievement in the College's history. Although the choice of style was not original, the accenting given to it through proportion, the lightness and subtlety of scale, the breaking up of masses, and the use of materials transformed many of its effects. Most important, the Norumbega Hill site and the adjustment of the buildings to it, and the symbolic expression

College Hall Hill (Severance Hill since 1927) with the Class of 1923 photograph in process. The photo shows Coolidge & Carlson's Tower Court as a dominating block set on the center of the hill.

Collegiate Gothic assumed in the context of Wellesley and of higher education raise the buildings to the top rank of work in this style.

Before Green could be started, let alone Pendleton, the College turned to the construction of an additional dormitory, Severance, in 1926 and then to the reconstruction of Stone (to become Stone–Davis) following the fire that consumed it during the course of renovation in 1927. For both, Day & Klauder were retained with Cram again serving as supervising architect. It may be recalled that the outcry over Coolidge & Carlson's Tower Court had led to the suspension of the projected west and east wings. Subsequently the trustees assented to erecting the west wing (Claflin). This left the east wing in limbo. The major criticisms of Coolidge & Carlson's Tower Court concerned its positioning on the crown of the hill and its insistent bulk. The insensitivity to site is well illustrated in the Class of 1923 photo, which shows Tower Court rising as a blunt, isolated block. In planning Severance, therefore, Day & Klauder seized the chance to mitigate this "scar." They strung the building along the rim of the escarpment of College Hall Hill, breaking the dormitory into a sequence of connected parts, some turned at right angles with prominent gables, others given different heights and window sequences (achieved on the inside with no fewer than twenty-one different floor levels). On the lower north slope, granite walling anchors the building to the hillside and provides a series of terraces opening from the main living areas toward Severance Green.

In the siting of Severance Hall, Day & Klauder thus managed three feats with peerless brilliance. They adjusted the dormitory to the descending topography by stretching it along the rim of the escarpment in a manner that exemplifies Olmsted's recommendation for building placement. They used the building to provide a superb backdrop to Severance Green, the College's community center. And they incorporated the earlier Tower Court as a central element of the new work in a manner that, paradoxically, elevates Tower Court to the role of an intended crown of an irregular composition. For the last, Day & Klauder's adroit transmutation of the failings of their predecessors is a rare achievement in the profession, a self-effacing triumph.

On the interior the Severance dormitory was treated with a distinctly domesticized Gothic. For the ceiling of the principal living room, boldly carved birds and beasts hold coats of arms to form the terminals of the timber roof. The space is scaled, however, to resemble more a club lounge than a Gothic hall. At Severance Hall, as at dormitories elsewhere in the women's colleges, much greater emphasis was placed on the public spaces for communal activities and the reception of callers than on the dormitory rooms themselves, which opened from austere corridors.

Two further buildings in other parts of the campus concluded the unprecedented work undertaken by President Pendleton. Alumnae Hall (1923) and Sage Hall (1931) were both designed by Cram, Ferguson and Medary (the partnership formed following the departure of the highly talented Goodhue). The genesis of Alumnae Hall (as it has been known since the 1950s) goes back to Caroline Hazard's years as president, when a Student Building was proposed. The name for the proposed building seems to have changed only in 1915 to the Student–Alumnae Building). Prior to that the students' recreation hall had been consigned to one of Mr. Durant's cow barns. The proposed building allowed for the staging of plays, social events such as receptions and ballroom dances, and lectures by distinguished speakers (then envisioned as requiring a large auditorium). Some office space for student organizations was also part of the building program.

The first idea placed the Student–Alumnae Building on College Hall Hill and a design was prepared by Pond and Pond of Chicago. Planned then to be located behind Shakespeare, it would have been part of the so-called "Linked Hills" scheme developed by Day & Klauder in 1916, which was intended to tie College Hall Hill with its old associations to Norumbega Hill with its new. When the Linked Hills scheme was abandoned, the

Severance dormitory in a view taken in
the mid-1930s showing the right part of
the dormitory with the left in shadow.
The composition provides an architectural
boundary for Severance Green and breaks
up the blunt bulk of Tower Court behind.
The original College road skirts the green
on the right, thereby extending its width.

Student–Alumnae Building was left without a site. Over the next year or so alternatives were sought, complicated in part by the need for an outdoor space for theater performances (in addition to the indoor auditorium). Suggestions for the outdoor theater had included the 1914 proposal to develop the hillside below Lake House for this purpose. The site finally chosen was adjacent to and fronted by the Valley that extended behind College Hall Hill (now the Service Lot). It was selected with the idea of meshing its functions with those of the proposed recreation building (finally begun in 1938), which was to extend the existing Hemenway Gymnasium.

Cram's design of 1922 for Alumnae Hall had to accommodate a building whose size was determined by the 1,500-seat auditorium it housed. This he devised as an upper story surmounting a vast recreation hall to be used for "Alumnae luncheons of 600 to 700 covers, the Senior Dance, and Class Receptions" in the words of the building program. The building's considerable bulk was lessened by ledging it into the hillside. Offices, a tea room, and a small library to "serve non-society girls including in that number the freshmen" were squeezed into two pylon-like features that formed the east façade. While access to the auditorium was gained through generous north-facing doorways on the upper level, the hall was approached from the east a story lower. The west-facing terrace opening from the ballroom formed the entry into the Hay Outdoor Theater (finally built in 1936), which utilized the

Alumnae Hall viewed from the east side, 1923. Designed by Cram's firm, the building eschewed Collegiate Gothic in favor of an eclectic Jacobean-Colonial style.

Severance living room shortly after completion of the dormitory in 1927. Comparison with Tower Court's Great Hall shows the increase in Gothic vocabulary, albeit at a smaller scale, particularly in the timber responds sporting feathered eagles holding armoreal shields that support the principal ceiling beams.

sloping hillside for its stone benching. Alumnae Hall was developed from an amalgam of Jacobean and Colonial styles. The choice is puzzling. Cram adjusted his design to link with Julius Schweinfurth's Hazard Quadrangle to the north rather than the Tudor-Elizabethan Tower Court to the south.

Similarly puzzling is Cram, Ferguson and Medary's design for Sage, which was to accommodate the zoology and botany departments that had been in temporary quarters since the burning of College Hall. Initial plans had placed both departments with the other sciences on Norumbega Hill. Cram urged their separation and location on the hillside to the north of Norumbega, close to the Whitin Observatory. Adjacent land for the Ferguson Greenhouses (constructed in 1922–1923) and for the Alexandra Botanic Garden (begun in 1925) made this site plausible. For the classrooms and laboratories, Cram designed a symmetrical building centered on an imposing two-story entry. It was built in two stages, with Sage begun in 1927 and the Zoology Building following four years later. Unlike the Norumbega complex where irregular, broken forms with rich decorative accents were exploited, Sage was designed in a minimal Gothic mode with a monotonous regularity of fenestration and balanced parts.

Both Alumnae Hall and Sage shroud Cram's considerable contribution to Wellesley. For someone who had built with brilliance in Collegiate Gothic at West Point, Princeton, and elsewhere, had espoused its language with proselytizing fervor, and had guided Day & Klauder faultlessly at Founders, Green, Pendleton, Severance, and Stone–Davis, the styles of Alumnae Hall and Sage strike one as puzzling, even banal. It cannot be argued that Cram was best in advisory roles and lacked creative capacity; both West Point and Princeton were his designs. It is true that he worked in styles other than Collegiate Gothic, at Rice and elsewhere. No satisfactory answer emerges from the written records and Cram himself is silent (for once). Surprisingly, the process for architect selection and for the monitoring of designs that had been so painstakingly instituted by the trustees in 1915–1916 was overlooked, for the terms of appointment of the supervising architect forbade taking on the role of project architect.

The construction of Pendleton ended Day & Klauder's work at Wellesley. It would also memorialize President Pendleton, whose death just weeks after her retirement in June 1936 coincided with the completion of work. Even when finished the new building fulfilled only part of the intended transformation of the hillside. As the aerial view photographed in 1936–1937

The Norumbega Hill complex, now the Academic Quadrangle, seen from the west after the completion of Jewett Arts Center in 1958 and the demolition of its predecessor, Farnsworth. The harmonizing of new with old and the superb siting of the complex marked the end of fifty years of work to create the College's Academic Center.

clearly shows, the western and southern sides of the hill remained in their 1880s guise (see page 162) with Norumbega (the last of the cottage dormitories) on the west and Farnsworth (the ponderous art building) skewed to face College Hall Hill on the south.

Day & Klauder's Scheme 24 had envisioned a design to complete the western and southern sides. But Wellesley's new president, Mildred McAfee (later McAfee Horton), had barely settled into office when the specter of another world war rendered such plans a distant prospect; she herself would be called to Washington in a military role to head the United States WAVES (Women Accepted for Volunteer Emergency Service), a division of the U.S. Naval Reserve. Another twenty years were to pass before her successor, Margaret Clapp '30, would complete what then became known as the Academic Quadrangle (displacing in usage the older name of the Academic Center, also referred to simply as Norumbega Hill). Jewett Arts Center of 1958 effectively concluded the intentions of Day & Klauder's scheme as did the Davis Museum and Cultural Center (1993), which added the parallel tier of architecture to the west. Sited where the Norumbega Cottage once stood, Jewett sealed the west side of the quadrangle with the Farnsworth Art Building screening much of the south side. From the Green this placement formed in effect an architectural backdrop while from the Quadrangle the partial closure provided the opening for a panoramic "window" toward the

Green Hall seen from the west.
Anchoring the Academic Quadrangle,
the building is fronted by an irregular
grove of oaks that canopy and close
the space during the growing season
with a panorama opening on the right
to Severance Green.

College's ceremonial sacred space of Severance Green. This superb site planning put the finishing touches on the center imagined by Cram and Day & Klauder decades earlier. Even though Jewett's modern style differed profoundly from Collegiate Gothic, it was designed respectfully, serving as a remarkably good-mannered neighbor by employing similar materials and making deft reference to the architectural forms used in the earlier groupings.

The fifty years of work on Norumbega Hill produced a sublime marriage of architecture to site. That a union formed from different styles succeeded so happily resulted in part from the high quality of the designs. The Academic Quadrangle takes its place among the best complexes in university and college building in North America. Not least remarkable is the patience with which the project was brought to completion and the commitment of generations of women to a transformation of the hillside from a dowdy and inchoate collection of small-scale timber and brick dormitories into a center for Wellesley.

Helen Lefkowitz Horowitz ends her memorable chapter in *Alma Mater* on this period in the College's history with the observation that "… the heroic vision of the women's college, which began at Bryn Mawr under M. Carey Thomas, found its most complete expression" in the rebuilding of Norumbega Hill after the College Hall conflagration. From the beginning, the hill had been intended to evoke unique and distinct values. As already seen, the impressive women—College leaders, faculty, and alumnae—who first envisioned the new Academic Center atop Norumbega saw the buildings as representing "… something of the splendid character of Wellesley … its faithfulness to duty, its justice, steadfastness and patience, its unselfishness in service, its aspiration." In their campaigns for the appointment of Cram whose "heroic imagination" could make this vision a reality, in their influence on the design of the architecture through their role as client and patron, and in their patient commitment to providing the money to realize it, these women embodied their own aspiring ideals at the same time that they brought them to fruition. To the faculty, almunae, and the administration led by President Ellen Fitz Pendleton the new style of architecture and its siting transcended utility. They intended the entire project to raise the observer to "a higher plane of thought and emotion."

CHAPTER EIGHT

THE ARRIVAL OF MODERNISM

The College's earliest modernist buildings are Bates and Freeman Halls, completed in 1952 and shown here before the third of the New Dorms, McAfee Hall, was completed nine years later.

NO SINGLE BUILDING on the Wellesley campus can claim as much historical significance and general admiration as does the landscape itself, and the buildings best loved within the Wellesley community have aesthetic properties that blend with those of the landscape. Thus the pronounced texture, warm colors, varied outline, and intricate detail of most of the College's revivalist architecture can be said to serve a broader purpose than mere period-style quaintness. But the specific appeal of the latter also remains undeniably, and unsurprisingly, strong at Wellesley. The ideology of the entire American campus tradition—indeed the very concept of campus—is steeped in cultural nostalgia.

As on many other campuses, the buildings least liked at Wellesley today are the modern ones, more precisely those that represent the modernist movement, which was the long-running main event in twentieth-century architecture. That the earliest of these buildings continue to be referred to, starkly, as the "New Dorms" no doubt subtly reinforces their implicit alien status. Half a century after its arrival at Wellesley, modernist architecture is still not part of the institution's fondest image of itself.

While Wellesley, in the early twentieth century, was still debating whether to build in a classicizing or a medievalizing style, modernism was already gradually taking shape as a comprehensive new approach to the theory and practice of architecture. Far from simply offering a new stylistic option, to be set alongside the revivalist styles, modernist theory rejected the very notion of style as an option and sought instead to redefine style by locking it into the other aspects of architecture. In theory, modernist style would be nothing other than the logical, candid expression of modern structure and modern accommodation to modern life—not an ornamental overlay disguising the present by evoking the past. Thus style should henceforth be understood as an outcome achieved by the architect, through practical expertise, rather than a predisposing taste exercised on behalf of the patron. In this new model, nostalgia was irrelevant, quaintness was out of the question, and the patron was challenged to acknowledge and to identify with the blunt realities of here and now—not an easy task for any institution upholding any form of cultural tradition. And how could such unadorned, plainspoken architecture be expected to blend into the aesthetic richness of Wellesley's landscape?

Wellesley admitted modernist architecture to its campus very reluctantly, at the same moment as did comparable institutions and with the same rationale as theirs: by default, as a consequence of sheer economic necessity. The end of World War II signaled a new era with new priorities, in which revivalist architecture was no longer deemed appropriate, above all because it no longer seemed affordable. Fostered by the war, changed conditions in both production and labor made elaborate custom-crafted buildings a luxury for even the best-endowed institutions.

Wellesley's financial condition at the end of the war proved to be troubling. In 1946, after two years of operating at a large deficit, the College opened its campaign for a Seventy-Fifth Anniversary Fund to meet a range of long-deferred expenses. The goal was $7.5 million, but only a little less than $4.5 million was raised by the close of the campaign in 1950. Just to counter inflation, the whole of this sum was allocated to increase faculty salaries and financial aid for students, leaving unfunded several major building projects also targeted by the campaign as urgent needs. A new library and new facilities for art and music would have to wait; for a new dormitory complex, which was already well into the planning stage, the College bravely decided to proceed with borrowed money.

The project had a special ambition: to allow all Wellesley students to live on campus. Strangely, this had not been the case since the late nineteenth century, no doubt in part because the longstanding debate at women's colleges over how their students should be housed had never truly been resolved at Wellesley, which maintained various housing options along with differing standards of living—most conspicuously for students on financial aid. Already in the 1880s, the College began setting aside some facilities as "cooperative" housing in which such students undertook much of the house-keeping. Opened in 1933, Munger Hall was expressly designed for this purpose by architect and Trustee William T. Aldrich. First-year students were also

Designed by Shepley Bulfinch Richardson and Abbott, the New Dorms complex made it possible, for the first time since the late nineteenth century, for all Wellesley students to live on campus.

segregated and as a class bore the brunt of a persistent housing shortage. This was aggravated, for all classes, during World War II, when the College lent Cazenove and Pomeroy Halls to the Navy for officer training and, in order to house the dislocated students, brought onto the campus a military-surplus barracks that squatted on the future site of the College Club until the New Dorms were completed. In 1946, almost four hundred first-year students were living someplace other than the dormitories proper, some of them in smaller structures (including the so-called Navy House) scattered across the campus, but most of them in nine frame houses—ill-equipped for fire prevention, among other shortcomings—that the College variously owned and leased in Wellesley village, nearly a mile from most of their classes. According to a promotional booklet produced for the Seventy-Fifth Anniversary Fund, the cost of operating the village houses had been running twenty-four percent higher, over the previous decade, than that of running the campus dormitories. Besides being more economical for the College and safer and more convenient for the students, the projected New Dorms would also "facilitate their adjustment" to College life. But in the larger view, what the institution actually hoped to bring about was a new way of life better adjusted to the financial and social realities of the times.

To judge from the design history of the New Dorms, neither patron nor architect started out with a very clear vision of how to achieve this. The Board of Trustees approached the task cautiously. They hired specialists in collegiate architecture, the prominent and familiar Shepley firm of Boston—architects of the College library, Lake House, and most recently a very plain addition to the infirmary, formerly Simpson Cottage—to produce a tentative first design in 1946. Illustrated in the Fund booklet, it is thoroughly unlike the final product and may have been intended as little more than an attractive visualization for potential donors. Even so, it is a puzzling document. It presents a massive symmetrical building on the plan of a comb with four teeth, each housing a hundred students. The style is stripped-down neo-Georgian, minimally detailed but nevertheless retaining pedimented gables and a central cupola. The building looks like a poor descendant of the Shepley firm's best-known local work, the Harvard Houses of the 1920s and '30s. But it also bears a general family resemblance to a much earlier Wellesley proposal by the same firm for the same purpose on roughly the same site. Included in the Beaux-Arts campus plan produced in 1912 by Shepley Rutan and Coolidge was a dormitory complex laid out in a U-shape in the vicinity of the old orchard near Homestead. By 1921, when the Beaux-Arts concept had given way to Ralph Adams Cram and Frederick Law Olmsted, Jr.'s recommendations for campus planning, these proposed "Orchard" dormitories were reconfigured by Arthur Shurtleff in an asymmetrical, irregular site plan that implied a medievalizing rather than classicizing style. This would have accommodated the steeply sloping terrain in a manner similar to the academic complex then rising on Norumbega Hill, whereas the earlier Beaux-Arts proposal would have favored a more flattened site. Corresponding to the latter concept, the Shepley firm's 1946 design is sited on a broad flat plane, with the slope in front strictly terraced along the whole considerable width of the layout, unlike anything else at Wellesley.

PROPOSED DORMITORY FOR WELLESLEY COLLEGE
Coolidge Shepley Bulfinch & Abbott - Architects

Dated 1946, the first design for the New Dorms seems an odd reversion to unsuccessful early twentieth-century proposals to classicize Wellesley's architectural image and to formalize its landscape. The neo-Georgian style of this monumental structure was a specialty of the architects, the prominent and long-established Shepley firm of Boston. Each of the four projecting wings was intended to house 100 students.

Thus the first design for the New Dorms was an odd reversion, in both architecture and landscape, to unsuccessful earlier notions seemingly without any particular, bankable appeal to alumnae donors. Possibly the trustees contemplated it as a suitable, cost-effective compromise between past and present, invoking revivalist nostalgia but in a style less dependent on expensive detail—neo-Georgian being comparatively plain—than Wellesley's preferred medievalism. In other words, perhaps it was a provisional attempt to fend off modernism. In any case, the trustees scrapped the design in 1948 in favor of further proposals "on modern lines," as noted in their minutes.

The trustees seem to have settled upon the Shepley firm without considering any others, but they did not settle so easily upon a modernist design. Nor did the architects themselves embrace modernism with much confidence. The firm had not previously ventured very often beyond its established revivalist territory, and this inexperience showed in a series of preliminary designs that are interesting to the historian precisely for being so awkward. The design history of the New Dorms is worth noting because it is characteristic: it provides a record of the moment and an example of the process in which modernism was assimilated by the American architectural and educational establishment. What Wellesley and the Shepley firm went through together looks in retrospect like a rite of passage.

Son of the firm's founder, the principal architect for the project was senior partner Henry Richardson Shepley, named for his famous grandfather. He graduated in 1910 from Harvard and in 1914 from the Ecole des Beaux-Arts, where his training was supremely well suited to the kind of architecture

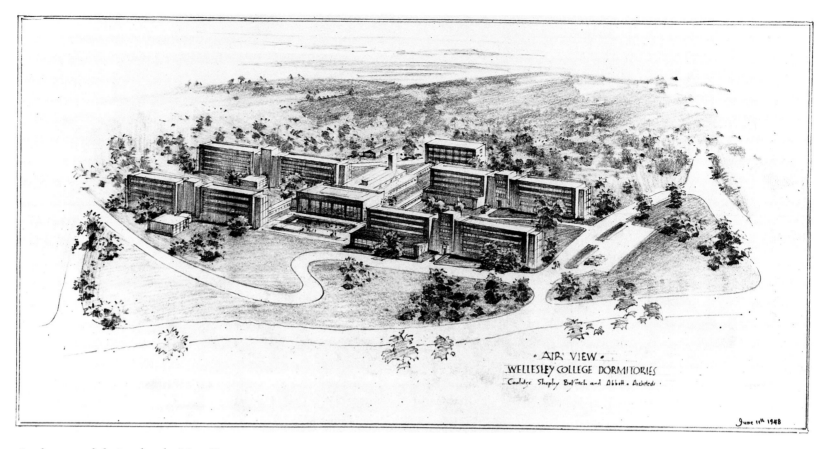

· AIR· VIEW ·
WELLESLEY COLLEGE DORMITORIES
Coolidge Shepley Bulfinch and Abbott · Architects ·

June 11th 1948

In the second design for the New Dorms, principal architect Henry Shepley adopted a typical modernist vocabulary of flat roofs, strip windows, and unornamented surfaces. Yet his longtime allegiance to Beaux-Arts planning principles is still evident in the pronounced symmetry of the vast layout, which would have required extensive leveling of the hilly site near the eastern edge of the campus.

he produced for most of his long career. In his designs for the New Dorms from 1948 onward, he adopted a typical modernist vocabulary of flat roofs, unornamented surfaces, strip windows, and window walls. But in the more fundamental aspects of planning spaces and composing masses, Shepley clearly retained a Beaux-Arts preference for using symmetry, hierarchy, and geometry to generate designs.

Most of the designs preserved in the firm's files as well as the College Archives comprise variations on three successive schemes, in a sequence that seems to show the architect gradually relinquishing his predilections, as the concept becomes less grand in scale and less assertive in shape. The first scheme calls for a single monumental building, not so unlike the neo-Georgian design, with four long dormitory wings extending in an H-shape from kitchen and dining rooms at the center, with servants' quarters at the rear. Though the living room at the front of each dormitory wing is treated somewhat differently, the arrangement is otherwise symmetrical. The next scheme sets the four dormitories into two separate, very large quadrangle-like blocks. Each is markedly asymmetrical in massing and articulation, but as a pair they mirror each other. In one variant they are juxtaposed on the site at ninety degrees, in another at an oblique angle. In the variants of the third scheme, which evolved into the final design, the complex is further broken down into looser arrangements of four separate components: three dormitory blocks and a block for kitchen and dining rooms.

How did the trustees' thinking contribute to the design development? Their Buildings and Grounds Committee rejected the first scheme in January 1949 for being "too extreme and severe" in its modernism but noted also that it would not "use the contours of the site chosen in a sufficiently interesting way." Perhaps the latter issue was meant to be addressed by the separate, more manipulable blocks of the second scheme, presented a few months later, which the committee liked. By the end of the year, however, this was abandoned as the result of a reassessment of the whole project, which led in turn to the third scheme.

Confronted with the disappointing results thus far of the Seventy-Fifth Anniversary Fund, the Board of Trustees and new President Margaret Clapp '30 decided in November 1949 that if the project were to proceed at all, it must be drastically scaled back. Having just taken office at the start of that semester, President Clapp in particular felt committed to bring to some state of completion so important an endeavor handed down by her much admired predecessor, Mildred McAfee Horton. Therefore the building program was reduced from four to two units housing 100 students each, with the construction of the remainder postponed indefinitely. More ominously, aesthetic considerations were also to be curtailed. In December, in a letter announcing the revised program to the deans, Clapp warned that the building "is to be functional, with, if necessary, beauty or symmetry on the outside sacrificed for good living on the inside"; the goal was "to have a dormitory stripped of all luxuries and in simple good taste." A month later, the chairman of the Buildings and Grounds Committee, Boston lawyer F. Murray Forbes, declared similarly: "The simplification of the new building is not expected to lessen the comfort or the cheerfulness of the living quarters, and, functionally, it will be up-to-date. The esthetic side is not being overlooked, but this, because of the financial restrictions, may be the one element of criticism which may not be escaped." This followed his announcement, at the same trustees meeting in January 1950, that the Shepley firm had made "a complete new start from scratch."

Over the next few months, the building program was modified once again, more optimistically, to distribute 400 students in three dormitory units, one of them to be planned with the others but built later. The redistribution followed from a decision to house two-thirds of the students in double rooms, whereas the earlier plans called mostly for singles. This was purely a "concession to economy—not in itself anything desirable," according to the committee. They also economized significantly by eliminating the servants' quarters included in earlier designs and planning for a sharp reduction in maid service, which was soon to be eliminated by attrition throughout the College. All students in the New Dorms—not just those assigned jobs for financial aid— would be required to contribute a few hours each week to housecleaning (this revived a Durant-era regimen ended by the College's second president, Alice Freeman). Another economizing feature in the building program had been conceived from the start of the project: each dormitory would have its own dining room, but all three would be served by a single kitchen, which would moreover be equipped to provide breakfast and lunch from a cafeteria counter. Dinner would continue to be served at table by student waitresses on financial aid. In sum, the updated way of life that the College sought to model at the New Dorms would be distinctly more egalitarian as well as more economical. By the time they opened, Wellesley had furthermore abolished the "cooperative" house system and also the segregation of first-year students.

The revised building program induced Henry Shepley to design with fewer and simpler components and consequently fewer elements of articulation from part to part. Both his earlier schemes, by contrast, were perhaps over-articulated, with a variety of demarcations and transitions providing, though clad in modernism, the kind of detailed hierarchy typical of Beaux-Arts planning. But the simplified layout made possible by the new program still required a fundamental hierarchical distinction between front and back: the kitchen and dining block would need an entrance and an access drive separate from those for the dormitory blocks. This had been a challenge throughout the planning process, given the limiting factors of topography and the existing road system; some variants of Shepley's earlier schemes would have required extensive roadwork. The architect had to deal also with two further issues of layout and siting that derived from particular concerns of the Buildings and Grounds Committee. Mindful of the long winter, they wanted the dormitories sited to provide students' rooms with optimal sunlight, and they did not want students to have to walk outside to reach the dining rooms.

The architect's solution was to space the dormitory wings at generous intervals in a staggered, asymmetrical alignment at right angles to a spine of kitchen and dining rooms set beneath them, tucked into the hillside. The spine was curved slightly to angle the dormitory wings outward in a fan shape, so that the spaces between them widened toward the south/southeast. Taking advantage of the site, this split-level arrangement was a neat, economical solution to the access problem as well: segregated by level, access to the front of the dormitory wings and to the back of the kitchen was provided in one compact area, at the heel of the fan shape, by two short drives branching off from Fiske Road as it climbed onward past Simpson Infirmary.

The contrast between this design, worked out from late 1950 into the following year, and Shepley's previous proposals is almost startling. His earlier schemes relied, in the traditional manner, on predetermined aesthetic priorities, to which the architectural problem solving was adapted. But the final design for the New Dorms took shape remarkably directly and thoroughly from the particulars and exigencies of the building program, the site, and, ultimately, the budget. It was a genuine modernist product, wrought wholly in the present.

In the parts as in the whole, the plan of the New Dorms is straightforward and economical. The result is a surprisingly interesting massing of the constituent volumes, as the parts themselves create, instead of being fitted to, the shapes. The monotony of the long slender dormitory blocks is relieved

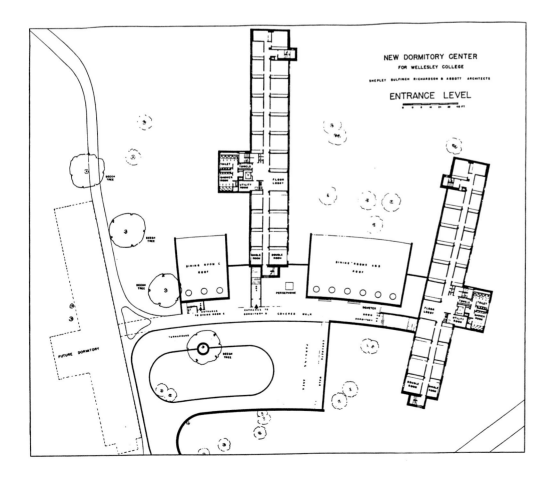

By 1950, the building program for the New Dorms had been considerably scaled back as a result of the College's financial woes. The plan as commissioned, seen here at entrance level, provided three dormitories, one to be built later, and eliminated servants' quarters included in earlier designs. Three dining rooms (two of them separated only by a moveable partition, so the whole space could be opened for dances) and the single kitchen serving them are set one story lower, tucked into the slope of the site.

The final design for the New Dorms was a straightforward modernist response to the challenges of the site, the building program, and the budget. The informal staggered layout and split-level massing of the complex subtly relax its bold geometry and help to settle it into the landscape. The dormitory wings fan out to the south and southeast to take advantage of winter sunlight.

by projecting elements that enclose a staircase at the front end of each block, a core of utilities partway down one side and another staircase on the opposite side near the other end of the block. All these rise an extra story at the top, along with small penthouses, adding variety to the flat rooflines. At ground level on the downward slope of the site, the dining rooms between the dormitory wings likewise project as separate volumes, emphasized by their higher ceilings. (Two of the three dining rooms are joined together, divided only by a folding partition, thus designed so that the whole space can be opened for dances.)

When the New Dorms are approached from the front, through the entrance court over the kitchen block, the size and mass of the split-level complex are downplayed. The three wings are joined by the curve of a slimly scaled covered walkway and, a little beyond it, the parallel brick wall that screens from view the tops of the dining rooms. The walkway steps down

toward Fiske Road. The curve of the walkway, the curve of the entrance drive, the slope of the site—all approaches to the complex are oblique, and thus all views of it are constantly shifting, so that the simple boxy volumes are enriched with sculptural values, not to mention the framing effects of the landscape around them. What the New Dorms lack in intricacy of detail is in some measure made up in the picturesque variability with which they present themselves to the viewer.

Most of the exterior is treated very simply. Windows are thinly framed in white against red brick walls, in deference to traditional treatments elsewhere on the campus. In the typical modernist manner, the size and shape of the windows vary in discrete groupings keyed to the different spaces and functions they serve. The dining rooms and other communal spaces along the base of the complex are opened to the view with window walls. On the ground floor of the dormitory wings, these are given a distinctive variation: in seminar rooms, apartments for heads of house, and other areas where floor-to-ceiling glass was unwanted, solid walls rise here and there but only to door height, with the glass of the adjacent window walls continuing across their tops. This continuous strip of glass across the top of the story adds emphasis to the building's characteristic modernist proclamation of its skeletal construction. Thus the naked reinforced-concrete columns that support these parts of the structure are conspicuously displayed set back just a little way from the glass walls. (In the upper stories the structural support is provided by a skeletal frame set within the walls.) The five-story dormitory wings are thereby shown to poise lightly upon the site. And yet, in an amusingly

Seen from the curving slope of the entrance drive (shown here before the third dormitory was built), the complex seems relatively lightweight and modest in scale. In the planning and construction of the New Dorms, great care was taken to preserve some of the most venerable trees on the site.

Though the New Dorms are thoroughly modernist in design, their materials and colors defer politely to Wellesley's prevailing revivalist architecture. The glassiest stretches of the exterior, serving the communal spaces along the base of the complex, are strikingly juxtaposed with fieldstone traditionally used for foundations, and its texture helps to link the buildings' stark shapes to the landscape.

complementary connotation, they are also securely tied to the site: the partial wall panels are clad in the same fieldstone, traditionally favored for foundations, used here for low retaining walls extending outward from the buildings to enclose patios.

The exposed, freestanding structural support and the unencumbered window wall it makes feasible are familiar hallmarks of modernism, enshrined by Le Corbusier, for instance, among his "Five Points of the New Architecture" in 1926. The first two of the New Dorms, Bates and Freeman Halls (named for the poet and Wellesley's second president), were completed in 1952, long after modernism's innovating phase. But their date is worth noting within the context of some much-publicized, standard examples of American modernism. The all-glass house in Plano, Illinois, that Mies van der Rohe designed for Edith Farnsworth is dated 1945–1951; in New Canaan, Connecticut, Philip Johnson's very similar house for himself is dated 1949; and Lever House, the canonical New York glass office building by Skidmore, Owings and Merrill, is dated 1951. Though extremely modest by comparison with these works, the glassy stretches of the New Dorms must have struck their first occupants as a still somewhat glamorous novelty.

The New Dorms are more closely related to significant modernist architecture arising at the same time in the Boston area. Alvar Aalto's Baker House on MIT's riverfront opened in 1949. It too is a tall red brick dormitory

that defers politely to its neighbors and, in a different way, takes advantage of a picturesque site. The well-known work that the New Dorms most resemble is the Graduate Center at Harvard, designed by The Architects Collaborative, the firm Walter Gropius founded with some of his students from the Harvard Graduate School of Design. Built to a small scale and a tight budget in 1949–1950, the Graduate Center is lower than the New Dorms and faced in cream-colored rather than red brick, and it occupies a flat urban site. But it is fundamentally similar as an airy composition of slim dormitory wings linked by covered walkways to a slightly curved commons building. There are similarities also in the detailing, such as the partial-wall motif, and there are still further reasons for supposing that the Graduate Center influenced the final design for Wellesley's New Dorms. The Shepley firm was also working at Harvard during the late 1940s, and Henry Shepley himself, through long association with the Graduate School of Design, had connections with Gropius. When Gropius applied for U. S. citizenship in 1937, Shepley served as one of his sponsors, along with the dean who brought Gropius to Harvard, where he chaired the Department of Architecture. If Shepley learned modernism late, he had the opportunity, at least, to learn it in the ambience of one of its pioneers. Younger architects in the Shepley firm were in charge of two Harvard projects spanning the same years as the New Dorms, Lamont Library of 1947 and Allston Burr Lecture Hall of 1951. The former is similar to the New Dorms but less thoroughgoing in its modernism, while the latter, now demolished, was designed in a slightly different, cooler and sleeker idiom.

Predictably, the Graduate Center design generated a certain amount of controversy within the Harvard community. A comparable conflict over a modernist commission for a revivalist campus had resulted in an embarrassing incident—marked by student protest and one professor's resignation—a few years earlier at Wheaton College, whose new president refused to build the winning design in a well-publicized competition, for an arts center, held by his predecessor. Wellesley fortunately had no such problem with its new president. Both Margaret Clapp and the Buildings and Grounds Committee certainly harbored some doubts about their project, however, which they sought to allay on a visit in the fall of 1949 to inspect a modernist dormitory recently built by Wellesley's trusted older sister, Mount Holyoke College. It is a rather awkward, halfhearted affair, comparable to Shepley's preliminary designs, but the Wellesley delegation was sufficiently impressed, or at least relieved, by it to ask Shepley to consult on pricing of construction with Mount Holyoke's contractor.

In this architect's rendering of the ground-story living room in Bates Hall, the most telling feature stylistically is the exposure of the skeletal structure: the concrete columns, set back from the window walls they make feasible. At the time, such large expanses of glass were still a somewhat glamorous novelty with which few students would have lived before coming to Wellesley.

From start to finish of the New Dorms project, Wellesley persisted in emphasizing the unavoidability of modernism as an economic necessity, and the Shepley firm did likewise. The latter's publicity was handled by Joseph P. Richardson, a younger cousin of Henry Shepley who was made partner in 1950. In an article in Wellesley's alumnae magazine, celebrating the opening of the first two dorms in the fall of 1952, Richardson wrote that the budget and program required that "not a square foot of space was wasted nor any money spent on purely aesthetic embellishment," so that modernism was "a foregone conclusion." He also justifiably pointed out that the materials, siting, and other aspects of the design nevertheless conformed to "the spirit of the College" and contributed to "a feeling already prevailing at Wellesley which is affected by neither period nor style."

The notion that modernist architecture was aesthetically lacking led to an "embellishment" of the New Dorms that Wellesley did not have to pay for. Trustee Dorothy Bridgman Atkinson Rood '10 and her husband John offered a sculpture by the latter and were persuaded to donate as well the expensive bluestone paving for its setting, the walkway linking Bates and Freeman Halls. (The bluestone did not wear well and was soon replaced with brick.) In a newspaper interview the sculptor asserted: "Modern architecture needs sculpture, because it is so plain, bold and unadorned." Rood chose as his subject Persephone, through which he wanted "to express the burgeoning of plants in the spring." The limestone sculpture is a bud-shaped, abstracted female figure rendered as bands of stylized vegetation defining a curvaceous open core, which in retrospect seems almost as suggestive, though hardly as impressive artistically, as the flowers of Georgia O'Keeffe. The freestanding figure is chaperoned, at a little distance, by a more subdued wall panel carved in relief and intended to evoke Demeter, Persephone's mother. The overall

In this 1952 photograph, Trustee Dorothy Bridgman Atkinson Rood '10 and her husband John Rood pose with his sculpture Persephone, *which they donated to help compensate for the modernist plainness of the New Dorms' exterior. Set near the entrance to Bates Hall, the abstracted, bud-shaped female figure was intended to evoke springtime.*

effect of the ensemble is essentially decorative and avoids the darker implications of the subject, so typical of the period's pyschosexualizing interest in myth.

The third dorm in the complex opened in 1961, with the name under which the former president had served for nine of her fourteen years in office. The building's original plan was somewhat modified by Richardson, who probably had a hand in the final design of the first two dorms as well. Built along the highest edge of the site, McAfee sits one story higher than the others and has a different layout on the ground floor. Its living room is located in a separate volume opening onto the front walkway. Richardson designed the living room to incorporate, rather surprisingly, two architectural antiquities he secured as gifts from the Hearst Foundation, a French Gothic fireplace and a Gothic ceiling from an Austrian town providentially named Wels. Explaining the acquisition of these "art treasures" in a memo to the chairman of the Buildings and Grounds Committee, he conveyed a characteristic attitude: "The contemporary nature of architecture today is imposed for economic reasons and the lack of craftsmen. Wellesley was therefore most fortunate to obtain these relics of the past, making possible for the girls not only to sleep and study in accommodations of today but also to meet one another and entertain in a true atmosphere of the past."

The New Dorms offered Wellesley students an array of novel amenities, most of them gender-related: on each floor a kitchenette and a lounge with built-in ironing boards and convenient electrical outlets for hair dryers; in the communal bathrooms, special basins with sprayers for shampooing; besides washers and dryers in the basement, a drying room with racks for hand laundry of delicate items; and built-in bookshelves and dressers, complete with mirrors, in student rooms slightly more spacious than was the norm at Wellesley. Students contributed to the planning of these features, which ensured the popularity of the New Dorms while they were indeed still new. But within a decade after McAfee opened, the dorms began to lose favor, for reasons that are not very hard to reckon. The style of student life changed considerably. The use of ironing boards, to take just one emblematic example, surely diminished sharply during the 1960s. More broadly, after modernist architecture had become commonplace and was taken for granted in the society at large, its presence at Wellesley seemed intrusively banal. To impatient eyes, the simple, restrained exterior of the New Dorms was liable to evoke too readily, though unfairly, the housing projects of the declining inner cities or perhaps the standard-issue motels scattered through chaotic strip developments at the cities' edges. By contrast, the conventionalized quaintness of

Students participated in planning the New Dorms' novel amenities, which included kitchenettes and lounges with built-in ironing boards and conveniently high-set electrical outlets for hairdryers. As indicated in this early photograph, the College recycled a good many older items in the furnishing of the New Dorms.

The New Dorms' neat built-in dressers and bookcases conduced to slightly more spacious student rooms than were standard in Wellesley's older residences. The walls were painted in cheerful pastel colors.

DOUBLE ROOM

Wellesley's revivalist architecture looked increasingly, charmingly rarefied as it aged, accruing a little authentic patina of its own. Despite a far better provenance, Richardson's token "true atmosphere of the past" in the McAfee living room could hardly hope to compete in nostalgic appeal.

The total cost of the New Dorms was about $3.8 million. The College borrowed $1.8 million from the John Hancock Insurance Company to cover most of the cost of the first two dorms and, while still repaying that debt, borrowed another million from the federal government in order to build McAfee. The project was a heavy burden that perforce brought the whole of Wellesley's finances into sharp focus, impelled a reorganization of fund-raising, and no doubt set President Margaret Clapp's frugality on permanent alert.

Wellesley's first modernist architecture was discreetly placed. In both the planning and the construction of the New Dorms, great care was taken to preserve the most impressive trees on the heavily wooded site, so that from the start the complex was integrated into the landscape. Thus it was framed and enriched in the approved picturesque manner but also all the more hidden away in its location near the periphery of the campus. Only a few years after the completion of Bates and Freeman Halls, however, the College commissioned a conspicuous modernist building for a commanding position at the very heart of the campus, on Norumbega Hill. The decision was surprising in several respects.

The history of the Jewett Arts Center is linked with that of the major addition to the College library completed in the same year, 1958. Both projects answered to long-felt needs, which had been addressed in a number of reports and tentative plans and were listed among the top priorities of the disappointing Seventy-Fifth Anniversary Fund campaign, but they finally took shape very differently from what had long been anticipated. At the start of the campaign, the consensus was that a new library should be built on Norumbega Hill. The College's library was drastically overstocked with 225,000 volumes in a building intended, when it was first expanded in 1915–1916, to house 150,000. To allow also for increased services and a reasonable span of further growth, the library would need at the very least to be doubled in size. This seemed to merit a wholly new building, which would be ideal as a more imposing replacement for Norumbega Hall, the last remaining cottage and sole wooden structure on the hill. Once the New Dorms were built, Norumbega would no longer be needed as a residential unit incongruously set within the academic and administrative center of the College. Relocating the library there would be an emphatic expression of its central importance. The old library building seemed well suited, in turn, to be taken over by the Department of Music, which had outgrown nearby Billings and Music Halls. As for the Department of Art, which for decades had been severely crowded in Farnsworth, its needs could be met with an addition linking the latter, remodeled, with the new library and thus completing the quadrangle-like composition suggested by the layout of the other buildings on Norumbega Hill.

Already in 1940, in a report to the standing faculty committee on the library building, Librarian Blanche Prichard McCrum had proposed such a scheme and helpfully provided a short list of recent college library buildings. Among them was a library addition at Mount Holyoke designed by the Boston firm of Allen, Collens and Willis, who were, as she noted, "Specialists in Collegiate Gothic." Six years later, with Seventy-Fifth Anniversary Fund-raising in mind, the Board of Trustees commissioned the successor firm of Collens, Willis and Beckonert to prepare tentative plans for the scheme and specified what had been assumed all along, that the new buildings should conform to the style of Green and Pendleton Halls.

With this last condition, however, the project ran into trouble with the art department, whose position on style was already on record. In December 1945, well before the architects were engaged, art history professor Serarpie

Der Nercessian had written to President Horton that "if we have an art building we should like it to be of the same material as the other buildings on Norumbega Hill and in general harmony with them. But we should certainly not want a Gothic façade which would add considerably to the expense and be entirely unsatisfactory for lighting and other purposes." In an undated letter written some time after plans had been submitted, she stressed again, "All of us in the department, without any exception, are very respectfully, but also very greatly opposed to a Gothic building which" for a number of reasons "could not be a building adequately planned for modern usage." These objections, along with the art department's understanding of architectural harmony on Norumbega Hill, were amplified and spelled out in yet another, somewhat more confrontational letter to the president written in May 1947 by art professor Agnes Abbott. After detailing many problems in the plans, she asserted the department's expertise in the matter by noting its pedagogical role in "developing an understanding and appreciation of sound architectural design," in which both the Collegiate Gothic style generally and these particular architects fell short. She warned that "further development of the present plans" was unlikely "to produce results which we should feel able to approve," even if these architects "were released from the specification that the exterior conform to the Gothic style."

At that point, the project came to a halt anyway, awaiting funding. In the spring of 1949, the trustees resumed discussion of it, though the financial prospect remained dim. The chairman of the Buildings and Grounds Committee reported that architect Willis had recently, on his own initiative, produced new studies and proposed, unexpectedly, that the exterior "could be designed on contemporary lines without damage to the general appearance of the Quadrangle"—perhaps his attempt to salvage what looked like a doomed endeavor. He was immediately asked to drop the studies, lest the College feel morally obliged to pay out any more to the firm, which had been engaged purely for preliminary work. Though the trustees now requested specifications from library and art building committees, in preparation for more decisive action in the future, they were in effect merely marking time.

Thus the failure of the Seventy-Fifth Anniversary Fund campaign forestalled what might have developed into an unpleasant dispute with the art department, which was committed to modernist architecture. What is most interesting about the episode is that the art department also wanted a building in harmony with its neighbors but, unlike the trustees, had a clear vision of how modernism could achieve this. Indeed, Abbott's explanation to President Horton in 1947 seems to anticipate the design of the Jewett Arts Center: the new building "should conform in material and in scale to the existing buildings"; "we should certainly want" its windows "to continue the measure and rhythm characteristic of the windows of the whole group"; and if its mass "were more broken up, more informally treated, and if it took better advantage of the site" than did the Collens firm's proposal, "it could be made not only to harmonize" but also "to offer a pleasing variety ... in much the same way that diverse styles have grown up harmoniously side by side in many European cities."

Just as earlier reports had done, the specifications supplied to the trustees by the library committee in 1950 called for a new building, but with no new funding in sight President Clapp soon ordered a reconsideration of the feasibility of adding to the old building. By early 1954 and after much consultation, she decided in favor of a major addition that would meet most but not all of the specifications yet cost significantly less than wholly new construction. Though a new building would be ideal, she regarded it as a luxury, an unwise allocation of whatever funds were to be raised in the foreseeable future. As with the Seventy-Fifth Anniversary Fund, her strategy was a reflection of her priorities: she favored faculty salaries over buildings. She later remarked, "An adequate library with an excellent faculty will make a better college than an excellent library with an adequate faculty."

In April 1954, a surprise gift from unfamiliar benefactors suddenly set the project into motion. Having come across an old brochure for the Seventy-Fifth Anniversary Fund while going through the papers of his late alumna niece, David M. Mahood was inspired to answer its call for a new library. In memory of Helen Ritchie Petit '28, he and her mother, his sister Helen M. Petit, offered $500,000 provided that the College could raise the remainder needed to start building soon. When brought up to date on the project, the donors fortunately agreed to an addition rather than a new building as long as construction began by June 1956.

The trustees easily settled upon the obvious choice by commissioning the College library's original architects, the Shepley firm, for the new work. The architect in charge of the project was James F. Clapp, Jr. (no relation to Margaret), who had supervised the design of Harvard's Lamont Library. He came specially recommended for his cooperativeness, or pliancy, by the director of Lamont, Keyes Metcalf, who was serving as consultant to Wellesley.

President Margaret Clapp '30

Metcalf claimed that in reality he himself had laid out the plan of Lamont, with Clapp merely doing the drawing.

Construction began on schedule thanks to a successful campaign in the name of the Development Fund, which had been established at the end of the Seventy-Fifth Anniversary Fund campaign. The latter's failing was ultimately that of inefficiency, so the rationale for the new entity was to combine and thus to coordinate what had previously been two independent fund-raising structures run by the Alumnae Association and the Board of Trustees. The organizational advantage of the new joint structure was confirmed by the speed with which a package of old and new financial resources was assembled to cover, with the Petit gift, the library project's cost of $1.6 million.

The Shepley firm remodeled the interior of the old building and added new construction that doubled the size of the library. The addition is a simple rectangular volume, extending west from the original reading room in order to make use of the downward slope of the site toward Longfellow Pond. This allowed the architect to squeeze four low stories into a structure rising no higher than the two-storied older structure. The continuity in height and the integrity of the shape are basic but effective means of unifying the exterior, in

Long overdue, a major expansion of the College library was commissioned in 1955 from the Shepley firm, architects of the original structure. The building committee balked at the glassy, rather conventional modernist treatment of the windows in this penultimate version of the ingeniously compact design.

Wellesley College Library
Shepley Bulfinch Richardson Abbott Architects

The revised window treatment of the library addition combines abstract modernist form with elements of traditional imagery. The alternating rhythm of the window frame motif as well as the diagonal checkered pattern in the wall panels subtly enliven an otherwise sober composition.

sympathy with the neo-classical style of the original building. At the juncture, the new structure commences with a spacious interval of blank wall, imitating in concrete the limestone cladding of the original building. This provides a neutral element of transition to the modernist style of the rest of the exterior, the west façade of which is now hidden within the later extension of this wing.

The design of the exterior was a last-minute revision, undertaken by Henry Shepley himself in May 1956, after the rest of the design had been approved. Up to that point, the greater part of the exterior was to be given over to strip windows of a conventional modernist type, with thin mullions and overall a lightweight, somewhat slick look the trustees were bound to dislike.

The revised design is far less glassy and, more interestingly, far less conventional in its modernism. Beyond the transitional blank wall, the unusual window treatment of the upper three stories, which project moderately over strip windows retained in the plainer ground story, combines elements of both modernist and traditional window types. The leading motif is an abstracted yet recognizable window frame composed of the same flat bands of limestone sheathing used to face the edges of the story slabs. Repeated throughout the design, it stretches the full height of each story. Its bottom edge coincides with the edge of the story slab, while its top is a separate band underlining the story slab above, with a deeply recessed line between the two.

The most telling detail is that the two bands of limestone are joined briefly at the center, where the recessed line is interrupted—as if by the head of a vestigial keystone in this vestigial neo-classical window frame.

These window frames are spaced in a regular rhythm that alternates from story to story, producing a checkered pattern of rectangles. The intervening spans are two-and-a-half times the width of the window frames; the proportional scheme of the whole design derives from, without copying, the older building. On the north façade, the intervals between the framed windows are themselves filled with glass, so that in this main view of the library, the effect is of old and new architectural conventions layered together—the vestigial neo-classical windows are set into modernist walls that are also windows. Across the west façade, the intervals between the windows are clad in traditional masonry in which a rather surprising diaper pattern (a gridiron set on the diagonal) is picked out subtly yet distinctly in blocks of white marble and light gray limestone. Because the diaper unit is square, its repetitions are offset from those of the rectangular pattern set by the windows—an effect that emphasizes the thinness of this ornamentation, as if it were merely a patterned wallpaper abruptly cut to fit. (The west façade treatment is still visible, at very close range, story by story, within the library stacks. During the later addition, most of the façade was simply left in place to serve as an interior wall, with the glass removed from the window frames.) The south façade combines the treatments of the other two in a symmetrical composition, with intervals of glass down the center and patterned masonry down the sides.

All in all, for the time and for the firm, the exterior of the library addition was quite a performance. On command from the Wellesley trustees, the Shepley firm adapted its not very longstanding practice of modernism to accommodate, without reverting to, its former practice of revivalism. The addition's modernized references to the old library could be considered paraphrases as distinguished from quotations. Slightly later, in two new Houses at Harvard, the firm again sought to augment its own heritage in an up-to-date yet deferential idiom, but their Wellesley design is subtler, finer, and more sophisticated.

Indeed, the Wellesley design reflects a much broader shift within modernist architectural practice at that moment, by no means limited to older architects whose tastes were still innately conservative. For instance, the use of the abstracted window frame, particularly in the composition of the glassy north façade, bears a certain resemblance to the exterior of a well-known work by the prominent modernist Eero Saarinen—his American Embassy in London, which was designed in the spring of 1956, just a few months before the revision of the Wellesley library exterior. Coincidentally perhaps, but not surprisingly, Henry Shepley, who was regarded as a distinguished elder statesman within the profession, served on the U.S. State Department's Architectural Advisory Committee and was thereby a juror in the competition for the embassy building. Saarinen's abstracted window frames are bolder, more thickly set, and livelier in their effect than those at Wellesley, but they too are repeated in a checkered pattern, and they were similarly inspired by their context, in this case the vernacular Georgian architecture of London. (A detailed account of the Saarinen commission is provided by Jane Canter Loeffler '68 in her superb, authoritative history of the whole span of the State Department's important patronage, *The Architecture of Diplomacy*, published in 1998.)

The effect of sheer, applied ornament in the masonry diaper pattern seems the most unlikely and idiosyncratic aspect of the Wellesley design. The pattern does not derive from the original library, but it is comparable to the diaper pattern set in bicolored brick on the towers of the Hazard Quadrangle. There is also a more general, inherent resemblance between its stepped diagonals in a muted color contrast and the pervasive stepwise texture of contrasting brick and mortar on buildings all around Severance Green. These affinities suggest that the architect's larger motivation was to include within the new addition's frame of reference Wellesley's prevailing medievalism as well as the anomalous classicism of the old library. In any case, the library addition's diaper pattern served to enrich and to enliven somewhat a comparatively stolid, monochrome building subjected to deep views through one of the loveliest spaces on the campus. Perhaps the pattern's best justification is merely this appropriate strategy of contributing to a picturesque view—a reflexive response to the ruling aesthetic of the place.

CHAPTER NINE

THE JEWETT ARTS CENTER

This view of the open stairway passage under the entrance to the Jewett Arts Center captures both the monumentality and the finely scaled detail with which architect Paul Rudolph sought to adapt his design to its setting.

THE JEWETT ARTS CENTER is, by any standard, one of the most important buildings at Wellesley. It is one of the very few that are widely known beyond the campus. For architectural historians, it has special status as a highly original, experimental work that launched a major career at an interesting point in the history of American modernism. In the history of the institution, it embodies conspicuously both the good fortunes and the longstanding formative influence of one of the College's largest and strongest academic departments.

Put simply, what provided the impetus for Jewett was concern for maintaining the beauty of the campus. The story begins at the same meeting in May 1954 at which the Board of Trustees first endorsed President Margaret Clapp's proposal to add to the old rather than build a new College library. This would in turn allow an alteration in the standing plan to meet the art department's needs with an addition to a remodeled Farnsworth Art Building—the library's loss of a site on Norumbega Hill could become the art department's gain. What the Buildings and Grounds Committee now recommended was that the Farnsworth addition be built as soon as funds were raised, but in such a way that it could be extended into a wholly new, self-sufficient facility, adjacent to the old, at some point in the future. The plan seemed prudent and fair, given the College's other commitments, and consistent with the strategy of building the New Dorms in phases, as funding allowed.

The problem with the plan was Farnsworth, and it was essentially an aesthetic problem. As the committee had taken into account, the trustees considered Farnsworth too sturdy to raze, even when a new art building was completed, although they also acknowledged, at the meeting, that no one thus far had proposed a new use for it once the art department no longer needed it. In truth, Farnsworth may have been venerable as one of the oldest buildings on campus, but it was distinctly unlovable. No one liked the look of it, particularly in its almost painfully awkward juxtaposition to the splendid ensemble of Founders, Green, and Pendleton Halls. The 1940s plan to complete the Academic Quadrangle in their Gothic style, linking Farnsworth through its addition to a large new library, might have lessened its impact. But by this point, revivalist architecture was no longer an option, and the new proposal's incremental approach highlighted the obvious question of what an addition to Farnsworth would look like. It would occupy an especially conspicuous site, on the edge of Norumbega Hill in full view of Severance Green, and in all likelihood it would stand there in its fragmentary state, attached to the end of Farnsworth, for some time before money could be found to extend it into a complete new building—at which point it would still be attached to something unattractive.

To one dissenting trustee on the Buildings and Grounds Committee, the outlook was so intolerable that she brought to the meeting of the full board a bold counterproposal. Jeanette Johnson Dempsey '24 argued that Farnsworth in effect prevented the College from realizing a great opportunity on an important site. Raising money to "repair an ancient mistake" would be difficult, she predicted, and the old building would be a constraint on the design of anything adjacent to it. Above all, the art department deserved better: how could aesthetic appreciation be taught in a building "so poorly designed, so atrociously built and so unmitigatedly ugly?" The College should aim high: for a department dealing in "beauty as its first reason for existence," she proposed that "we engage the services of the best possible modern architect now available in this country. Only the creative genius of a great architect can give us the satisfying quality of inherent beauty." Tackling head-on the issue of style, Mrs. Dempsey invoked both the suitability and the affordability of modernist architecture: "It should not be an elaborate building or over-expensive in materials. Our new dormitories have shown us how appropriate to the campus the simplicity of modern architecture can be." And she further suggested that in choosing an architect the College should seek the advice of three distinguished and closely connected professionals who were longtime champions of modernism: Alfred H. Barr, Jr., who had taught briefly at Wellesley, as she pointed out, before founding the Museum of Modern Art in 1929; Smith College professor Henry-Russell Hitchcock, well known for his work on that museum's influential 1932 exhibition and related book

The International Style; and Wellesley's resident expert, already involved in the project, art history professor and director of the College museum John McAndrew, who had been curator of architecture at the Museum of Modern Art in 1937–1941.

Mrs. Dempsey's enthusiasm for modernist architecture undoubtedly owed something to her younger brother, the architect and critic Philip Johnson, who might easily have been a fourth expert on her list. He had served the Museum of Modern Art in a number of ways, was a close ally of Barr, and the co-author with Hitchcock of *The International Style*. Mrs. Dempsey may have thought that it would be impolitic to mention him, but probably not because she supposed he could be a suitable candidate for the Wellesley commission. More likely, she bore in mind that her brother and McAndrew, once friends, had long ago fallen out. Johnson was disdainful of McAndrew's work at the Museum of Modern Art, while McAndrew was disgusted by Johnson's pro-Nazi activities from the mid-1930s into the early days of World War II.

But where would Wellesley find the money for such a project? Mrs. Dempsey made an unusual, conditional offer. If she "could be assured that the architect would be outstanding" and every effort would be made to have "a beautiful building," she volunteered to raise funds for it "quietly and without recourse to alumnae or regular donors to the College," given that all normal fund-raising for the next year would have to be devoted to the library addition, to meet the deadline set by the Petit gift, its chief source of funding.

There was no immediate response to Mrs. Dempsey's offer, however. The trustees were not prepared to take any action on the art department project and referred the whole matter back to the Buildings and Grounds Committee. Trustee Mary Cooper Jewett '23 left the meeting with a sense of alarm. When she returned to her home in Spokane, Washington, she told her husband that "the Wellesley campus was going to be ruined by 'a wart on Farnsworth,'" using a vivid turn of phrase she remembered long afterwards, in this quotation from the transcript of a 1973 oral history interview preserved in the College Archives.

The result of Mrs. Jewett's report to her husband was extraordinary but not entirely surprising. George Frederick Jewett quickly decided that this was the occasion for the substantial gift he had been planning to make for some time, an opportunity to fund completely a major project remaining from the Seventy-Fifth Anniversary Fund campaign—to which the largest single gift had been made by Mrs. Jewett, who also funded two seminar rooms in the New Dorms. Mr. Jewett's Wellesley connection now spanned three generations, from his mother and two aunts to his recently graduated daughter, and the family's contributions to the College, in service as well as money, had long been generous. To meet the College's need at a moment of crisis would be a privilege accorded by the family's wealth, based in the timber industry of the Northwest. President Margaret Clapp '30 announced the gift of an art building at the annual meeting of the Alumnae Association in June, just under a month after the impasse of the trustees meeting: it would be "a beautiful, simple, appropriate building" named for Mary Cooper Jewett.

Choosing an architect would be a momentous endeavor. Initially, all parties agreed that the choice should be made through a closed competition among a small number of invited architects. This idea had been discussed since the late 1940s, when the Collens firm's preliminary studies for the Norumbega Hill complex were scrapped, and the project was stalled for lack of funds. The trustees were then persuaded by fund-raisers that a competition would stimulate the interest of potential donors. But it appealed also as a cautious way of dealing with the unfamiliar, untested quality of modernist architecture. The topic was discussed again at the board meeting in May 1954. A few days later, Trustee James Lawrence, Jr., an architect himself, wrote to President Clapp explaining that he favored a competition in part because it would be a safeguard. By way of example, he offered his assessment of Eero Saarinen, who had lately "been mentioned fairly frequently" but whose recent work at Brandeis and MIT Lawrence strongly disliked. "He is undoubtedly an able and accomplished architect, but I feel his reputation far outruns him.... In other words, all have their low moments but a well run competition such as is proposed would guard Wellesley against them." And he gamely included Saarinen in presenting his own "very tentative list" of candidates for the still hypothetical commission. His other choices were all local architects (unlike Saarinen) with strong academic connections: Walter Gropius's firm The Architects Collaborative; Hugh Stubbins, a colleague and successor to Gropius at Harvard; Anderson and Beckwith, architects teaching and also designing at MIT; and the Shepley firm.

Lawrence's inclusion of the Shepley firm, which had not yet been commissioned for the library project, illustrated another appealing aspect of a closed competition: it could include the tried-and-true candidate as a dependable backup choice. John McAndrew worried that the trustees might indeed fall back on the familiar and, in his opinion, inferior Shepley firm, whose New Dorms evidently did not impress him. "They have never done anything distinguished as far as I know," he wrote to his art department colleague Agnes Abbott in June 1954. "I hope that they are not really particular favorites or friends of either Lawrence or Forbes"—a shrewd shorthand reference to the close-knit Boston elite to which the Shepley firm belonged and from which Wellesley perennially drew its trustees. (For example, the Forbes in question was Alexander, who succeeded his father, F. Murray, as chairman of the Buildings and Grounds Committee.) McAndrew went on to speculate that perhaps the firm could be diplomatically eliminated on the basis that the College already had a recent major work by them and sought architectural variety for pedagogical purposes. A similar, realistic wariness of parochial conservatism among the trustees had very likely stirred Mrs. Dempsey in her call for a truly important architect.

The list of competitors McAndrew submitted on behalf of the art department after the Jewett gift was announced overlapped with Lawrence's earlier list. Along with Saarinen and The Architects Collaborative, it included Marcel Breuer, Gropius's colleague and sometime partner from Harvard as well as the Bauhaus long before, who was now based in New York; and also from New York, Edward D. Stone, who with Philip Goodwin had designed the Museum of Modern Art's new building in 1939, during McAndrew's tenure as curator and with his participation. (McAndrew and Barr designed the sculpture garden, later redone by Philip Johnson.) With the exception of the Shepley firm, all the candidates on both lists were thorough modernists with good credentials, at the very least. Thus the trustees and the art department were probably not really very far apart in what they expected of a competition. Certainly McAndrew was experienced: during his years at the Museum of Modern Art, he had served as a juror on the ill-fated Wheaton College arts center competition and organized exhibitions based on it and two other competitions promoted by the museum.

The plan faded away, however. By August the Jewetts had let it be known that, while they were not opposed to a competition, they were inclined to think it might be more trouble than it was worth, considering that its fund-raising rationale no longer held. One objection they hinted at had by this point occurred to other parties as well. A closed competition entailed paying the invited candidates for their entries, an extra expense that was no longer justified as an investment in publicity value. The candidates' presumed

Architect Paul Rudolph

fame would not in itself count for much. Reporting the Jewetts' views to the art department and the Buildings and Grounds Committee, President Clapp said that they felt, "as I am sure all of us do, that a building appropriate to our campus and for our teaching needs is what we want, whether or not the architect is famous."

This last point must have irritated McAndrew no less than Mrs. Dempsey, and it may have been what prompted him to try a new tack with the Buildings and Grounds Committee. By early November 1954, the competition plan had stalled, and the committee was debating how to proceed. McAndrew suggested that they drop the competition and consider just two candidates, both relatively young, one already rather famous, the other not. He cleverly dubbed them "the best" architects under fifty and forty, respectively. They were Eero Saarinen (born in 1910) and Paul Rudolph (born in 1918). Saarinen's career was in full stride, having begun in partnership with his eminent father Eliel. He already had an impressive resumé of conspicuous commissions, especially on campuses, and he was hard to fault as a suitable candidate for the Wellesley job, as James Lawrence had conceded months earlier. Rudolph, on the other hand, was distinctly a dark horse, a name not likely to be recognized outside the profession. Though he had won prizes and a few institutional commissions still in the planning stages, he had thus far built nothing more substantial than a three-bedroom house in far-off Sarasota, Florida, where his practice was based. McAndrew was persuasive, however. The committee decided to keep two other candidates in the running as well—Stubbins and Stone—but apparently in a secondary category, after Saarinen and Rudolph. Three months later, Rudolph had the job.

This was the most unpredictable, most adventurous commission in Wellesley's history. How could the Board of Trustees, by definition a cautious, usually conservative body, have entrusted such a significant project, to be paid for by so important a donor, to an architect who was such an unknown quantity to them? Certainly Rudolph made a remarkable impression at his interview in December 1954, yet in one respect he had the advantage over Saarinen even before the interview. Quite simply, Rudolph was attractive to Wellesley not despite his relative obscurity but because of it: he would be so grateful for the commission, so likely to be accommodating, so anxious to do a good job. At the same time, his talent and his promise were vouched for by the expertise of McAndrew, whose word was in effect an insider's tip on a winner. In her 1973 oral history interview, Mary Cooper Jewett (then Mrs.

Gaiser) explained that Rudolph was chosen "because he was an up-and-coming young man. And frankly they thought it would be a great opportunity for him," whereas "one of the more famous, well-established architects would think of it as just one more job and perhaps not be as thrilled about the opportunity, or as innovative." The Wellesley project did indeed prove to be a great opportunity for Rudolph, who immediately thereafter, in 1958, became chairman of the architecture department at Yale and received the first of the commissions that made him famous, the Yale School of Art and Architecture building. Though very unlike the latter in most respects, in building type Jewett could be said to have served as a rehearsal for it.

McAndrew undoubtedly saw the Jewett commission as a great opportunity also for himself, as something he wrested from what he regarded as the predictable niggling approach of the Wellesley administration and trustees. In mid-December 1954, before departing for the holidays, he wrote to President Clapp to convey in advance the art department's preference for Rudolph, who would be interviewed by the Buildings and Grounds Committee the following week. The deciding question, he said, must be which candidate "is likely to produce the most distinguished design. The problem is one of *quality*, and I hope that we will not be sidetracked into getting anything but the best. We have no first-rate buildings, and I think one would add to the standing of a liberal arts college." This last unflattering comment hints that perhaps Wellesley as much as the architect should be thrilled about the opportunity. It illustrates the connoisseur's conviction, both inspiring and chiding, with which McAndrew and his old friend Barr, among others, had successfully claimed a place for modern art and architecture in the American cultural establishment.

By declaring Rudolph "the best architect under forty" McAndrew the connoisseur was also staking a certain claim as an historian. Throughout his career he had followed the modernist movement closely, beginning with his student pilgrimage to Europe in 1929 (he traveled part of the time with Philip Johnson) to see the Bauhaus and other exemplary buildings when they were still brand-new. In his exhibitions and publications at the Museum of Modern Art, McAndrew called attention to later tendencies within modernism as well as expounding its fundamental principles. He believed in its flexible and progressive character and by the early 1950s he and many other critics saw in Rudolph's work promising evidence of modernism's further development, which he could encourage by bringing the architect to Wellesley.

*John McAndrew, director of
the College Museum*

McAndrew and Rudolph had been personally acquainted for some time, though how they met is unclear. They might conceivably have met soon after their wartime military service, when McAndrew came to Wellesley and Rudolph returned to the Harvard Graduate School of Design to finish his master's degree under Gropius; after undergraduate studies in Alabama, he had been enrolled at Harvard only a year before enlisting in the Navy. Certainly there were many later occasions when their paths could have crossed. Though based in Sarasota, Rudolph traveled frequently and was well connected in architectural circles and in touch with McAndrew's former colleagues at the Museum of Modern Art. In the early 1950s he wrote for various architectural journals and lectured and served as visiting critic at a number of architecture schools, including Harvard. He designed the installation of a furnishings exhibition at the Museum of Modern Art in 1952, and he was scheduled to design another exhibition there, Edward Steichen's immensely popular *Family of Man* photographic survey, just after his interview at Wellesley.

Rudolph's interview in late December 1954 was a great success, as President Clapp reported immediately to the Jewetts. She saw mixed traits of strength and deference in his manner, no doubt fulfilling her expectations of someone up-and-coming rather than famous. He "is confident and modest, stutters a bit yet talks rather fluently. He made an excellent personal impression." More importantly, he responded with enthusiasm to the picturesque aesthetic of the campus and indicated that he could "relate happily" to Wellesley's Gothic architecture "in a modern medium, without affecting the integrity of his own design." This had implications for one of the main issues discussed at the interview, the siting of the new building, which was not yet firmly decided. One reason was that the trustees were awaiting the completion of the Shepley firm's initial feasibility studies for the library addition before committing fully to that project, though the outcome was not much in doubt. Furthermore, though the Jewett gift was intended to avert an eyesore on Norumbega Hill, it inspired some consideration also of other, more spacious but less central sites, in particular Tupelo Point and the western slope of Observatory Hill. The Jewetts for a while favored the latter and suggested that the Norumbega Hill site might be reserved for a student center. But President Clapp, the art department, and Rudolph himself held that art at Wellesley should retain its location at the heart of the campus, and this opinion prevailed. When Saarinen was interviewed shortly afterward, it

With the completion of the Jewett Arts Center in 1958, modernist architecture attained a prominent position at the heart of the Wellesley campus.

counted against him that he favored Tupelo Point so that, as Margaret Clapp recalled in later years, he could "build something completely modern where it wouldn't be clashing" with Gothic.

The art department had long envisioned a modernist building in harmony with its revivalist neighbors, and this was evoked again in the new building program, which was revised by McAndrew from the document supplied to the Buildings and Grounds Committee in 1950. He called for a structure "neither monumental nor loosely rambling, not a single big-scale block but rather a free massing of component parts in sympathetic relation to the landscape and harmonious in scale and materials with its architectural neighbors (though in style not so much their contemporary as our contemporary; one might say an attractive grandchild who has the old family looks but does not wear the old family clothes)."

Well before the commission, Rudolph, too, had been pondering how modernist architecture should respond to its surroundings. The issue was one of the main themes in a lecture entitled "The Changing Philosophy of Architecture" that he gave at the convention of the American Institute of Architects in Boston in June 1954. It was enthusiastically received and soon published in architectural journals. Addressing widespread concerns within the profession, the lecture condemned the increasing standardization and banality seen in the postwar building boom. In particular, Rudolph urged architects to take more responsibility for the urbanistic effects of their buildings, for the sake of greater variety and expressiveness in public spaces. He contrasted American cities' monotonous lineup of glass boxes with the "picturesque grouping of buildings" and the piazzas, courtyards, and interesting spatial sequences he had admired abroad, especially in Italy. There American architects could learn that "it is possible to design a building which is complete in itself but is also related to its neighbors." Thus Rudolph summoned up much the same notion of harmony within variety, inspired by European example, as had Agnes Abbott in her letter to President Horton seven years earlier.

The sparse and shapeless resort community of Sarasota was hardly the place for Rudolph to put these ideas into practice. What he had in mind at the time of the lecture was an important commission he had just received from the U.S. State Department, for an embassy in Amman, Jordan, a project eventually cancelled ostensibly because of a change in American foreign policy. In great contrast to the light and airy beach houses he had been designing in

Sarasota, the building he proposed for the embassy was closed and inward-looking, focused on a courtyard and with relatively few, slit-like windows on the exterior—a design inspired by local architectural traditions. Though the State Department in principle favored this kind of architectural diplomacy, essayed also in Saarinen's London embassy two years later, Rudolph's design was criticized for looking defensive and lacking grandeur, among other things. The State Department's Architectural Advisory Committee approved it reluctantly, after revisions, in January 1955, with member Henry Shepley reportedly having quipped that Rudolph seemed to be "out-Arabing the Arabs" (a piquant detail from Jane Canter Loeffler's account of the project in *The Architecture of Diplomacy*).

The cultural cues were less problematical at Wellesley, where Rudolph found moreover a splendid opportunity to shape a public space. When he started work in the spring of 1955, his first priority was to lay out the building to make the most of the site itself, which he studied carefully. The art department had suggested a position slightly lower down the slope of Norumbega Hill, but Rudolph chose instead the rim, for continuity with Green and Pendleton Halls. Commanding the view from Severance Green, the building's major component would be a three-story block of offices, classrooms, study rooms, and departmental library. Toward the west end, a shorter wing housing a gallery and an auditorium would project back toward Pendleton. As noted in the building program, the 300-seat auditorium needed by the art department for its largest classes would be used for musical events as well, and this inspired the Buildings and Grounds Committee to instruct Rudolph to leave room on the site for a future music building and to situate the auditorium accordingly. The gallery then fell into place at the entrance to the complex, as a link between the main block and the auditorium. Rudolph did not initially envision this link as a bridge over an exterior stairway, however, but assumed that the main access through the Academic Quadrangle would be routed from the stairs squeezed between Founders and Farnsworth.

Conceded at last by the trustees, the demolition of Farnsworth would open up the quadrangle to a particularly fine deep view of Severance Green and Lake Waban, and Rudolph realized—as he explained later, when the building opened—that this could be the single most consequential aspect of the whole design. While his building would complete the Academic Quadrangle, his treatment of this opening would redefine the character of its space and in so doing enlarge its significance at the center of the campus.

The siting of the Jewett Arts Center finally provided an appropriately firm enclosure at the west end of the Academic Quadrangle. Complementarily, the demolition of the Farnsworth Art Building opened a new vista linking the quadrangle with Severance Green. This photograph was taken before the main road through the campus was re-routed to the north side of Norumbega Hill in 1961.

From something inward looking and vaguely cloisterish, the quadrangle would become a grander, stage-like platform. The depth of the view would be subtly perceived to complement the loftiness of Galen Stone Tower and indeed the whole citadel image of the complex. This effect would extend the scale of the landscape below. Framed on one side by the art wing, the view would bypass the original focus of the campus, College Hall Hill (which Farnsworth faced), to seek the elusive furthest stretches of Lake Waban through the screening treetops of Severance Green. In its boldness this view would constitute a modernization, and a new triumph, of the picturesque landscape aesthetic of the Wellesley campus.

All this Rudolph accomplished through his site plan. He aligned the art wing at a slight angle inward toward the end of Green Hall, counter to Farnsworth's outward skew, and he cut the slope in parallel, bringing its edge well into the footprint of Farnsworth. Seen from below, this new alignment redefined the space of Severance Green, by firming up its enclosure with a lengthy continuous backdrop while also directing attention to its link, at the open edge, with the space of the quadrangle.

As executed, the open edge is simpler than in Rudolph's original plan. He envisioned the whole area at the end of the art wing as part of a larger paved expanse, adorned with a hypothetical monumental sculpture and extending back toward the center of the quadrangle, with three straight paths radiating beyond, to the center and ends of Pendleton. Rudolph's aim was to clarify the site, to bring out, in a typical modernist strategy, the crisp geometry underlying the revivalist trim of Green and Pendleton. At the same time, the formality of the plan was undoubtedly Italian in inspiration, reflecting urbanistic themes in his lecture the previous year. Rudolph was not the first planner to call forth such associations on Norumbega Hill: decades earlier, President Caroline Hazard and architect Ralph Adams Cram had envisioned Italian hill towns on the site.

Rudolph's first proposal for the building itself was also Italian in its inspiration. It is the most remarkable of the several preliminary designs preserved in the College Archives and a compelling and significant document of the architect's stylistic experimentation as fostered by the Wellesley commission. Dating from the summer and early fall of 1955, the design survives in three perspective views, slightly variant in detailing. It emphasizes the horizontal mass of the art wing through strong contrasts in the treatment of stories. The first story is deeply recessed behind an arcade of widely spaced heavy columns supporting clusters of ribs. The second story has a continuous band of slim windows set into a simpler wall arcade of thin, closely spaced supports under corbel arches. The wall of the third story continues upward to serve as a high parapet along the roof, screening a complex skylight system, so that its total height is almost that of the lower two stories combined. It is treated as a continuous patterned surface, seemingly textured but essentially

In this early site plan for Jewett, architect Paul Rudolph envisioned new paths to focus the open space of the Academic Quadrangle on a piazza at the east end of the art wing. The angled ends of the auditorium (shown here before music and theatre facilities were added to the building program) were intended to echo the alignment of Pendleton Hall.

flat. The third story is windowless except for a bank of slim openings set on either side of the wing at its juncture, toward the west end, with the other, lower wing at one side. Along the roofline of the art wing, spiky terminations of the skylight system project at the intervals of the first-story arcade.

None of these features is a quotation from any historical source, yet the art wing's exterior as a whole is unmistakably a modernist paraphrase of a famous late Gothic building in Venice, the Doge's Palace. The distinctiveness of the latter's exterior lies in the contrast between the bold planar mass of its top half and the two lacy open arcades beneath it, the upper one doubling the rhythm of the lower. Its unexpected juxtaposition of opposites appealed especially to nineteenth-century architects (and their mentor John Ruskin) who were trying to reconcile ornate historicizing decoration with simple modern building types—not unlike what Rudolph was attempting in response to Gothic Revival. Two further similarities: the straight top edge of the Venetian building is trimmed with spike-like ornaments, and its broad upper wall surface is decorated with a diaper pattern. Though hard to read in the perspective views, the patterning on Rudolph's third story seems likewise to be diapered—as would be the exterior of the library addition, designed the following year by the ubiquitous Henry Shepley.

There is further evidence of Rudolph's Venetian inspiration. In 1998, Trustee Margaret Jewett Greer '51 recalled in a casual conversation with the author that her father's way of characterizing what struck him as extravagant in the architect's taste was to say that Rudolph "wanted to build the Doge's Palace." Even after that design for the building had been abandoned, Venice persisted in Rudolph's conception of the Academic Quadrangle itself. In an interview in the College newspaper when the Jewett Arts Center opened in October 1958, he said he hoped to create on the still unfinished site "the effect of space as in the Piazza San Marco." These associations would have resonated with the art department generally and especially John McAndrew, who spent many summers in Venice writing a book on its architecture, and whose devotion to the city would lead him, after the disastrous floods of 1966, to found an extraordinary organization still vital today, Save Venice, Inc.

Though all the concerned parties—the art department, the Buildings and Grounds Committee, the president, and the Jewetts—were initially impressed by Rudolph's proposal, it soon foundered on their growing unease, principally with the paucity of windows. The general effect, because of the prominent third story, of an almost windowless building on a site with such

splendid views seemed perverse. Yet the design was in keeping with the building program, which specifically called for three windowless classrooms for showing slides in art history courses and at least six studio classrooms for art courses that were to have only skylights or high, north-facing windows. Thereafter Rudolph would have to reconcile the demand for more windows with the requisite rationing of natural light.

The building program was very soon expanded when the Jewetts increased their gift to include new facilities for the music and theatre departments. The expansion would be named in memory of Mr. Jewett's mother, Margaret Weyerhauser Jewett, a special student in music in the 1880s, while his wife's name would now apply to the art facilities. By early November 1955, Rudolph produced a new layout in which classrooms, offices, a music library, and a theatre workshop were wrapped around the auditorium, considerably widening that portion of the building's lower wing and extending it close to the western end of Pendleton. The narrower gallery and main

Rudolph's initial idea for the exterior of the art wing of Jewett was to paraphrase in modernist terms the distinctive façade of the late-medieval Doge's Palace in Venice, which contrasts richly articulated arcading on the lower stories with a bold expanse of wall surface above. The design as seen in the preceding illustration is slightly variant in its detailing.

entrance corridor remained set back between the two larger blocks and further downplayed as a linking element. The increased size of the complex called for additional access, from the western edge of the site where the basement was exposed along the slope of the hill, and this took the form of a broad open stairway passage excavated under the gallery and entrance link. Granting it almost as much ground as the whole art wing, Rudolph scaled the stairway to its function as a major new route into the Academic Quadrangle as a whole. In his enthusiasm with this further opportunity to shape a significant spatial sequence, he steadily elaborated the design into a complex symmetrical composition, angling in and out of light and shade, with no less than four smaller staircases along the sides, rising opposite to the measured ascent of the one grand stair. No doubt Rudolph conceived it as a fitting counterpart to the complicated medievalizing stairs and roadway snaking up the ramparts on the eastern side of Norumbega Hill.

From late 1955 onward, Rudolph's design for the layout and basic massing of the Jewett complex—unlike its exterior articulation—remained essentially fixed except in the elaboration of the exterior stairway and also in two other respects. In his first proposal, the architect had shaped the auditorium as an elongated hexagon, with its sides continuing the walls of the gallery/entrance link and each end angling outward in a prow-like shape, which he retained in the later extension of the wing. He may have used this

The grand scale and elaborate symmetrical staging of the open stairway passage under Jewett's main entrance were calculated in response to the size and symbolic importance of the Academic Quadrangle as a whole.

shape in hopes of good acoustical properties inside the auditorium, but he was certainly thinking also of its exterior effect. As explained in correspondence in the College Archives, the oblique angle of the prow shape was chosen to establish an element of alignment with the angled siting of nearby Pendleton and thus subtly but perceptibly to relate the two buildings. The prow shape at the other end of the auditorium, visible above the lower link, determined in turn the shape of the open stairway below, when that was added to the design. Rudolph repeated the shape throughout the stairway and up into the entrance itself. He also tried out the prow motif elsewhere, changing his mind more than once. The most prominent additional applications in the finished building are at the ends of the art wing. The treatment at the eastern end, with symmetrical staircases serving fire exits, has the look of a ceremonial setting, rather like the interior of the auditorium. It was intended to match the formality of the adjacent piazza in Rudolph's site plan. It also seems to evoke the style of Frank Lloyd Wright, whose work was ever more widely popularized during the 1950s, in the last decade of the celebrated architect's very long life. In addition to all the Wright-influenced ranch houses of the period, there are countless prow-ended churches, deriving from Wright designs such as Pfeiffer Chapel at Florida Southern College in Lakeland, which Rudolph knew well. Worth noting near Wellesley, at Brandeis University, the 1957 Slosberg Music Center by Wallace K. Harrison and Max Abramowitz has, like Jewett, a prow-ended red brick auditorium with lower rooms lining its perimeter, though the design is much plainer overall and makes no gestures toward any kind of revivalist architecture.

Another basic element of massing with which Rudolph continued to experiment was the roof treatment of the auditorium, conceived to contrast dramatically with the flat roof of the rest of that wing. His first and most ingenious proposal was a row of eight-part vaults, quite Gothic in effect, devised from interlocking triangles. Most of his later designs were variations on a simpler folded roof topping a clerestory. In all but his final design for a flat-roofed clerestory, he retained some form of zigzag profile derived from the gables marching across the façade of Pendleton. These were the inspiration also for the more sharply pitched tent-like skylights in his final design for the roof of the art wing.

The design history of Jewett, as compared with other Wellesley buildings, is unusually well documented in the College Archives. The reason is twofold: the art department took great care to collect and to preserve the relevant papers in its possession; and more importantly, John McAndrew and Agnes Abbott maintained an exceptionally active role in the development of the design and consequently generated, for about two years, a steady stream of correspondence related to it. Abbott's long-term commitment to a modernist art building, beginning in the 1940s, might seem surprising, given that her own admirable work as a watercolorist was stylistically conservative. Yet she and McAndrew were staunch partners in the project, and she was more often the art department's spokesperson to the other parties.

Following standard practice, Rudolph worked in association with a supervising local firm, Anderson, Beckwith and Haible, but even from a distance he kept up a lively exchange with the art department and other parties at Wellesley. The main topic of discussion was the exterior articulation of the building, with which he was constantly preoccupied. His basic strategy, after the first proposal was abandoned, was to emphasize verticality through repetition of a prominent structural bay, which would relate more clearly to the neighboring buildings than had the horizontal mass of the Doge's Palace paraphrase. He retained from the latter's lower-story arcades, however, an ambition to make use of the most fundamental, defining aspect of Gothic architecture generally, its elegant, exposed skeletal structure. Admittedly, there is virtually no such thing at Wellesley, whose conspicuous Collegiate Gothic image is in fact layered onto distinctly modern construction. Yet there is an obvious, oft-noted affinity between authentic Gothic structure and bare-boned modernist architecture that appealed to Rudolph and inspired him to pursue a distinctive structural support as the key to his exterior design for Jewett. In one early scheme he tried a Y-shaped column (recycled in two later commissions), but he soon fixed, or perhaps fixated, on another motif derived from Gothic structure: an open cluster of columns, the number of which would vary depending on what the cluster supported. In the most complicated and cumbersome of the variants he proposed, each first-floor cluster in the art wing, with two upper stories to support, would have comprised six sturdy columns (each octagonal in profile) in a cluster fully six feet in diameter. McAndrew and Abbott regularly criticized, suggested improvements upon, and were often required to explain to other parties this and further features of Rudolph's evolving, freely inventive design. In its final form, and largely at the instigation of McAndrew and the consulting engineer, the cluster became a single column bulging out into four lobes. Its effect is surprisingly close to Gothic prototypes more directly copied elsewhere at Wellesley but used more often for decorative rather than structural purposes.

Much as Abbott had proposed years before, Rudolph gave to the bay system on Jewett's exterior the same interval as that of Pendleton, which Jewett's lower wing also matches in wall height. This continuity in scale is the most important factor establishing a harmonious relationship between the new and old buildings. At the same time, it sets up an instructive counterpoint, exploited by Rudolph with considerable wit, between modernism and Gothic revivalism. The heaviness and solidity of the latter he countered with modernism's characteristic lightness and openness. Whereas Green and Pendleton skirt the Academic Quadrangle with exaggerated foundations—

Rudolph's window treatment at the quadrangle level of Jewett wittily reverses the pattern of solids and voids in nearby Pendleton Hall. Emphasizing the clean lines and transparency of the new building, this early photograph exemplifies the modernist outlook of the period.

emulating a more massive construction than they actually employ—Jewett appears to hover, with the top of its basement story well recessed under the slim cantilevered floor slab of the first story. The building's skeletal structure is on display throughout, offering itself to analysis and conducing to an effect of airiness. Rudolph's treatment of the first-floor windows is a particularly amusing variation on a motif seen also in the New Dorms. Vertical strips of glass are set to coincide rather than alternate with supports standing free of the nonstructural wall. In the art wing, the wall is set a little behind the distinctive four-lobed columns. The positions are reversed in the music and theatre wing, with the wall set out to the edge of the floor slab, a little in front of paired columns of the much simpler sort used in most of Jewett's interior. One result of the arrangement is that this wing ends up with rather irreverent-looking all-glass corners. In both wings, the vertical strip windows alternate with glass-topped partial walls, which in turn set up a larger reversal when they are seen, from the quadrangle, in comparison with Pendleton. Surrounded on three sides by glass, the partial walls of the art wing in particular are similar in size and proportion to the windows, surrounded by wall, in analogous positions on Pendleton. In a final amusing turnabout, Rudolph gave to the narrower vertical windows of the music and theatre wing a curious V-shaped projecting profile. It is a variation on Jewett's prow-shape motif, but in this context it also tends to mimic in glass the deeply splayed stone mullions in Gothic Revival windows all over the quadrangle.

The most conspicuous of Jewett's features are the aluminum sunscreens, enameled a light stone color, that are cantilevered beyond the window walls of the art wing's upper stories. Providing another play upon the layering of structure and non-structure, the narrow voids between them are aligned with the columns well behind them. In the long view across Severance Green, the screens assert both the composition and the character of Jewett in a particularly suave manner. Rudolph first planned to double their rhythm, with two narrow screens for every structural bay, but the effect was rejected as too busy. In retrospect, the screens may seem a slightly faddish trait of the building's period style, a predictable but not wholly apt response to a tricky practical issue. The architect himself touted them as a form of "man-made ivy" mitigating the newness of the building. As with the distinctive columns, however, their design was troublesome and developed only slowly from Rudolph's initial proposal, received with much skepticism, that they be made of brick.

Jewett's mottled red brick and stone-colored concrete aggregate are closely related to the materials of Pendleton and Green Halls. But Rudolph proposed a number of different applications and additional materials that did not survive in the final design. He planned for a long while to sheath the complicated columns in either brick or tile or to use a finer, whiter concrete aggregate, and in various proposals for the auditorium clerestory and roof he envisioned tile, copper, and stone. In these and in other respects, the design

Along the south side of Norumbega Hill, broad retaining walls provide the art wing with a monumental podium, suitably scaled to deep views from Severance Green. The open colonnade and the cantilevered sunscreens establish a strong rhythm that calls attention to the structural module Jewett shares with its neighbors, while the steeply pitched skylights echo their prominent gables.

history reveals Rudolph's persistent taste for a richer, more intricately detailed and textured Jewett than was built. Partly to cut costs, the design was gradually simplified as it developed over the course of many exchanges with the art department and the other parties, all of whom were satisfied with its state of completion and anticipated price by early January 1957. But when the cost estimates on the working drawings came in soon afterwards, they were three-quarters of a million dollars higher than the roughly $2.75 million in the budget at that point. For the next several months, all parties prepared, debated, and voted on lists of large and small cuts, inside and out, that

The architect referred to the fine-textured aluminum sunscreens of the art wing (seen in this drawing with a variant treatment of its east end) as "man-made ivy" that would mitigate the newness of Jewett by disguising the window walls of the upper stories.

The original doors at the main entrance
to Jewett were plain, flush panels in
rectangles of wood rising to the full
height of the foyer—a typical modernist
treatment calling attention to their role
in the building's abstract composition
of lightweight planes.

Never much liked, the doors proved
increasingly unpopular as they warped
and jammed over the years. In the
1980s they were replaced with the
conventional glass doors seen here.

simplified the design a good deal more and slightly reduced the size and amenities of the building. The greatest single blow to the design, however, was still to come and would be dealt singlehandedly, and perhaps somewhat underhandedly, by Margaret Clapp. To help relieve the budget crisis, she committed the College to take over from the Jewetts the cost of the landscaping, including paths and piazza, with the reasonable stipulation that most of it be postponed. She thoroughly disliked Rudolph's new layout for the Academic Quadrangle, thinking it too formal and urban, and it was never executed.

Quite apart from the issue of expense, much of the simplification of Rudolph's design reflected a difference in taste. The prevailing opinion at Wellesley, once the building was completed, was that the enforced economies had actually improved it, and this attitude was not merely a predictable case of putting things in the best possible light. Jewett's design history suggests strongly that probably all the client parties, including McAndrew and Abbott, were uneasy with aspects of Rudolph's preliminary designs that seemed to them too fussy or too flashy to suit the institution. What they wished for, in this important commission, was a delicate balance: a building not as plain and utilitarian-looking as the New Dorms but not overly splendid either. The situation was not peculiar to Wellesley, with its presumed New England restraint, but was in fact symptomatic of a larger trend. During the later 1950s, within the architectural profession generally, there was a very lively debate about the ongoing transformation of modernist architecture, and it came down to much the same question of balance as at Wellesley: how much was too much? For what Rudolph, Saarinen, and many other innovative architects were attempting was a synthesis, itself a delicate balance between the fundamental values and priorities of modernism and a brighter, livelier, more sensuous and responsive aesthetic—friendlier to the past, among other things. Rudolph's distinctive column, for example, was typical of a very widespread ambition to devise new, customized forms that were inherently both decorative and structural and not, as in revivalist practice, merely decoration laid over structure. Such strategies were not in themselves novel. (Among recent buildings illustrated in *What Is Modern Architecture?*—a little primer by John McAndrew published by the Museum of Modern Art in 1942—there are several details that look forward to Rudolph's work at Wellesley.) They were increasingly conspicuous, however, and for some critics the balance was tilting too far toward decoration. The overall tendency was popularizing, and its friendliness upset a kind of architectural etiquette, in which sobriety was equated with authority. The rhetoric of the debate sometimes took on overtones of gender stereotyping, as in one English critic's jibe that Saarinen's London embassy belonged to "the 'Ballet School' in U. S. architecture." (Decades earlier and with the best of intentions, Ralph Adams Cram had devised a "feminine Gothic" he thought suitable for Wellesley.) But the fundamental difference at issue lay in the perception not of gender but of class distinction, which is so often the bedrock of taste, at Wellesley as elsewhere.

The simplification of Rudolph's design did indeed bring it somewhat closer to the New Dorms, but Jewett nevertheless remains far more complex, refined, and thorough in its expressiveness. Even small details such as the extra moldings on the edges of the story slabs and in the exterior stairs contribute decisively to the textural richness with which the building answers its neighbors. Inside the building as well, the architect's skill and aesthetic ambitions are still amply evident, despite considerable but mostly respectful remodeling to serve Jewett's changing functions over the years.

Inspired by the donor, Rudolph was most ingenious in his treatment of the exhibition spaces. George F. Jewett (who died in November 1956) had wanted art to be encountered by all who used the building and not simply those entering the gallery. Thus Rudolph designed the entrance corridor itself as a gallery, without windows, and supplied the gallery proper, behind the corridor, with sliding wall panels at either end so that it could be opened to

The former gallery in Jewett was designed for the short-term display of changing selections from a far smaller collection than the College museum now has. The emphasis on horizontality, especially in the ceiling treatment, lent to the elongated, relatively low space an emblematic modernist dynamism. Enclosed at the ends merely with sliding wall panels, the gallery was intended to serve frequently as an open corridor encouraging casual, everyday encounters with art.

The most unusual space in Jewett, and perhaps the most potent pedagogically, was the sculpture court, in which some of the museum's choicest treasures were literally set into the path of all the art wing's routine traffic and daily life.

serve also as a kind of broad, art-filled corridor. This appealing notion of casual, daily access to art (back in the days before security measures assumed much priority at small college museums) inspired also a third space, which remains the finest in Jewett. Designed as a sculpture court, it is a mezzanine space set between the first and second stories of the art wing and rising to the full height of the second story. In effect, it is an elaborated landing, branching out in two stages from the building's main stairs. The emphatic symmetry of its composition, motivated by the large square mosaic from ancient Antioch originally set into the floor, induces a sense of occasion amid the routine traffic through the space. (The mosaic is now installed in the Davis Museum and Cultural Center.) Yet the firmness of the sculpture court's composition is complemented by the airiness of its enclosure, a sequence of planes layered through space, from the half-story walls along its central axis out to the sun-screens along the building's perimeter. The resulting modulation of natural, altering daylight contributes to an environment exceptionally well suited to the display of sculpture. The sequence of planes plays a part also in the room's gratifying scale, an effect that is produced by the generous range of dimensions Rudolph used, starting with his characteristic fine details. This, too, is flattering to sculpture.

The Jewett Arts Center, the library addition, and the New Dorms—all together an enormous undertaking within a single decade—are the most impressive architectural achievements of Margaret Clapp's presidency. Among the lesser buildings built during her tenure, the most interesting is Acorns, a new dean's residence completed in 1956. Overlooking Lake Waban from a wooded site behind the library, it is a rather Wrightian ranch house, modest but more sophisticated than the suburban norm. Clapp's continuing concern for the needs of Wellesley's faculty resulted in new off-campus housing and also the College Club, opened in 1963, from which a superb view of the lake helps to compensate for a forgettably banal design. Facing College Road, the Shepley firm's 1964–1965 addition to the Stone–Davis dormitories is a heavy-handed bit of neo-medievalizing whimsy, its effect more carousel-like than crenellated. Though hardly in the same league as Jewett, it was evidently intended likewise to answer to Wellesley's trademark architecture, the Collegiate Gothic complex on Norumbega Hill.

A notable motif here and throughout Jewett, the layering of slim planes through space enriches the modulation of abundant natural light. Also evident in this view of the cantilevered main staircase is the architect's characteristic attention to detail, which contributes to the building's agreeable scale. The adjacent sculpture court now provides a setting for students' works and other curricular endeavors.

ARCHITECTURE SINCE 1970

FROM THE 1950S ONWARD, the College's fund-raising organization was increasingly sophisticated, ambitious, and efficient, and it set and met a series of impressive goals. The characteristic social and political ferment of the 1960s—less disruptive at Wellesley than on many other campuses—also contributed to a stronger, more secure institution in the long run, for it led to dramatically broadened participation in policy making and thus a greater cohesiveness in the College's pursuit of both change and continuity: a new commitment to diversity along with an emphatic reaffirmation of women's education.

Caught short at its seventy-fifth anniversary, Wellesley celebrated its centennial confidently, with two major building projects among other achievements and goals. By 1971, the College library had exceeded eighty percent of its capacity—the standard limit for efficient reshelving in an open-stacks collection—and was growing at four percent annually. In all its other needs also, the short-term solutions of the 1950s expansion were outdated. The situation having been anticipated, the planning for another addition to the building went quickly and smoothly. In January 1972, with no other architects in the running, the commission went to Shepley Bulfinch Richardson and Abbott. Again the architect in charge of the project was James F. Clapp, Jr. At a cost of $5.3 million, the addition was completed in 1975, whereupon the library as a whole was rededicated in the name of former president Margaret Clapp '30, who had died the previous year.

In plan, the new addition continued the axis of the previous one. The stacks were again extended to the west. Extended eastward from the original reading room were new workspaces for library staff and the more specialized resources and services, with the reserve reading room tucked into the lowest level and entered from a little terrace facing the convenient new student center, which had been remodeled from Music Hall in 1969 and named in memory of Vice-President Robert J. Schneider. The exterior of the new library addition followed the previous design in deferring to the original north façade, now flanked on both sides with windowless setbacks quite in keeping with its neo-classical composition. The 1950s addition's unusual window treatment, instead of turning the corner at the west end, was now also symmetrically flanked with windowless walls and thereby transformed into a secondary compositional focus along the north façade (see illustration on page 106).

Keeping to the same height and the same integral massing as the previous work, the new addition actually augments, in most respects and in modern terms, the fundamental character of the original library, emphasizing those traits of sobriety, solidity, and predictability which institutional and corporate clients had so long appreciated in neo-classicism. Indeed the look of the new addition is typical of a great many large-scale buildings put up by government, academe, and business during the 1960s and '70s. Locally, such work is conspicuous along the riverfront campuses of Harvard, MIT, and Boston University, while the most ambitious example is the dramatic and still controversial City Hall completed in Boston in 1968. The architectural idiom has usually been labeled Brutalism, which sounds more pejorative today than it did at the time. Though the true derivation and original usage of the term are more complicated, it soon came to refer above all to the prominent use of exposed reinforced concrete, *béton brut* in French. Neither the material itself nor the exposure of structure was in any way new, but they were newly exploited for effects of heaviness and sculptural mass in great contrast to the lightness and thin planes most characteristic of modernism previously. The inspiration was the surprising post-World War II work of modernist pioneer Le Corbusier, in which he used this cheapest of materials, requiring only very simple building techniques, to create a richly expressive, highly personal style of modernism that was paradoxically somewhat archaic-looking. More or less rough, depending on the technique, the textured surface left by the wooden molds in which the concrete was poured weathered rapidly, giving an interesting patina of age even to the most prosaic new buildings. Somber yet sensuous, Brutalism appealed already during the 1950s to American architects like Paul Rudolph (who embraced it wholeheartedly just after he completed the Jewett Arts Center) for the same reasons as had centuries-old architectural ensembles in Italian cities, and it appealed all the more widely as the characteristic tastes of the 1960s emerged.

Upon the completion in 1975 of remodeling
and further expansion by the Shepley firm,
the College library was named in memory
of Margaret Clapp. The window walls at the
east and west ends of the new construction
are shaded with hefty concrete partitions
in a manner derived ultimately from
Le Corbusier's late works. In the foreground
of this view of the east end, curved forms
in the paving and landscaping provide
a pleasant counterpoint to the assertive
rigidity of the architecture.

Along the north and south sides of the library addition, the concrete was carefully finished to blend in with the limestone sheathing of the original building, but the prominent window treatment at the east and west ends is distinctly Corbusian in both texture and form. The glass wall is set back behind sturdy concrete partitions, on the egg-crate principle, which serve as sunscreens integrated into the building's structure instead of being, as Jewett's are, non-structural elements lightly attached to the building. The circle motif cut into the partitions was intended to temper somewhat the structure's gritty monumentality. The motif also shapes a last vestige of Longfellow Pond and reappears in various applications inside the building, most notably in the light wells added along the sides of the original reading room. An influence from the Pop Art movement, the bright, unmodulated colors of the new carpets and furniture were likewise an attempt to compensate for the drabness of the concrete surfaces. According to the architect, reflections of vivid purple carpeting would also lend warmth to the shiny metal ducting of the new climate-control system overhead, necessarily exposed in the stacks because of the very low story heights established in the earlier addition.

All these stylistic traits are highly characteristic of the period, and most of them appear also in the far more ambitious and interesting design of the Science Center, completed in 1977. Like Jewett, the Science Center is well known and much admired within the architectural community. The Boston Society of Architects gave it an extraordinary award in 1988 for being the best building of the whole of the previous decade in the Boston area. But within the Wellesley community, the Science Center is unappreciated, to say the least. Ever since it opened, the great majority of students, faculty, and alumnae have judged that, while its interior is appealing, its exterior is an eyesore, an affront to the style of the campus and an inexplicably insensitive act of patronage. This response is unfair and also ironic, given that the boldness not just of the building but of the whole new endeavor behind it was assumed to be good public relations for the sciences at Wellesley.

Admittedly, the Science Center was designed, very painstakingly, from the inside out. Because it was not destined for a site as demanding in its institutional symbolism and architectural quality as that of Jewett, little priority was given to its exterior. The situation was just the reverse: the building program for the Science Center, unlike Jewett's, made overwhelming demands on the design of the interior, and even the production of the building program itself was a formidable task.

By the late 1960s, when planning for the new building began, Wellesley's science facilities were inadequate, outdated, and, in some particulars, actually unsafe, despite remodeling and renewal of equipment. They were located in Pendleton, Green, and Founders Halls as well as Sage Hall and the Whitin Observatory, and this dispersal was in itself highly inefficient and limiting. The obvious course was to abandon the facilities in the Academic Quadrangle, where conditions were the worst, and build anew in the vicinity of Sage and the observatory. As planning commenced, the choice of site was soon narrowed down: the optimal location for a building of any size would be on the slope south of Sage, so as not to block the telescopes of the observatory to the north, and sufficiently westward along the slope to avoid blocking sunlight to the greenhouses toward the east. Thus for purely practical reasons, the Science Center was sited on a hillside, almost in accordance with the planning ideals of Ralph Adams Cram and Frederick Law Olmsted, Jr., though it extends down the whole slope and thus appears to rise from the meadow.

The move would bring together nine academic departments: astronomy, biological sciences, chemistry, computer science, geology, history of science, mathematics, physics, and psychology. But the goal of the project went beyond the already considerable task of addressing their distinct needs. The larger rationale for the Science Center was to join the departments into a new entity, the purely economic and administrative advantages of which were clear enough. The most important benefit, however, would be to foster the increasingly interdisciplinary character of the sciences themselves during a period of extraordinary development. The curricular and pedagogical implications were profound and only partly foreseeable, yet they would somehow need to be accounted for in the building program. In effect, the Science Center was to be designed for a faculty in flux, redefining itself in order to restructure in an open-ended way a major component of a Wellesley education. The project was necessarily idealistic and experimental.

The planning began in 1969 with the appointment of a faculty committee representing all nine departments, from which extensive data would be gathered. In 1970, the College engaged the services of a local consultant, Burgess Standley, an engineer whose specialty was program planning for science buildings. In 1971, President Ruth M. Adams revived briefly the long-forgotten notion of a supervising architect for all College building projects and hired a New York architect named Walker Cain, who took part in preliminary planning for both the library addition and the Science Center.

By January 1972, plentifully supplied with expertise, the trustees' Buildings and Grounds Committee was ready to choose an architect for the Science Center and apparently decided not to compound the complexity and novelty of the project by experimenting also with patronage. Of four firms interviewed, the two leading contenders were the tried-and-true Shepley firm—already the committee's choice for the library addition—and another, quite similar long-established Boston firm, called at that time Perry, Dean & Stewart (later Perry, Dean, Stahl & Rogers). The committee decided on the Perry firm in late January, one day after the Board of Trustees awarded the library commission to the Shepley firm. The board approved the committee's choice for the Science Center a few weeks later.

Specialists in exactly the same realm of institutional architecture as the Shepley firm and best known for rebuilding Colonial Williamsburg in the 1930s, the former Perry, Shaw and Hepburn had worked very briefly at Wellesley once before, having submitted in 1946 a tentative design, quickly rejected, for a new library on Norumbega Hill. Long since converted to modernism, by 1972 the firm had roughly the same number and type of recent science buildings to its credit as did the Shepley firm. What persuaded the Buildings and Grounds Committee may have been the architects' avowal of what they called a "systems approach" to design. This involved computers, still uncommon in the architectural practice of the time, and sounded appropriately scientific.

The chief architect for the Science Center was a younger member of the firm, Charles F. Rogers II, whose planning method was indeed highly sympathetic to the experimental nature of the project. Put briefly, his approach was more conceptual than visual and emphasized process as much as product. He translated the whole of the building program into a kit of distinct components, whose assembly—that is, the structure, the plan, and the massing of the building—would be determined experimentally, in effect, subject to a range of priorities producing a number of options at successive stages in the process. This method required the clients' constant participation, for which the size of the original faculty committee proved unwieldy, so a smaller delegation, called the Check and Answer Committee, took responsibility for dealing directly with the architect.

Virtually the only constant factor in the design itself was a conventional assumption that it would consist of modules in a gridiron. Ideally the module would integrate structural elements with the routing of supply and exhaust services required by the laboratories, which were the most complicated components of the building program. This would provide greater flexibility as the uses of the building inevitably changed over time. Among the priorities determining the initial layout, the most important and demanding were what the original faculty committee called "propinquities," meaning the desired spatial interrelationships among the various departments. These in themselves formed a kind of three-dimensional gridiron of vertical and horizontal vectors. One example of the resulting challenge to planning was noted in the minutes of the Check and Answer Committee for May 1972: pedagogy required easy access between chemistry and physics laboratories, yet the former would ideally be at the top of the building, where fumes could be exhausted most efficiently, whereas experiments conducted in the latter would ideally be at the bottom of the building, where the floor was most stable.

In the layout of the Science Center, architect Charles F. Rogers II ingeniously exploited an awkward juxtaposition of old and new structures by creating between them an atrium that proved to be the most popular feature of the complex. The illustration shows the plan at ground level.

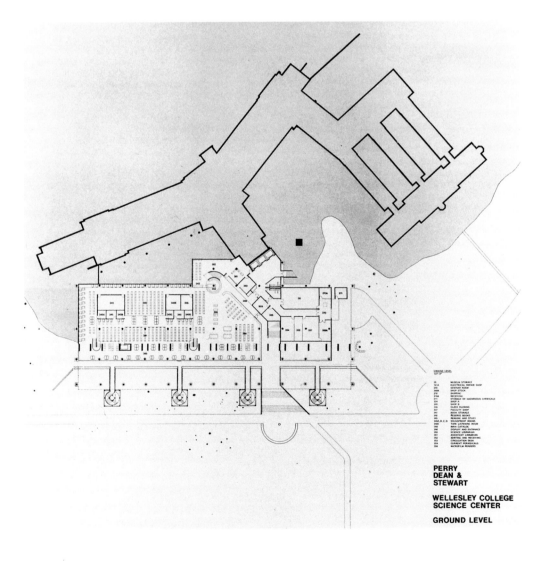

PERRY
DEAN &
STEWART

WELLESLEY COLLEGE
SCIENCE CENTER

GROUND LEVEL

Time has bestowed upon the Science Center a certain patina that enhances its underappreciated architectural dignity, and the maturing of the trees along its façade and the increasing rusticity of the restored meadow below have subdued the building's industrial aspect.

Another fundamental and critical consideration in the overall design was the new building's connection with Sage, which was to be remodeled. Ideally the new building would provide easy access between the two without being hindered by the layout, the limited mechanical capacities, and especially the story heights of the older building. The solution, which was decided in principle early on, was to link the upper stories of the two buildings only with bridges across an atrium. The latter soon became the most novel and ingratiating aspect of the whole design. Nicknamed the "Focus" and also the "Street"—it would incorporate the charming old streetlights from the path behind Sage—the atrium would be the vibrant social center of the complex, a combination traffic interchange, lounge, and administrative clearinghouse, and a compelling emblem of the interdisciplinary ideal of the building program. In the final design, the two-story reading and reference area of the new Science Library (formerly five departmental libraries) was situated between the four-story atrium and the front of the building, so that the two spaces overlap to provide a monumental yet informal, welcoming effect of openness at the entrance.

Rogers's method produced several alternatives for the overall plan and massing of the building, varying in the number of stories and the orientation to Sage. Most of them were more complex and broken-up than the simple rectangular block of the final design, which was the most efficient and economical solution. Potentially overwhelming in its bulk, the resulting long, twelve-bay façade is much reduced in scale by the deep recession of both ground and top stories and by four projecting bays housing fire exit staircases (an unexpected and yet familiar application, given that the back of the building is enclosed by the atrium and Sage, like many an urban tenement hemmed in at the back of its lot). The building's entrance stairway, set asymmetrically and negotiating the slope at a pronounced angle to the façade, also inflects strongly the rhythm of the long block. The overall effect of the composition is surprisingly engaging. The enclosing framework is monumental without being heavy, and it holds interest in the long views to which the building is subjected. The proportioning of the parts, if not their vocabulary, is elegant.

The aggressive exposure of all the flues and other mechanical elements atop the Science Center proclaims the function of the building and is no doubt the most incriminating evidence that the exterior came second to the demands of the interior. The architect himself once remarked that half of the building's enormous cost ($15 million) lay in its mechanical fittings, and the client might as well see where the money went. On the whole, the façade seems little more than the structural grid of the building exposed where it comes to a halt and simply filled in with glass and translucent plastic panels (the latter controlling natural light in the laboratories). Yet a second glance reveals that Rogers in fact emphasized and exaggerated the structural details. In particular, the ends of beams project beyond or are oversized for the loads they support, and in this respect, though they thus serve in part as sun-screening devices, they are actually more ornamental than structural. The same is true of the pronounced contrasts between round posts and rectangular beams where they intersect in the projecting open bays supporting the stair-cases, for which task the bays themselves are blatantly much larger than they need to be. These features tend to suggest, quite misleadingly, that the building was put together from prefabricated standard units, and they certainly evoke something of the "systems approach" taken to the design, a concept of the building as a blunt assemblage of parts.

In short, Rogers clearly cultivated the utilitarian, industrial image that offends so many Wellesley sensibilities. But at the same time he pursued aesthetic effects whose provenance ought to be more easily discerned than it apparently is by most Wellesley observers. The complicated layering of the façade—so very unlike any factory's, despite the smokestacks—and the many fine-scaled details in the treatment of the glass and plastic panels, the railings, and, for that matter, all the business on the roof create a composition no less sculptural, intricate, and, in its way, picturesque than the most florid passages of Gothic Revival in Green Hall or Tower Court. The façade's extraordinary modulation of light and shade is more dramatic and more intimately integrated with landscaping than in any other building on campus. The building's ultimate ornament is the embroidery of trees growing right up against the façade and even *within* it, natural and fabricated columns side by side. All this was the architect's explicit strategy, planned from the start; some of the trees were actually preserved in situ during construction. With the maturing of the trees and especially with the recent, ongoing restoration of the meadow to its original unruly lushness, the industrial image has receded considerably. The scenic effect is increasingly brooding, almost in the vein of Piranesi's eighteenth-century views of once grand Roman monuments overtaken by rank nature, and brings to mind such resonant themes as time and change, progress and entropy.

The conventional wisdom at Wellesley has long held that the Science Center is somehow related to the highly publicized Pompidou Center in Paris, designed by Renzo Piano and Richard Rogers (no relation to Charles) also in the early 1970s, but there is scarcely any resemblance between the two. The Parisian arts center borrows industrial imagery merely as a generic emblem of modern culture and a provocative form of packaging with no significant relation to the spaces and functions within the building. It is altogether shinier, more metallic and lightweight than the Wellesley building, and ostentatiously anomalous in its setting. The Science Center, far from snubbing its neighbors, was originally intended to be partly sheathed in brick, which was dropped from the design to keep costs down. The only meaningful similarity between the two buildings is the use of bright color, in both cases to emulate for purely symbolic purposes the functional color-coding used in much modern technology. This was hardly a new idea in modernist architecture, and in the composition of the Wellesley façade the color plays a comparatively small role, yet it has always been one of the most startling and disliked aspects of the design.

To judge from the extensive documentation preserved in the College Archives, the planning of the Science Center did not elicit, or at least sustain, much discussion of what the exterior would ultimately look like, and the color obviously came as a surprise to many parties, including science faculty members. As the exterior was nearing completion in late 1975, Assistant Professor of Chemistry Nancy Harrison Kolodny '64, serving in the new position of administrator of the Science Center, was obliged to write to President Barbara Warne Newell and, a month later, also to the Vice-President for Business Affairs Joseph Kiebala explaining the colors and, more especially, assigning the blame for them. She pointed out to Newell that the building specifications reserved to the architect the right to choose exterior colors. She wrote to Kiebala that she had, at his request, "investigated the color decisions," which she explained had been made by the architect seemingly in consultation with at least one of a handful of faculty members serving as a "color committee" concerned primarily with interior decor. Rogers had already been called in to explain his choices to the Buildings and Grounds Committee. Reporting in turn to the Board of Trustees, committee chair George Kidder explained that the blue was supposed to be "Wellesley blue" whereas Rogers had taken the orange from the fire escapes and window frames of the popular Schneider College Center; the inspiration for the green must have been self-evident. Kidder noted that the architect had defended the colors as appropriate to "the type of futuristic activity which will take place within the building." At least for a brief period, the colors were undoubtedly a serious issue, for Rogers had "urged the Committee to wait until the glassing is complete around the stair towers before expressing concern," and Kidder himself then "urged that the Trustees wait to see the final result before looking to change." Around the same time, the College's public relations office arranged for Kolodny to give a tour of the building to a journalist who had made fun of it in the *Wellesley Townsman*. She must have been persuasive, for he recanted generously in a follow-up article, carefully explaining the rationale for the colors among other things. But when Kolodny herself later wrote about the Science Center, in an article (based on a talk to the Boston Wellesley Club) in the winter 1977 issue of the *Wellesley Alumnae Magazine*, she did not attempt to discuss the style of the building nor did she mention the exterior color. As usual in the magazine at that time, the numerous illustrations were reproduced from black-and-white photographs.

The problem with color was that it posed a challenge (not unlike some of Rudolph's ideas for Jewett) to the College's sense of architectural decorum. Bright exterior color was acceptable on the Schneider College Center, because the building was small, inconspicuous, rather whimsical-looking anyway and, above all, lighthearted in its function. But the Science Center was perceived as altogether too important and expensive an edifice to be allowed to flaunt the frivolity of bright color, which seemed like a final, gratuitous impertinence added to an already provocative modernist design. No doubt the latter was tolerable—as long as it looked sober—mainly because it could be blamed on the awkward demands of both the building program and, as ever, the budget.

Interior color was an altogether different matter—a typical distinction in decorum. Rogers used far more bright color inside the Science Center, where it clearly delighted rather than offended the majority of the College community. In compensating for the chilliness of the technology and the grimness of the concrete, it countered as well the persistent forbidding stereotype of science. This was obviously the motivation for the treatment of the atrium, in which playfulness seems taken to an almost bizarre extreme, as if to embrace the irrational in contrast to the premise of the building as a whole. The many different materials, the tilting diagonals of the upper-story bridges, the shifting reflections in the mirrored windows of Sage, the fragmentary views into the latter where other windows were removed, and the complicated staircases, balconies, and entrance sequence are all rather bewildering elements that exaggerate the oddness of the triangular space left between the new structure and the obliquely angled older building. The design induces

a nonstop yet aimless perusal that is entertaining, when time allows. The experience is familiar from shopping malls, and this may account for some of the enduring popularity of the atrium.

Though tucked away on a suburban campus, the atrium of the Science Center is interestingly related to a major shift in the urbanistic thinking of the period, which has had a long-lasting and profound impact on American cities: instead of wholesale demolition, the preferred strategy has become adaptive rehabilitation of old structures as foci for new development, often accommodating or even generating tourism. As in San Francisco's Ghirardelli Square and Boston's Faneuil Hall Marketplace—two famous examples, the latter contemporaneous with the Science Center—the contrasting materials and styles of old and new construction in the atrium are briskly juxtaposed rather than blended, and even awkward elements of the retrofitting are left in view on the assumption that they may well contribute some unplanned aesthetic interest of their own (exemplified also in the new College library addition, in the architect's prediction of color reflections on the shiny ducting). At the same time, artifacts of superseded technology or outdated design—such as Wellesley's old lampposts—are recycled as quaint sculpture. The design principle is collage, and the aesthetic is that of the found object and the vernacular, ready-made component—thus the rather contrived kit-built look of the Science Center. That Rogers declared he had consulted, for color, something so trivial as the new exterior detailing of Schneider College Center is characteristic too of the anti-elitist, popularizing mood and improvisatory strategy of the new urbanistic trend.

In 1991 the Science Center was expanded to a design by the same firm. The addition links the other wing of Sage to the east end of the 1970s block. Its plan is similar to the latter, but the vocabulary and the materials are significantly different, and the design is less interesting. Largely hidden by trees and greenhouses, the shed-like exterior of the addition is sheathed in aluminum. The interior is shiny and brightly colored. In general, the addition is harmonious with the 1970s design, though to the specialist's eye, the architectural imagery in some of its details reflects an important new stylistic development exemplified more conspicuously, and in quite different terms, in the Keohane Sports Center of the mid-1980s.

The architectural history of Wellesley from the New Dorms to the main block of the Science Center offers a surprisingly good sampling of modernism's course over some thirty years. Wellesley's next major building is

Nicknamed "the Focus," the atrium between Sage Hall and the main block of the Science Center is a soaring, cheerfully bizarre precinct whose eclectic decor is regularly and lovingly augmented by offerings from its devotees, in this case seniors celebrating their imminent graduation. In the background of the photograph, their paper streamers crisscross the space as if in tribute to the tilted bridges linking the unaligned upper stories of the two structures.

no less useful in marking the following period, in which much, though hardly all, of what modernism was understood to be was widely rejected. The resulting architecture was conveniently labeled post-modernist, but in reality it delivered an alternative to modernism rather than a fatal blow. Seeking ultimately to establish some standard of cultural authority in architecture, its proponents argued that modernism was aesthetically too austere and exclusionary to be broadly meaningful, and they called for the revival of traditional, explicit imagery and ornament. Post-modernism turned out to be almost, but not quite, the revival of revivalism. Though the distinction is subtle, it is readily apparent at Wellesley.

The first building erected during the presidency of Nannerl Overholser Keohane '61 was bound to become one of the most popular on campus. After many decades of neglect, Wellesley's formerly superior sports facilities, in egregious contrast to its other offerings, ranked at the very bottom when compared with those of the College's competitors. This was particularly embarrassing at a time when exercise and fitness were enshrined in the national culture as never before, and unprecedented numbers of young women participated in athletics at all levels, with the acknowledgement and support of the Title IX federal legislation dating from 1972. Indeed, Wellesley's inferior facilities seemed to be implicated in a worrisome decline in applications for admission. Very soon after she took office in 1981, President Keohane called for action. By 1985 and after a vigorous campaign that raised some $16 million, Wellesley had a highly rated new Sports Center, which was named in honor of Keohane in 1993 as she departed to take charge of Duke University.

An unusual choice for Wellesley, the architects were the New York firm of Hardy Holzman Pfeiffer Associates, the only non-local firm among the five finalists selected from some twenty candidates. The Hardy firm was the favorite of several non-Bostonian trustees who knew the architects' work in other parts of the country. Betty K. Freyhof Johnson '44, who was now the first woman chair of the Board of Trustees, had recommended the firm for the Science Center a decade earlier, when she chaired the College's National Development Fund Committee. She noted then that she had been impressed with Hugh Hardy when he designed a Cincinnati theater on whose board her husband presided. There were also more recent trustee connections with the firm, which was well known for large-scale institutional work. Characteristically, Hardy's initial presentation at Wellesley was superbly prepared, showy, and assured in a manner that appealed strongly to many corporate clients.

President Nannerl Overholser Keohane '61

The building committee assigned to the project by President Keohane, however, was not at first very enthusiastic about Hardy and his partners, above all because they had never designed an athletics facility. Though their architectural style was more adaptable than distinctive, it tended toward strong contrasts in bold geometric forms and colors. Serving on the committee as a consultant, former dean of the MIT architecture school William L. Porter pointed out that the firm's approach to design was "exhibitionistic" in exposing structural and other components. Having noticed such traits herself, Keohane expressed concern that the firm's previous work reminded her of the Science Center, which she evidently did not admire.

What the Hardy firm produced at Wellesley is surprisingly subdued and not as impressive aesthetically as it is functionally. On the whole, the design of the Keohane Sports Center seems banal, underlining rather than overcoming the ostensible limitations of shed-like building types. Brick sheathing, which the architects preferred to the aluminum siding imposed by the budget, would have made the field house and pool building less drab but would not have improved their composition. The layout and massing of the complex are disappointingly unimaginative, given the high standards set by the campus, and the proportions seem needlessly awkward. The forms carry imagery, to be sure, but they are in themselves inexpressive.

The most interesting feature of the exterior design is the treatment around the main entrance to the complex, at the south end of the remodeled 1938–1939 Recreation Building. Here the architects provided a typical post-modernist assemblage of references to traditional architecture, in particular Wellesley's Gothic Revival buildings. The most explicit example is the polygonal mini-tower housing a staircase. Crenellated and diaper-patterned in multicolored brick, it emulates in a whimsical way the towers of the Hazard Quadrangle (diapering appears also within the stylistic hodgepodge of nearby Alumnae Hall). Rather than subtly paraphrasing in the modernist manner, the little tower quotes directly from the past, as does revivalism, but unlike the latter it communicates ironically, without seriously attempting to pass for something other than itself. The Gothic Revival image is worn lightly, as a thin veneer whose details are deliberately imprecise copies, such as the peculiar, oversized brick. In this respect, the post-modernist strategy can be enjoyed as a highly sophisticated joke that points out, by exaggerating, revivalism's own inevitable failure to recreate the past. Most of the other elements within this grouping and also elsewhere in the complex are more generic in their reference to traditional architectural imagery. Thus the numerous gables, though they

relieve the monotony of the shed structures, and the big, cartoonishly drawn windows seem merely inattentive rather than wittily subversive responses to their surroundings.

A final, non-judgmental comment: as it happens, the Keohane Sports Center embodies a well-known catchphrase in post-modernist architectural theory. One of the latter's criticisms of modernism was that it idealized too far the integration of form and function and consequently failed to acknowledge that there are often good reasons, as well as admirable precedents, for a building's exterior to communicate something more complicated and specialized than its interior might seem to warrant. In a provocative 1972 book called *Learning from Las Vegas*, architects Robert Venturi, Denise Scott Brown, and Steven Izenour categorized and promoted this strategy under the memorable label "the decorated shed."

In addition to the Sports Center, the expansion of the Science Center, and extensive renovations within the dormitories, Wellesley undertook yet another major building project, long overdue, during Keohane's presidency. The College museum had outgrown its quarters in the Jewett Arts Center astonishingly quickly. For several years straddling the opening of the building in 1958, John McAndrew took pains to enlarge and especially to upgrade the collection. With the help of his wealthy wife Betty Bartlett McAndrew, he himself donated some of the choicest among these new acquisitions. (McAndrew resigned as director in 1959 but remained an important presence in the museum until his retirement in 1968.) In a snowballing effect, the enthusiastic response to improved offerings in new exhibition spaces stimulated more ambitious programming, publicity, and fund-raising, including the formation of the Friends of Art support organization. Within twenty-five years the number of objects in the collection quadrupled, yet most of them were destined, most of the time, to languish and in some cases to deteriorate in improper makeshift storage. Even when the Jewett Arts Center opened, storage and workspace had been very skimpy, in part because of the final round of cost-cutting during the design. The facilities proved inadequate in other ways also, as higher standards—barely foreseen when Jewett was built—for both conservation and security were established in the museum world generally, which was undergoing a transformation during the 1960s and '70s. The enormous proliferation of museums was accompanied by greater specialization within the museological professions. As was typical of small college museums, the Wellesley museum had always been administered

In 1993, the Nannerl Overholser Keohane Sports Center was named in honor of the departing president who had overseen its completion eight years earlier. The complex was designed by Hardy Holzman Pfeiffer Associates. Shown here, the most notable aspect of the exterior is the postmodernist treatment around the main entrance, where new construction joins the revamped Recreation Building. The picturesque assembly of diverse colors, shapes, and textures makes witty use of motifs borrowed from nearby revivalist architecture.

by the art department, and the directorship and curatorial duties remained part-time adjuncts to teaching. Though suitable and effective under previous conditions, the arrangement was inherently somewhat improvisatory and increasingly strained by the expansion of the collection and the program. In 1969 the College hired its first full-time museum director, and in 1982, after a prolonged and strenuous debate, the museum became an independent administrative unit reporting directly to the president and aspiring, at least, to fully professional policies.

Soon after she became director in 1972, Ann R. Gabhart '61 began pleading the case for new facilities. By 1986, when she resigned to pursue a second career as a ceramist, she had overseen feasibility studies for a new building and for conversion of the older facilities to departmental needs. Gabhart's assistant director, Susan M. Taylor, was appointed director and began preparing a definitive building program. The search for an architect began in 1988, when the project was truly launched by a gift of $5 million from Trustee Kathryn Wasserman Davis '28 and her husband Shelby Cullom Davis. Longtime benefactors to Wellesley, both were experts in international affairs, and they conceived an expanded mission for the new building to serve as a cultural center as well as a museum. This would entail a cinema, with attached café, to broaden the building's teaching uses and constituency. These were funded by Trustee Emerita Dorothy Dann Collins '42 and her family. Among other major donors to the project, the Jewett family was once again very generous. The total cost, including the rehabilitation of Jewett (at long last fully air-conditioned) and also the western half of Pendleton Hall, into which studio art facilities had expanded a decade earlier, was finally about $20 million.

The building program was carefully defined in great detail. Mindful of the practical shortcomings of Jewett but also the stimulus it had provided for the development of the museum, Taylor was particularly concerned that the new building should accommodate further growth as well as advances in museum technology. At the same time, Jewett set a high standard for architectural significance and inspired a comparable, distinctive approach to College patronage. Ideally the new building should provide, as had Jewett, a timely creative opportunity for a notable architect whose star was still rising —though in this case the magnitude and complexity of the project would require a more experienced candidate than Paul Rudolph had been at the time of the Jewett commission. Thus the committee appointed by President Keohane in 1988 would be sympathetic to smaller firms than might otherwise have been thought suitable. Nevertheless, some of the largest and best-known firms working in the United States and also abroad were included among the nearly two hundred initially contacted, of whom about a hundred applied for the job. The extraordinary breadth of the search, unprecedented at Wellesley, derived from very extensive canvassing of alumnae and other interested groups. It was certainly motivated by a desire to attract the best range of candidates but also, and ultimately more importantly, by a commitment to maximize the involvement and sense of shared purpose—not to mention financial support—throughout the College community. In this regard, it was intended to reflect conspicuously the institutional ethos, which had changed considerably from the days when the trustees could simply call up a single firm, as in the case of the New Dorms, with little concern for public relations.

After much review and consultation, the committee winnowed the list down to six firms (including one headed by an alumna and another with a woman principal), all of whom made presentations on campus, and then to three firms whose aesthetic priorities and experience in museum design seemed particularly apt: the Kallmann McKinnell Wood firm of Boston, designers of Boston City Hall twenty years earlier; and two architects with smaller offices, Peter Rose of Montreal and José Rafael Moneo of Madrid, who were the final, close contenders. Both had recently designed striking museums intimately fitted into older architecture, respectively the Canadian Centre for Architecture in Montreal and the National Museum of Roman Art in Mérida, Spain. Over the course of the selection process, Taylor, her committee co-chair Trustee Suzanne Kibler Morris '44, Professor Alice T. Friedman (director of the architecture program in the art department), and other members of the committee variously visited these and further works by the finalists along with a good many recent museums by other architects. After Moneo was chosen and commenced planning in the spring of 1989, he joined Taylor in an ongoing, detailed study of other museums.

Moneo was an increasingly prominent and influential figure at the time, chairing the architecture department at the Harvard Graduate School of Design. The Wellesley commission was his first in the United States. With his practice still based in Madrid, he undertook the project in affiliation with the Cambridge firm of Payette Associates. The supervising architect he chose

from his own office was Victoria Kiechel, a young woman whose constant presence and accessibility on campus proved a boon to Wellesley architecture students. In 1996, three years after the Davis Museum and Cultural Center opened, Moneo won the prestigious Pritzker Prize for architecture.

There was a consensus from the start that the look of the new building should respect that of its neighbor. President Keohane's letter announcing the project required candidates to declare their "knowledge of and empathy with" Jewett. The remarkable enthusiasm and consistency of the response, even if discounted somewhat for mere flattery induced by the letter, took the committee by surprise. Time had burnished Jewett's reputation. From the vantage point of post-modernism, Rudolph's contextual references looked prophetic, and many candidates—including Moneo—testified to the impact of the widely published building's originality on the architecture students of its era. Several supplied appreciative reminiscences of Rudolph as a teacher at Yale. In short, the selection process further confirmed Jewett's historical status, while the commission itself would serve as an homage to Rudolph by prompting a later generation to respond to his work as he had responded to earlier architecture at Wellesley. (Instead of first presenting the case in this light to Rudolph himself, by way of explaining the patronage concept, the committee inexplicably invited him to apply along with everyone else, which he did. Rejecting his application was in effect a backhanded compliment.)

Because all parties agreed that for pedagogical purposes the new building must be adjacent to Jewett, there was little flexibility in siting it. The parking lot to the west of Jewett was far preferable to an intrusion upon Severance Green to the south, which had been recommended by the local firm that produced the feasibility study. Moreover, the west side of Jewett had always been judged the least successful and was further disadvantaged by its dreary setting. Crudely done, the inevitable expansion of parking space had long since obliterated most of Rudolph's original design for the lot's paving and landscaping.

The site plan Moneo devised was ingenious and elegant. He laid out the complex in an L-shape open toward Jewett and Severance Green, with one leg along the western edge of the site and the other extended toward the front end of the music wing of Jewett and linked to it by a bridge, echoing the old gallery over the Jewett stairs. This arrangement segregated the homely loading docks for both the museum and the Jewett auditorium in a compact service area left along the north of the site and allowed the remainder of the

Designed by José Rafael Moneo and completed in 1993, the Davis Museum and Cultural Center is an imposing yet compact edifice adroitly fitted onto a cramped site behind the Jewett Arts Center. While proclaiming its own strong identity, the new building also maintains fundamental continuities with the old. The landscaping of the plaza was designed by Laurie Olin in 1994.

open space to be transformed into a plaza, deliberately in the vein of Rudolph's unexecuted plan for the Academic Quadrangle. But Moneo's most inspired stroke—actually the prime motif for the whole design—was to cut a stairway passage, aligned with Jewett's though smaller and slightly asymmetrical, through the western wing of the new complex, so that the two buildings frame a single extended spatial sequence from the boundary road upward into the Academic Quadrangle. On the opposite axis, the site is traversed, as before, along the back side of Jewett with a driveway, newly paved in continuity with the plaza. The use of the driveway as a bus stop influenced Moneo's distinctly urban-looking treatment of the plaza, which he lined with low flat-topped bollards intended to double as seats for waiting passengers.

Moneo's site plan also served to make manifest, in typical modernist fashion, the three main components of the building program as discrete units in a neatly functional arrangement. The broadest and tallest block, comprising the major public spaces of the museum, dominates the corner of the L-shape. The museum offices, storage, and workspaces, including a study room for prints and drawings and a classroom, are gathered in the lower wing extending toward Jewett. The bridge from the latter makes these backstage areas directly accessible for everyday academic uses, most notably the roster of conference classes within the art department's largest offering, the introductory art history survey. The other low wing, with its separate entrance across the open stairway passage from the main entrance to the museum block, is the entirely appropriate location for the Collins Cinema and Café at the level of the plaza. Its second story provides an additional gallery linked to the museum block by the bridge over the stairway passage.

The extreme clarity of the layout and massing gives the design an aura of inevitability that mitigates the awkwardness of the site. Yet Moneo's masterful concept had also a somewhat Procrustean effect upon the working-out of the program. The formal integrity of the main block required a problematical arrangement of its interior—namely a four-story stack of galleries—to accommodate all the exhibition space needed. Unanticipated in the building program, such a setup runs counter to the conventional wisdom in museum planning for two reasons: a vertical orientation tends to curtail the sequences in which works of art can be presented, and museumgoers ordinarily dislike negotiating more than two stories.

On the other hand, this unorthodox arrangement lent itself to Moneo's unusual, slightly sepulchral vision of the Wellesley museum. He spoke of it, in an interview published by the museum, as "a coffer that keeps so many memories of the alumnae" embodied in works of art that "they have chosen, that they loved" and eventually left to the museum, where their gifts are preserved "as in a sanctuary." His appraisal of the collection primarily as relics of a sort might be thought to reveal a certain European condescension toward the intrinsic merits of Wellesley's still relatively modest holdings. At any rate, it was joined to his concept of the viewing experience within the vertical stack of galleries. The arrangement inevitably called for a central atrium, to bring in from the top the natural light emphatically requested in the building program. Moneo envisioned along one side of the atrium a prominent staircase with openings through which the viewer would ideally see, across the central space, the collection arrayed as a whole, so that the viewer "is at once the owner of the collection, visually mastering it completely." The gratification thus evoked derives above all from the accumulative aspect, the piling up of the collection, an attitude reinforcing the notion of the museum as a treasure chest. Its contents being prized as relics of generations of alumnae devotion, the museum would constitute a shrine-like precinct in which the viewer's possessive identification with the collection partakes of something ritualistic.

In actuality, the museum interior is less overtly dramatic and idiosyncratic than Moneo's characterizations might suggest and surprisingly well adapted to the gallery program. The atrium links the three upper stories, which house long-term displays of the permanent collection in a mostly chronological sequence ascending from contemporary to ancient art. For good practical reasons, temporary exhibitions are purposely segregated at the lowest level, one story below the entrance, and also in the gallery over the cinema and café. The exhibition spaces ringing the atrium are pleasantly, unexpectedly varied. On the second and third stories, conventionally enclosed galleries are sheltered behind the staircase taking up one side of the atrium. Opening off the main exhibition space on all three stories, a small additional gallery, sized to the museum's slim non-Western holdings, is tucked around one corner of the elevator stack. On the whole, the scale of the interior is certainly generous but not as thoroughly monumental as the exterior bulk of the building predicts. The top story is the grandest interior space, its ceiling

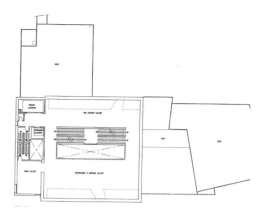

In the plan of the Davis complex, shown here at the third story, the three major components of the building program— the museum's galleries, its other spaces, and the combined cinema and café—are functionally and cleanly demarcated in the bold integral forms characteristically favored by the architect.

angling upward to five sawtooth clerestory monitors slanted to let in northern light. Assigned to this story as works least subject to fading, the ancient and medieval sculptures—none very large—and the pottery are inevitably somewhat overwhelmed, the more so because the interior design is minimally detailed. Oddly, their presence seems also slightly subdued by the remarkable and otherwise admirable evenness of the light, which the atrium bestows with serene effect upon the stories below.

The atrium itself is subtly scaled and proportioned, just assertive enough to unify the three stories without also being distracting. The adjacent staircase, however, seems miscalculated. Though it complements the atrium opening with a neat matching enclosure of the same size and shape, the over-complicated, symmetrically doubled switchback stairs squeezed within it are daunting, disagreeably confining, and strangely disorienting. Their rigors hardly enhance the atrium views supplied at the landings along the central axis. No doubt Moneo intended a processional effect of grandeur and solemnity, its slow pace enforced by the steps' low risers. In striking contrast, as if emphasizing a demarcation between the mundane and the exalted, the museum's entrance lobby at plaza level is low-ceilinged, asymmetrical, and extremely plain. Accordingly, the stairs leading down to the special exhibitions gallery, which can be viewed from the lobby landing, and up to the first story of the atrium have risers of normal height.

Somewhat as in the case of the Science Center, the Davis complex gets a mixed review on campus: the interior is much admired, but the exterior is problematical. Despite the suavity of the site plan, the beautiful abstract geometry of the massing, and the obvious, respectful references to Jewett (among others, the sharp triangular shapes on Davis's roof and the palette of

The central motif inside the museum is the atrium linking the three stories devoted to the display of the permanent collection. The atrium's scale and proportions are superbly calculated to unify the interior without also distracting from its contents, and the resulting distribution of natural light from the top story is admirable.

Robert Irwin's Filigreed Steel Line *was created in 1980 in response to its site, which was chosen by the artist on commission from the College museum. Reflecting and blending into the ceaseless play of light and shade around it, this unconventional sculpture also serves as a framing device, calling attention to the splendid view underlined by its low straight edge.*

colors and materials), the overall effect is uningratiating, essentially because of the building's scale. Instead of lessening the impact of its sheer size, Moneo's treatment calls attention to it. Elements of contrast are few and far between, so that the subdivisions of the composition are themselves large in scale. Moreover, they form no significant patterns or regular rhythms that are carried throughout the design, and in this respect Davis stands alone at Wellesley. Rhythmic repetition is found only in a few isolated, self-contained units, such as the museum offices' strip of windows, which are derived from those nearby in the music wing of Jewett, or the white-enameled steel beams applied decoratively to the main block of the museum. Moneo seems to have endeavored to give each side of the building its own unique, boldly asymmetrical design—even the steel beams are not repeated exactly on opposite sides. Another factor accentuating the huge bulk of Davis is the insistent flatness of the building's broad surfaces, quite opposite to the range of layering, lightening effects in Jewett. The only significant projecting elements are the two hefty bay-window variations (their profile a version of Jewett's prow motif) set like cyclopean eyes on opposite sides of the top story to provide the museum, rather grudgingly, with dramatic views of the landscape. Unfortunately, the building's conspicuous surfaces are not in themselves as rich and attractive as Moneo originally intended. Budget constraints substituted concrete for limestone sheathing along the lower stretches of the building, and neither the concrete nor the brick sheathing was executed with much finesse.

To some extent, the self-conscious monumentality of Moneo's design reflects the museum's newfound ambitiousness and serves to proclaim, with justifiable pride, its increasing importance both within and beyond the campus. But for the most part, the building's overweening scale and character convey the architect's predilections and, notwithstanding his modernist vocabulary, reveal a typical post-modernist nostalgia for the architectural grandeur associated with cultural institutions of a much earlier era. In sensibility if not in look, Davis has much in common with numerous other museums of recent decades (for a local example, the Sackler Museum at Harvard) that evoke more explicitly the Beaux-Arts ancestry of the building type. Perhaps Davis's discomfiting presence on the site should be attributed to Moneo's having unwittingly raised the ghost of its unmourned predecessor in the Beaux-Arts mode, the Farnsworth Art Building.

Apart from Davis, two other projects commissioned by the College museum deserve special mention for their contribution to the campus environment—not buildings but unconventional outdoor sculptures, low-spread and geometric, evoking the tradition of landscape architecture. They were created for specific sites, to which they respond with both subtlety and assurance, and they rank among the best of all works of art at Wellesley, indoors and out. Conceptual artist Robert Irwin's *Filigreed Steel Line* of 1980 adorns the edge of Severance Green near Clapp Library and Lake Waban. With remarkable economy of means, it calls attention to its setting by mimicking the dappled shade of trees and the shimmering reflections on water. In 1992, sculptor Michael Singer and architect Michael McKinnell (of the Kallmann firm) completed an untitled collaborative project near a path in the woods along the western shore of the lake. A multi-part composition of stone, stucco, bronze, and discreet landscaping, it suggests at first glance the remains of a secluded early homestead, then reveals gradually an array of exquisitely crafted variations on the theme of transformation. In an instructive way, these two works exemplify complementary pleasures in the art of landscape: the Irwin celebrates immediacy, the Singer/McKinnell meditates on change.

In 1992, sculptor Michael Singer and architect Michael McKinnell completed an intriguing untitled work inspired by the secluded site they selected in the woods west of Lake Waban. Though its crisp composition is recognizably modern, its imagery reprises a favorite feature in eighteenth-century landscape design, the faux ruin, adapted here to New England building traditions. (Photograph copyright David Stansbury)

CHAPTER ELEVEN

LOSS AND RECOVERY
IN THE WELLESLEY LANDSCAPE

Turned into a playing field in the 1980s, Munger Meadow was originally connected on its far side with the valley in front of Alumnae Hall. The causeway with the main College road was constructed in the 1920s.

THE 1921 MASTER PLAN based on Frederick Law Olmsted, Jr.'s 1902 letter (discussed in Chapter 5) governed decisions on the landscape and new building placement at Wellesley for the next forty years. By the 1960s, however, the principles on which the plan was based had faded in the collective memory. Successive administrations dealt with the new challenges facing the College in a piecemeal, *ad hoc* basis, seemingly oblivious to any overarching vision of the campus.

At the forefront of the challenges was the car. To a large extent the car had been held at bay at Wellesley until the post-World War II years; it was denied to students (except after spring vacation of their senior year), and faculty were enjoined to be resident in College housing as also were many of the staff. The economic boom of the 1960s changed this. Further factors increased parking needs in the 1970s such as the adoption of new programs like Continuing Education (the Davis Scholars as they are now known), the Stone Center for Developmental Services and Studies, and the Center for Research on Women. From 300 parking places in 1940, the car claimed more and more Wellesley meadow and woodland for macadam; by 1970 1,066 parking places were recorded and by the mid-1990s the number reached 1,730 (400 for students, the remainder for faculty and staff). Thirty-six designated parking areas within the historic core of the campus served for parking (with yet more spaces lying outside the core). The most notorious of these, the Service Lot behind Tower Court, consumed an entire valley with the valley floor hard-capped and occupied by 298 parking places.

With the car came traffic. Efforts to reduce the use of the campus by non-College users led in 1961 to a third redesign of the entry and circulation system. The designers were Innocenti and Webel of New York City, although

*The Campus in 1910. The original
circulation system remains in place with
the principal entrance at East Lodge
(right side, no 27) leading across the
meadows, in front of the chapel (no. 19),
along the north side of Severance Green,
and thence to College Hall (no. 11).
Wellesley's center remains College Hall
with its mix of residential, administrative,
classroom, and laboratory functions. To
accompany the expansion of the College
undertaken by President Hazard, the new
dormitory group, named in her honor
(nos. 4, 5, 6, 7), dominates the upper center
of the plan. The older, smaller "Cottage"
residences dot the periphery of Norumbega
Hill (nos. 12, 13, 14, 15).*

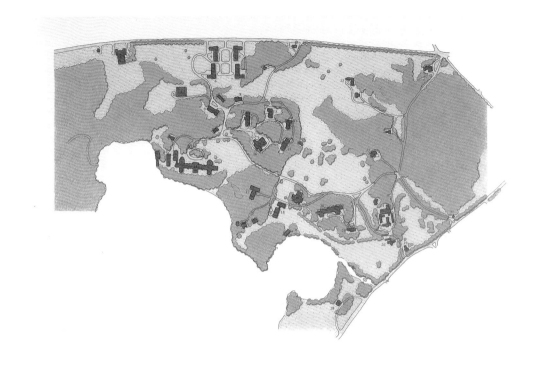

*The Campus in 1950. The original entrance
at East Lodge was closed in 1921 and
replaced by the new entrance at Fiske
House (upper right) adjacent to the town.
College Hall, which burned in 1914, has
been replaced by Tower Court, Claflin,
and Severance (nos. 14, 15, 16). The new
center of the College has been established
on Norumbega Hill with Founders,
Green, and Pendleton (nos. 20, 19, 18).
The botany department has expanded
into Sage (no. 26) along with the greenhouses. The botanic garden and arboretum
now occupy the upper-right portion
of the campus.*

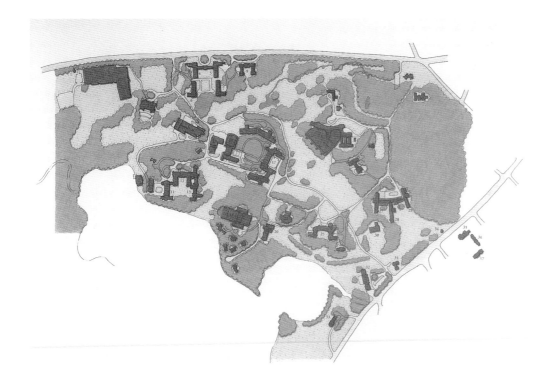

President Margaret Clapp '30 herself took a decisive role in the system's layout, rising at dawn one spring morning to personally stake out its route and ignoring professional recommendations. The principal entrance had first been located on the east side of the College (by East Lodge in 1875), then on the north (by Fiske House in 1922). Now it was placed on the west side accessed from Route 135 (the idea of relocating the Class of 1916 gates and enhancing this entrance fell victim to budget tightening). The new circulation system, moved from its original location in front of Houghton Memorial Chapel, cut through the southern border of the Middle Meadow (in front of the present Science Center), and swung north around the back of Norumbega Hill. The road took the form of a parkway and was set along the valley floor of the campus. The changes brought unforeseen consequences. The revised circulation meant that entire building groups got "turned around." On Norumbega Hill, for instance, traffic was directed west to east (the opposite of the buildings' orientation) thereby rendering meaningless the Green Hall east façade, approach road, and the medievalizing metaphor behind them (see Chapter 7). More injurious, the new road system severed any meaningful connection between circulation and the experience of site, it excised nearly twenty percent of the Middle Meadow and fifteen percent of the Upper Meadow, and, worst of all, its greater efficiency led to more traffic, increased speeds, and the demand for yet more parking spaces. To complement the new system and render access more direct, buildings such as the College Club (1963) and the Science Center (1977) were oriented to the new main road, whereas earlier building placement on ridges had looked to vistas across the landscape.

To a degree, parking replaced the landscape as a priority in the period from 1960 to 1990. The receding importance of the landscape may be tracked in decreasing staffing for landscape work (the grounds crew declined from 40 in 1936, to 26 in 1946, to 23 in 1966, to 13 in 1982, one worker in the present day for every twenty-three acres within the historic core and the equivalent outside). At the same time, paradoxically, the College was increasing its overall maintenance needs through new programs and buildings. Other evidence of the loss of the landscape's priority included a budget that consistently fell in line behind those of other projects, thin expressions of interest in the grounds from either faculty or staff, and the lapse of a separate Grounds Committee within the Board of Trustee Buildings and Grounds structure. On occasion it was even left to the town of Wellesley to intervene, on those projects where it exercised some control, in efforts to raise the College's standards such as with the siting of the new Keohane Sports Center, or the expanded parking adjacent to the College Club, or the nomination of the College (including the landscape) to the National Register of Historic Places in 1988 (subsequently declined by the trustees from fear it might restrict their powers). Perusal of the College maps from these years confronts one with the reduction of the campus to buildings, roads, and parking lots. From map to map pathways

Wellesley College map, 1995. The map shows buildings, roads, and parking lots. It omits topography, paths (for the most part), and any sense of woodland or meadow.

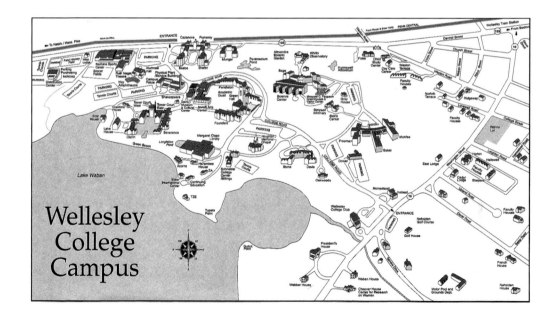

Wellesley College map, 1943. By contrast to the 1995 map, the College is shown with barely a single road. Major emphasis is given to topography and the placement of residences in reference to it. The main entrance in the lower left corner corresponds to circulation patterns between 1921 and 1961. Vignettes of the College's history frame the image.

vanished as did woodlands and topographic features; the landscape gradually dwindled to become the space between the buildings. An earlier map from 1943 offers a nearly complete contrast, showing the College with hardly a single road and giving preference to the wooded hillsides and separate building complexes.

In this period of 1960–1990, perforce, the College's attention was focused on multiple demands resulting from inflation, spiraling energy uses and costs, tuition increases, rising faculty pay scales, intensifying competition for able women students (following coeducation at peer Ivy League colleges in 1970), racial tensions, security issues, enrollment concerns, divestment, and other matters. The impact was most noticeable in the siting of the major building project of the 1970s, the Science Center. Necessary as this structure was and distinguished as its architecture turned out to be, the Science Center was designed without consideration of its relationship to established landscape principles (or even consultation with a landscape architect). Instead of adhering to the rim of the escarpment, the Center was sited down the hillside from Sage Hall and descended all the way to the valley floor. The effect was the displacement of landscape by architecture, with the latter "rebellious against it" in architect Ralph Adams Cram's forgotten phrase.

The best that can be said of this period is that the lawns were mown, granite curbing installed, new building access constructed (to bring the College in compliance with legislation like the Americans with Disabilities Act [ADA]), lighting improved, and some small-scale landscaping undertaken. For the last the trustees continued to turn to leading figures in the profession: Fletcher Steele in the early 1950s, Diane Kostial McGuire in the late 1970s, Carol Johnson '51 in the 1980s and 1990s. But funding for larger landscape projects was meager and more usually simply absent. Lacking commitment from the trustees, a voice from an action group, or faculty articulation of the role of the landscape in the education of the College's students, these designers' wide-ranging talents went largely unused.

If some of the Wellesley landscape's decline in the thirty years from 1960 may be blamed on neglect, an equal amount was due to ignorance. The concept of the landscape as a conscious construct based in an historical past with its own values and associations had disappeared. Shrunk to the status of an amenity, the landscape ceased to exercise meaning. The paralyzing amnesia underlying such reductionism was jolted in 1984 with the publication of alumna Helen Lefkowitz Horowitz's study of the Seven Sisters, *Alma Mater.* Horowitz '63 used architecture and landscape as themes to examine the Sister colleges' academic and social development. Both landscape and architecture were shown as intertwined expressions of identity complete with conscious intentions and ideals. Nowhere were these ideas clearer than at Wellesley. A still wider context emerged from studies of the American campus as an architectural type. Published the same year as Horowitz's book, Paul Turner's *Campus* illuminated the distinctive typology of university design. Other books followed rapidly, such as Thomas Gaines's *The Campus as a Work of Art* (1991), Richard Dober's *Campus Design* (1992), Ilene Forsyth's *Michigan Law Quadrangle* (1993), and the series, published from 1994 onward, of guidebooks for individual campuses from Princeton Architectural Press. The broadened perspectives these works offered only magnified the qualities of Wellesley that Gaines and others ranked with Princeton and Stanford at the top of campus designs in North America.

Even before Horowitz's insightful book, the establishment of the Grace Slack McNeil Chair in American Art in 1975 led to a number of students at the College turning to study the history of its landscape (and architecture) using the rich and well-organized College Archives for their research. Trustee attitudes were also changing. Descendents of the great families who had guided the College throughout its history, such as the Hunnewells, Forbes, Lawrences, Stones, and Jewetts, voiced concerns that prompted new attention towards the landscape and led among other things to the reconstitution of a separate Grounds Committee in the late 1980s. Somewhat tardily, faculty provided an additional impetus with members of the Departments of Biology, Philosophy, Psychology, English, Geology, and Art incorporating the College landscape in their teaching and research. It was from the biology faculty that the plea came to return the meadows to a state of biodiversity, as they had been a hundred years before.

This change of perspective was helped by the rising tide of interest in ecology and the environment, as well as a growing awareness of historic landscapes and parks. For the first, it should be recalled that the ecological movement was launched by women like Marjory Stoneman Douglas '12. Her book, *The Everglades: River of Grass* (1947) had spearheaded protection of the great Florida ecosystem and served as a prophetic voice for a new attitude to the environment; it preceded by fifteen years Rachel Carson's more widely known *Silent Spring* (1962). For historic landscapes and parks, the nation-wide revival of interest in the work of Frederick Law Olmsted, some stemming from the restoration of Central Park in New York under the direction of Elizabeth Barlow Rogers '57, created a new climate of understanding for the qualities and contributions of the landscape at Wellesley.

Underlying these changes was a shift in what might be called the educational culture. Wellesley changed in the post-World War II years, just as it had in the 1880s and again around 1920. The College now defined itself as a "Research College" with a geared-up professionalism highlighted for its faculty and students, a trend that reflected, in part, a shift from the humanities toward the social sciences. One manifestation of this new identity was a decline in the 1970s and '80s of a residential faculty and staff, as already noted. Living off campus, both groups claimed an independence from the institution; in consequence they placed more pressure on the College administration to provide accessible parking than to undertake environmental improvement. This trend showed signs of reversal in the late 1980s as the soaring housing and real estate market made the College's subsidized housing newly attractive.

By the mid-1990s the Board of Trustees confronted three facts with regard to the landscape: there were few available sites for new buildings, the landscape itself was demonstrably in need of attention, and the cleanup costs connected with the toxic wastes from the former Henry Woods Paint factory (at the west end of Lake Waban, an area that later became known as Paintmill Pond) were posing a massive financial dilemma. The process for dealing with these matters began with the commissioning of a new campus master plan, the first in seventy-five years.

For possible building sites the choices were severely limited. New construction between 1975 and 1995 of large-scale projects such as the Science Center and its subsequent extension, the Keohane Sports Center, the Davis Museum and Cultural Center, and the cogeneration plant, had seemingly seized the few available spaces. As the trustees pondered demands for another dormitory (to offset the chronic crowding in the existing ones), a student center, a book storage facility, and more playing fields, the crowding of the existing campus made it hard to see where they might be placed.

The second troubling issue, the condition of the landscape, alarmed a growing body of opinion. Degenerating hillside plantings, thinning trees, unrepaired walkways, soil deterioration, flawed drainage, rampant bitter-sweet vines and poison ivy, overgrown vistas, and eroded banks and lake edges were some of the more obvious manifestations of several decades of deferred maintenance. Compounding problems were the ubiquitous cars and the ever-expanding parking areas to accommodate them.

The primary critics of the College landscape's losses were the current and former students. No other users quite shared their perspective. To them the College remained a walking campus. They experienced the landscape in all seasons. It shaped their daily routines, exercise, sports, class celebrations, entertainments, leisure strolls, and the like. As alumnae, their associations with the College landscape became a central memory of their education, just as the Durants had intended. Their periodic returns to Wellesley for reunions and other business often left them expressing strong views about the landscape's deterioration and loss of complexity as it became ever more suburban and maintainable.

The third and more dramatic problem emerged slowly. In 1848 the Henry Woods Paint factory had been established on the western shore of Lake Waban, then called Bullard's Pond. It developed into one of the largest producers of paint pigment in the country, complete with its own rail head. The plant comprised twenty-four acres, about five with lake frontage (the buildings and smokestack are visible in old photographs). During its sixty-plus years of operation, the plant's manufacture of paint pigment depended on a high lead and chromium content. As elsewhere during the nineteenth and early twentieth century, waste products were simply dumped; in the case of the Woods factory (calculated at around six tons a day) onto the land, into Waban Brook, or into the lake. For the last, contaminants in the form of lead, chromium, and cyanide deposits quickly killed fish as well as the swans that the Hunnewells periodically tried to establish on the lake. For the first fifty years of the College's existence, the lake was, in fact, a dead body of water. The paint factory went out of business in World War I. To protect itself from developers the College bought the property in 1932.

Nothing happened for the next fifty years. The waters gradually cleared, fish and wildlife, including swans, returned and swimming is now permitted with regular monitoring by the Health Department. In the early 1980s the Department of Environmental Protection (DEP) notified the College about high levels of metals found in the soil around the original site and asked it to address the problem. The College fenced the site and undertook scientific studies to establish the extent of the polluted area. Thousands of soil sediment and water samples analyzed between 1982 and 1998 mapped the location of the contamination, which includes the twenty-four acre site, adjacent wetlands, Waban Brook, portions of Lake Waban, and some isolated campus locations where contaminated soil was apparently deposited as fill. What could not be established scientifically was the degree to which the site posed a risk to public health.

In 1991–1992 the College spent $2.5 million to truck surface soil to landfills in Québec Province, the closest hazardous-waste land fill. This still left the contaminents in the lake bottom as well as in surface and sub-surface soil. Within a few years the DEP pressed for the removal of the lead chromate residues. Making matters worse in 1997 the Massachusetts State Highway Department proposed a storm water runoff plan for a portion of Route 9 (one of the main east-west arteries in metropolitan Boston) entailing the diversion of waters into Morse's Pond (next to the College's land known as the North Forty), which, in turn, flows into Lake Waban. This posed the risk of disturbing contaminants at the bottom of Paintmill Pond, which would then enter adjoining wetlands, Waban Brook and Lake Waban. To seize the College's attention the DEP proposed to undertake the cleanup itself if Wellesley failed to do so, at a much greater cost.

President Diana Chapman Walsh '66

As in the past, it took a new president to provide momentum for change at the College. In 1993 Diana Chapman Walsh '66 assumed office as Wellesley's twelfth president. Walsh had come to the presidency from chairing Harvard's School of Public Health and moved quickly to confront the Paintmill Pond matter. Based on new studies she turned the problem on its head. Instead of exhaustive legal combat with the DEP, which had dominated the College's earlier thinking, she suggested reorienting the problem. Paintmill Pond needed to be viewed as an opportunity rather than a disaster. Cooperation with agencies like the highway department and DEP might even alleviate cleanup costs, while emerging ecological restoration technologies developed in part for the "Big Dig," the massive Central Artery/Tunnel project in Boston (1994–2005) could permit design ideas to address the College's needs rather than drain its finances.

The parking problem received an unexpected contribution from *Wellesley* alumnae magazine (Spring 1995). Before the new president arrived on campus an article had been commissioned by the then editor, Phyllis Méras '53, from a gifted city planner and architectural historian, Jane Canter Loeffler '68. Taking a wide view of parking issues, Loeffler urged the College to undertake more integrated planning as part of new building siting and program development. The response from the readership showed widespread agreement with Loeffler's ideas.

To assess the condition of the landscape with its long record of deferred maintenance the president appointed a visiting committee. Its chair was Elizabeth Barlow Rogers '57 whose skilled twenty-year restoration of New York's Central Park, Olmsted's most famous city park, along with the founding of the Central Park Conservancy to maintain it with private monies, had earned her national admiration. The visiting committee's report (1996) confirmed the views of the alumnae. Declaring Wellesley "the most beautiful campus in America," the report concluded that the College was "not doing a good job of maintaining and improving it." The committee was not afraid to be specific: "the lack of systematic tree pruning and clearing of overgrown understory vegetation, an inadequate budget for the necessary annual main-tenance and replanting of shrubs and groundcover, the loss of meadows by planting trees will-nilly in the wrong places, the multiplication of dirt trails ('desire lines'), soil compaction and erosion, eyesores like the access road near Bates and Freeman to the cellular phone towers (themselves encroachments upon the campus grounds) and the Davis Museum and Cultural Center parking lot (avoidable through site planning within the context of a comprehensive landscape plan), the forlorn and seedy appearance of the residential quadrangles, the entitlement of automobiles to a great deal of roadside parking space and the gradual eating away of former green space by parking lots—all these campus 'woes and wounds' filled us with dismay." In a memorable metaphor Rogers declared that "the legacy of the landscape was being spent down and not replenished." The report alerted the administration to the urgent need for a detailed management and restoration plan to arrest the landscape's further decline.

By rare good fortune the trustees' Grounds Committee was chaired from 1993 to 1999 by Margaret Jewett Greer '51. With the support of other trustees she pressed the need for a new master plan. The College contacted the major landscape architecture firms in the country and selected a short list: Hargraves Associates, Sasaki Associates, Laurie Olin, and Michael Van Valkenburgh Associates. In May 1997 the work was awarded to the last. A committed plantsman and ecologist with an articulate design philosophy, Van Valkenburgh combined teaching at Harvard with an active landscape practice. He had designed parks in Columbus, Pittsburgh, Minneapolis, and on Martha's Vineyard, restored Harvard Yard in 1994 (a project honored with an award from the National Trust for Historic Places), and completed landscape projects at Vassar and the Universities of Iowa and Virginia. His associate Matthew Urbanski would serve as project designer for the Wellesley plan.

As with the College's 1921 Master Plan, the charge given the landscape architects comprised both the landscape and the potential sites available for new buildings. Again following the earlier model, committees were formed to work with the architects. These totalled thirty-five members composed of trustees, administrators, faculty (retired as well as serving), staff, grounds crew, students, and alumnae. Adapting to this unfamiliar but typical Wellesley process, Van Valkenburgh's team discussed the firm's evolving ideas at five meetings open to the College community and in eight working papers amounting to nearly five hundred pages of text and drawings posted on a web site and available for comment.

Before tackling present needs, let alone future ones, Van Valkenburgh wanted to grasp what had led to existing conditions. A bedrock principle was that his firm's proposals would develop from a Wellesley context rather than draw on stereotyped solutions in fashion within the profession. Van Valkenburgh commissioned an early working paper from Elizabeth Meyer on the history of the College landscape. A professional landscape historian and chair of the School of Landscape Architecture at the University of Virginia, Meyer wrote her distinguished history in the College Archives during the summer of 1997. There was bountiful material at hand. A chronology of decisions pertaining to the Wellesley landscape could be reconstructed from trustee minutes, treasurer's reports, departmental records, and drawings and plans extending throughout the College's history, as well as photographic records (both official and from donated alumnae scrapbooks), and the inventory compiled for the College's 1994 nomination to the National Register of Historic Places.

Separate problems formed the basis for later Van Valkenburgh working papers. One looked at the entry and circulation system; another at parking; others at signage, lighting, infrastructure (few people realized its extent involving maintainence of seven miles of road, nine miles of pathway, two-and-a-half miles of tunnel for steam lines, electrical wiring, and computer cabling, and chilled water for air-conditioning); and a final report addressed the condition of plantings, trees, and soil.

For circulation, it was clear in hindsight that the 1961 road changes had made matters worse. The new road, laid along the valley floor, resulted in traffic moving at speeds judged to be unsafe for pedestrian use, while its routing away from centers of College life deprived drivers of a sense of way-finding. Furthermore, the explosive growth of surrounding suburbs in the 1980s meant increased traffic using the College as a favored shortcut (forty percent of present use is estimated as unconnected to the College). Furthermore, pressure for parking resulted in some roads and the meadows on occasion being used as parking spaces, thereby forming a metal screen between the students and the landscape. Since few drivers moved their cars once they arrived at the College, the problem was one of car storage more than of vehicle shifts from one parking area to another.

Van Valkenburgh's study of campus plantings revealed serious problems with trees, understories, and ground covers. Many trees were reaching maturity at the same time (without adequate replanting for future generations), and there was a dangerously narrow range of species. This was the opposite of Wellesley's richly cultivated natural landscape of the 1870s or the 1920s. The narrow range of species left the College's trees particularly vulnerable to diseases.

Early in the century invading fungi decimated the American horse chestnut; in the 1960s it was the American elm's turn; and in the late 1990s the wooly adelgid devastated the hemlocks. Further problems were identified along the lines of the report of the Visiting Committee. Compounding everything was the decline in the number of grounds staff, now half what it had been twenty years earlier, and the lack of a management and committee structure for the landscape.

Van Valkenburgh's final report to the trustees was presented in October 1998. Distilled into fifty-two pages of text, drawings, and cost estimates (from the five hundred pages of working papers), the 1998 Master Plan, as it became known, provided summaries of the firm's recommendations. These fell into two overall categories. The first addressed the renewal of the landscape and a management plan for its future. The second dealt with the capital costs occasioned by the parking recommendations, new construction, and a revised circulation for traffic.

To enable the College to undertake the renewal of the landscape, the architects broke down the area within the historic core into twenty-six stand-alone projects. These ranged from the residential quads, to the lake-edge paths, to the meadows, and so forth. Thus organized, the College could tackle over one decade the degeneration caused by many decades of deferred maintenance. Van Valkenburgh advocated several principles to govern this work: the priority of the dormitory landscapes (the quadrangles and their approaches), the return of diversity to the landscape through a wider variety of plantings and a different management strategy, the selective installation of irrigation using Lake Waban water to free up labor (hand-watering was a regular feature of ground-crew responsibilities into the mid-1990s), a reduction of foundation plantings that skirt buildings with yew and juniper (thereby reducing maintenance, increasing safety, improving the visibility of buildings, as well as returning to historic intentions), the substitution of perennial native plants for annuals, the clearing of historic vistas from hilltop building areas, a replanting program to replace diseased or storm-damaged trees and plants, the restoration of the meadows from their condition as lawns, the enhancement of pathways and walks and their adjustment to student use, and improvement of landscape compliance with the ADA requirements for wheelchair accessibility.

The goal of the 1998 Master Plan was renewal more than restoration. A return to a past implicit in the idea of restoration pure and simple is neither feasible nor possible. Conditions of landscape work and use have changed along with Wellesley students and their culture. Renewal incorporates both continuity and change. This is best seen in Van Valkenburgh's suggestions for one of the major components in the College's mosaic of landscape types, the belt of meadowed valleys that extends from Dower across the Science Center site, then turns around Norumbega Hill and finally terminates at Munger Meadow. In the present these are variously drained, mown, filled, transformed into playing fields, and used as ancillary parking. Thus compromised, the meadows are deprived of their role in charting seasonal change, supporting biodiversity, hosting wildflowers and wildlife, exhibiting a palette of color shifts synchronous with the calendar, and fostering, in short, "the related harmony of the forms of life they enclose," to borrow the words of ecologist and writer Marjory Stoneman Douglas '12.

The ecological concerns are more apparent now where suburban forces have removed the rural character of much of the landscape. Olmsted, Jr.'s instinct to preserve the meadows as a major structuring device of the campus was prescient in this respect. Born out of a desire to preserve the topographical complexity of the campus that was quickly disappearing elsewhere, Olmsted was also swayed by practical considerations. The meadows were the natural drainage ways of the landscape and were therefore less suitable for building (due to conditions of the water table and soil type). Van Valkenburgh accepted these ideas. Were the meadows to be managed as wet meadows once again, a somewhat rougher and less controlled look would return to the landscape, replacing the homogeneity that now prevails, the "suburbanization" critiqued by alumnae from the 1930s forward.

To rectify the chronic shortage of staffing and to maintain the landscape with its added buildings and parking adopted in the 1970s and '80s, Van Valkenburgh recommended a sixty percent increase in the grounds crew, reestablishing its level to that of the 1960s. The need was also recognized for some kind of committee structure to set priorities and establish goals for the campus and to pass up ideas to the Board of Trustees.

In 1999 and 2000 work began on four of the renewal projects called for in the plan: the Hazard and the Green Hall Quadrangles, the south front of the Science Center, and the College Club viewshed. The Hazard Quadrangle is the largest of the Wellesley dormitory complexes and provides residence for nearly 600 students. Per the master plan, new roads, brick paths, lighting, and drainage were installed; irrigation supplied to a redesigned and traffic-reduced interior; and 100 new trees along with 650 herbaceous woodland

*The Lower and Middle (or Science Center)
Meadow, along with the Upper Meadow
lying on the other side of Norumbega Hill,
retain their role as the major structuring
device of the campus landscape. Framed by
irregular, tree-shrouded slopes, and with
waist-high grasses throughout the summer
and fall, the meadows provide an image of
nature embodying biodiversity, freedom,
and empowerment.*

Among the first renewals of the landscape, the interior courtyard of Green Hall has been returned to its original 1931 form, and to community use for leisure and aesthetic enjoyment. Thirty-one parking spaces placed there in the 1960s have been eliminated. In their stead a central grassed area is now bordered by perennial flowers and spring-blossoming trees. The courtyard has been named in memory of Jane Freund Harris '41.

perennials (hay-scented fern, bugbane, and the like, with understory shrubs like bottlebush buckeye) planted around its hillsides. The Green Hall Quadrangle was transformed from car storage for thirty administration cars to become once more an oasis for those working in the Academic Center and a viewing area for the meadows. Removal of the cars was the first reduction in parking at the College in sixty years and voluntarily agreed to by the users.

The largest capital challenge to the College was—and still is—posed by the Paintmill Pond site. Since no place in North America could be found to accept the approximately thirty acres of polluted Waban Brook and Lake Waban bottom soil, Van Valkenburgh proposed an idea devised for the Big Dig in Boston, where the same problem had arisen. This was to excavate the polluted area and encapsulate it on an adjacent site in huge impermeable plastic holder-bags. These could serve as a base, topped by six feet of sand and top soil, for the College's much-needed enlarged athletic facilities, including playing fields with earthworks seating for spectators (see page 278). Tree plantings would serve as windbreaks and reduce visibility of the fields from the lake. At the same time the wetlands that originally formed the site would be reconstructed, and the watercourse forming the link between Morse's Pond and Lake Waban restored (both had been altered when the paint factory was established in 1848). Working with the Massachusetts DEP, the College has developed a remedial plan on which work is expected to start in late 2000.

For future buildings, the architects first looked at the tempting North Forty site, forty-seven acres lying unused northwest of the College. Part of the Durant Indenture, purchased in 1870 "for College purposes," the land is tightly constrained by deed restrictions and town regulations. Furthermore, its separation from the College by Route 135 and the railway line would pose formidable bridging and road work to link it to the campus. Together these obstacles led to the eventual rejection of the North Forty as a feasible site.

1998 Master Plan, east side of the campus. Artist's rendering showing potential site of a new dormitory (added to the back of Freeman and Bates) and recommending return to the original entrance to the College with a new roadway running down between Homestead and Dower. (Courtesy of Michael Van Valkenburgh Associates)

Service Lot today. The entire valley is filled with 298 parking places and six tennis courts. One of two sites being considered for the new Wang student center to be connected to Alumnae Hall, the valley would be returned to a grassed and tree-enclosed form. The cars would be stored in a parking structure pushed into the hillside under the present main College roadway.

More plausible for new buildings are the east and west sides of the College. For a future dormitory Van Valkenburgh suggested two possible locations: an extension to the New Dorms (on the east end of the campus), or a new building on the promontory above the Boat House (on the west end), which was first suggested as a building site by Olmsted, Jr. in 1902. The first could take advantage of adjacency to the College Club (for summer program use), the second to the Keohane Sports Center and proposed playing fields. For the student center two alternatives were again suggested: an extension and renovation of Schneider College Center, or a new building adjacent to or linked to Alumnae Hall. The former lacked parking but offered a central location, the latter joined students and alumnae in a building complex linked to an older ideal (see Chapter 7) and it offered extensive parking.

For the endemic parking or car-storage problem, the ongoing test facing the College has to do with its willingness to assert the priority of the landscape in the lives of its students, rather than accommodate the landscape to the exigencies of a car culture. Existing conditions bring to mind a parking-dominated ambience, which in turn reflects a suburban world of landscaped parking places. To restore the landscape to Wellesley students Van Valkenburgh proposes removing 600 to 800 cars from the center of the campus. To achieve this two parking structures would be needed: one for cars congesting Norumbega Hill and the Service Lot to be located in between the Power Plant and Alumnae Hall, the other, for cars around the Science Center, to be located on Water Tower Hill. The bulk and impact of these structures could be reduced by pushing them into the hillsides (thereby "hiding" three of their four sides), by breaking up their shape, and by extensive plantings.

In particular one aspect of Van Valkenburgh's plan offers the College a most dramatic recovery of landscape. Service Lot consumes an entire valley. Once deemed among the most beautiful valleys at the College, it is framed by dramatic contoured hillsides with superb views towards Lake Waban. Until 1922, the lot formed the culmination of a continuous three-quarter-mile valley scheme extending from Dower, around Norumbega, in front of the Hazard Quad. Compromised by the construction of the Power Plant in 1903, by the road causeway in 1921 (which severed the continuity of the valleys), and by the leveling of the northern side for the construction of Alumnae Hall (achieved with the fill from the foundations dug for Founders), Service Lot's degradation was completed by the extension of the Power Plant in the 1930s and the advent of parking after World War II. With 298 parking places, 6 tennis

courts, and adjacent spaces in front of Alumnae Hall for 60 cars added in the late 1980s, Service Lot surrenders a superb valley to passive car storage. Yet the valley remains intact and constitutes a potentially priceless asset. With parking removed it could be recovered for active landscape use, in conjunction with the proposed student center.

On the related matter of traffic, the landscape architects proposed a partially redesigned road and entry system. New entrances on the east and west side of the College would return entry to the original 1875 locations, a choice that would bring back to the road an experience of site as well as clarifying way-finding. To make the campus roads less appealing to non-College users and to encourage "traffic-calming," some existing roads would be removed and circulation would be less continuous; the major removal would be the road that skirts the east side of the Founders Parking Lot, with a return to the original College road that ran in front of the Houghton Memorial Chapel. A notable gain resulting from this scheme would be the restoration of the Lower and Middle Meadows lost in the 1961 road construction. On the west side of the campus the present entrance by the Hazard Quad dorms would be replaced by a new road running between Alumnae Hall and the swimming pool in the Keohane Sports Center, which would exit by the old West Lodge. For the Science Center a new road entering from the north from Weston Road and leading directly to the proposed Water Tower hillside garage would remove from the main campus roadway the traffic for nine academic departments as well as delivery and supply vehicles.

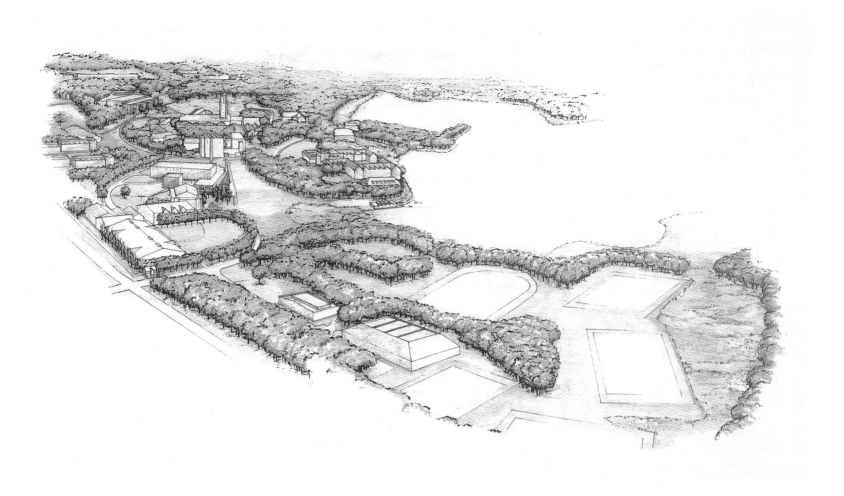

1998 Master Plan, west side of the campus. Artist's rendering showing in the foreground the new playing fields proposed over the Paintmill Pond site, and in the middle ground the transformed Service Lot shown now as a green valley. The west entrance to the College would return to the original location, next to West Lodge, shown on the left. (Courtesy of Michael Van Valkenburgh Associates)

Prepared with a twenty-year lifespan in mind, the 1998 Master Plan for Wellesley's campus presents the College with bold and challenging ideas. The plan, honored by an award in 1999 by the American Society of Landscape Architects, reaffirms the Durants' concept of the campus as structured around the existing valleys which become the organizing elements of the landscape. The uniqueness of this vision and its emphatic difference in the Durants' era—and still in large part today—from the landscape of men's colleges was first articulated by Frederick Law Olmsted, Jr. And it was this conception of the land that served as the basis for the 1921 Master Plan prepared by Shurtleff, Olmsted, and Cram. Distinctive to that plan was the principle of the adjustment of architecture to the landscape, with new buildings to be placed on the rim of the hills and shrouded with trees, and the valleys to be left inviolate.

Present and prospective needs can be adjusted to this historical perspective. The same holds for Olmsted senior's great urban parks, constructed at much the same date as the College's founding, which distinguish cities like New York, Boston, Buffalo, and Montreal. Like urban park users, students and their culture remain capable of adaptation. The Wellesley campus with its variegated landscape, sequestered walks, secret nooks, shaded trails, whispering trees, abundant wildlife, and expansive waters offers timeless opportunities for future generations as well as for personal development.

If as John Brinckerhoff Jackson, the renowed essayist of the vernacular landscape, argues, landscape is history made visible, then the unique qualities of Wellesley offer much for study. As the principal physical legacy of the founders, Henry and Pauline Durant, the landscape remains central to the experience of place and bears witness to the relationship of nature to the education offered by the College. The bonding of the students and alumnae with the Wellesley landscape has much to do with the manner in which identity and ambience complement each other.

The Wellesley landscape is a place for women. Personal development occurs against the backdrop of a landscape marked by an acceptance of a pre-existing topography, by varied contiguous parts, by irregularity. Such forms recall notions of freedom and individuality with important roots in the nation's historical culture. If the Durants provided the paradigm, the women who rapidly took charge of their own education labored to protect and enhance it, in the process serving varied roles as patron, client, critic, and architect.

Wellesley's ambience is not merely unlike that of men's colleges and universities; it is also one distinguished by an encounter of site and setting that expresses different values and meanings. The resulting sense of place allows for the discovery of self, the development of identity, and the process of empowerment in a space free from competitive male pressures during a critically formative period. It is in this sense that the Wellesley campus takes on meaning as a women's landscape. The struggle to maintain a distinctiveness for the Wellesley environment forms a moving story set against a long sequence of well-intentioned attempts to impose an order of regularity, homogeneity, and formality—most made by a profession that considered the College's rough, variegated landscape in need of remediation. Against formidable odds and powerful professional advice, the vision of the founders remains to serve the ideals they fostered 125 years ago.

A detail of the minstrels' gallery in the living room of Claflin dormitory, designed in 1916 by Day & Klauder

COLLEGE PRESIDENTS[1]	DATES	BUILDINGS AND PROJECTS	ARCHITECTS
Durant Estate era	c. 1850	Homestead (Durant Cottage)	unknown
	1862	Barn and Stables	Theodore Voelckers
	1863	President's house (Webber) acquired	unknown
	1869	East Lodge	Hammatt and Joseph E. Billings
	1869–1870	West Lodge	Hammatt and Joseph E. Billings (?)
	1871–1875	College Hall	Hammatt and Joseph E. Billings
Ada Howard 1875–1881	1875	Conservatory	unknown
		Boiler House	unknown
		Engineer's Cottage	unknown
	1879	Gray House (c. 1850) acquired	unknown
	1880	Music Hall (Billings Hall)	Ware and Van Brunt
		Stone Hall	Ware and Van Brunt
		Ellis Cottage acquired	unknown
	1880–1890	Golf House	unknown
Alice E. Freeman 1881–1887	1881	Waban Cottage acquired	unknown
		Simpson Cottage	Van Brunt and Howe
	1885	Norumbega (Decennial) Cottage	W. Frank Hurd
	1886	Elliot House acquired	unknown
Helen A. Shafer 1887–1894	1887	Freeman Cottage	W. Frank Hurd (?)
	1888	Wood Cottage	Allen and Kenway
	1889	Farnsworth Art Building	Rotch and Tilden
	1890	Superintendent's House	unknown
	c. 1890	Crawford House (Claflin Annex)	unknown
Julia J. Irvine 1894–1899	1894	Fiske House (c. 1820) acquired	unknown
		Chemistry Building	W. Frank Hurd
	1896	Competition for Houghton Memorial Chapel design	Heins & La Farge A. W. Longfellow, Jr. Peabody & Stearns Shaw & Hunnewell
		Durant Barn renovated for exercise room	unknown
		North Lodge	unknown
	1897–1899	Houghton Memorial Chapel	Heins & La Farge
	1898	Shakespeare (Elizabethan Hall)	Warren, Smith & Biscoe
	1899	Ellis Cottage (appears on 1899 map)	unknown

1. Dates under names indicate tenure of presidency

COLLEGE PRESIDENTS	DATES	BUILDINGS AND PROJECTS	ARCHITECTS
Caroline Hazard 1899–1910	1899–1900	Whitin Observatory	Henry Ayling Phillips
		C. E. House (Phi Sigma Kappa house)	Charles A. Cummings
	1900	Tau Zeta Epsilon house	Warren, Smith & Biscoe
		Wilder Hall	Julius A. Schweinfurth
	1901	Zeta Alpha house	Ralph E. Sawyer
	1902	Campus master plan proposals	Heins & La Farge
			Frederick L. Olmsted, Jr. / Warren, Smith & Biscoe
			C. Howard Walker
		Slater House (Agora, International House)	Shepley Rutan and Coolidge
		Oakwoods (home of President Hazard)	Angell & Swift
	1902–1903	Dormitory (Hazard Quad) competition	Coolidge & Carlson
			A. W. Longfellow, Jr.
			Julius A. Schweinfurth
	1903	Noanett House	unknown
		Power Plant	unknown
	1903–1904	Psychology Building	T. M. Clark
		Pomeroy Hall	Julius A. Schweinfurth
	1904	Billings Hall addition (Scheider College Center)	Angell & Swift
	1904–1905	Cazenove Hall	Julius A. Schweinfurth
	1906	Whitin Observatory house addition	Angell & Swift
		Laundry Building	unknown
	1907	Botany Labs	unknown
	1908	Beebe Hall	Julius A. Schweinfurth
		Simpson addition	Shepley Rutan and Coolidge
	1908–1909	Shafer Hall	Julius A. Schweinfurth
	1909	Mary Hemenway Gymnasium	Julius A. Schweinfurth
	1909–1910	College library (Margaret Clapp Library)	Shepley Rutan and Coolidge
Ellen Fitz Pendleton 1886 1910–1936	1912	Siting proposals for dorms and science center	Shepley Rutan and Coolidge
	1913	Siting proposal for Student–Alumnae Building	Shepley Rutan and Coolidge
		Servants' Dormitory Building (Lake House)	Shepley Rutan and Coolidge
	1914	College Hall destroyed by fire	
		Child Study Center (Ann Page Memorial)	Kilham and Hopkins
		Ark, a.k.a Hen Coop	unknown
		Geology Building	unknown
		Middle Meadow scheme for academic buildings	Coolidge & Carlson
			Arthur Shurtleff
	1914–1915	Tower Court	Coolidge & Carlson
	1915–1916	Master plan for the "Academic Center" (including Scheme 19)	Day & Klauder
	1916	College library addition	Henry O. Whitfield
	1916–1919	North wing of Hazard Quad	Julius A. Schweinfurth
	1917	Scheme 24, Academic Center	Day & Klauder, with architect Ralph Adams Cram supervising
		Claflin Hall	Coolidge & Carlson with Day & Klauder

PRESIDENTS	DATES	BUILDINGS AND PROJECTS	ARCHITECTS
	1917–1918	Founders Hall	Day & Klauder
	1920	Matheson House	unknown
		Zoology Building addition	unknown
		Washington House acquired	unknown
		Little House acquired	unknown
		Gray House renovated	unknown
		Ridgeway acquired	unknown
	1920–1921	Agora (Slater) addition	Eliza J. Newkirk (later Rogers)
	1920–1923	Class of 1916 Gates/Fiske Gateway	Putnam & Chandler
	1921	Campus master plan	Arthur Shurtleff
			Frederick Law Olmsted, Jr.
			Ralph Adams Cram
		Little House renovated	Eliza Newkirk Rogers
	1922	Hallowell House	Eliza Newkirk Rogers and
			George F. Marlowe
		Gray House renovated	unknown
		Pauline Durant's greenhouse demolished	
	1922–1923	Alumnae Hall (formerly called	
		the Student–Alumnae Building)	Cram and Ferguson
		Ferguson Greenhouses	Day & Klauder
	1923	Horton House	Eliza Newkirk Rogers and
			George F. Marlowe
		Homestead addition	Eliza Newkirk Rogers
		Barn renovated into dorms (Dower named in 1925)	unknown
	1924	Whitin Observatory addition	Roland W. Sellew
		Service Building	Walter O. Cain Associates
		Harambee House (Alpha Kappa Chi)	Eliza Newkirk Rogers
		Laundry Building (Distribution Center)	unknown
	1925	Alexandra Botanic Garden	Helen Davis
	1926	Power Plant addition	
		President's house addition	W. T. Aldrich
		Severance Hall	Day & Klauder
	1927–1931	Sage Hall	Cram, Ferguson and Medary
	1927	Nursery School	unknown
		Stone Hall destroyed by fire	
	1928	Stone–Davis Hall	Day & Klauder
	1929	New Tau Zeta Epsilon	Eleanor Raymond
		Wood Cottage demolished	
	1929–1931	Green Hall	Day & Klauder
	1930	Shepard House	Eliza Newkirk Rogers
		President's House renovated	Day & Klauder
		Wilder Hall demolished	
	1931	Sage Hall addition	Cram and Medary
		Nursery School addition	unknown
		Ark, a.k.a. Hen Coop, demolished	

COLLEGE PRESIDENTS	DATES	BUILDINGS AND PROJECTS	ARCHITECTS
	1933	Munger Hall	William T. Aldrich
		North Gate Lodge demolished	
		Ellis Cottage demolished	
	1934–1936	Pendleton Hall	Day & Klauder
		Freeman Cottage demolished	
	1935	Chemistry Building demolished	
		Alpha Kappa Chi demolished	
	1936	Hay Outdoor Theater	
Mildred McAfee Horton	1937	Nursery School addition	unknown
1936–1949	1937–1938	Recreation Building (Sports Center)	William T. Aldrich
	1941	Simpson Infirmary addition	Coolidge Shepley Bulfinch and Abbott
	1944	Cedar Lodge acquired	unknown
	1946	Schematic design for library complex on Norumbega Hill	Collens, Willis and Beckonert
	1947	Navy House (Navy building purchased and moved to campus)	unknown
Margaret Clapp '30	1952	Bates Hall	Shepley Bulfinch Richardson and Abbott
1949–1966		Freeman Hall	Shepley Bulfinch Richardson and Abbott
	1955	Hurricane survey and long range planning study	Fletcher Steele
	1955–1956	Acorns	Walter S. Pierce
	1956	Physical Plant Office	John H. Kreinheder
		Norumbega demolished	
	1957	Farnsworth Art Building demolished	
	1956–1958	Jewett Arts Center	Paul Rudolph
		College library addition	Shepley Bulfinch Richardson and Abbott
	1959–1960	Weston Terrace	Smith and Sewell
	1960–1961	McAfee Hall	Shepley Bulfinch Richardson and Abbott
	1961	System of roads revised	Umberto Innocenti and Richard Webel
	1962–1963	College Club	Heyward Cutting / Geometrics Inc.
	1963	Boat House	Heyward Cutting / Geometrics Inc.
		Navy House demolished	
	1964–1965	Stone-Davis Hall addition	Shepley Bulfinch Richardson and Abbott
	1965–1966	Whitin Observatory addition	Morehouse and Chesley
Ruth M. Adams	1966	President's House renovated	Cecil L. Wyide
1966–1972	1968–1970	Billings Hall (Schneider Center) renovated	Donald Gillespie
	1970	Harambee House renovated	Walker O. Cain Associates
Barbara Warne Newell	1975	Clapp Library addition	Shepley Bulfinch Richardson and Abbott
1972–1981		Pendleton renovated	Cambridge Seven Associates
	1974–1978	Sage Hall addition, Science Center	Perry, Dean, Stahl & Rogers

COLLEGE PRESIDENTS	DATES	BUILDINGS AND PROJECTS	ARCHITECTS
Nannerl Overholser Keohane '61	1982	Dower renovated	Ann Beha Associates
		Power Plant addition	R. W. Beck / Hart Engineering
1981–1993	1983	Houghton Memorial Chapel relandscaped	Carol Johnson Associates
	1984	Greenhouses renovated	Arrowstreet
	1985	Sports Center (later named for Nannerl Overholser Keohane '61)	Hardy Holzman Pfeiffer Associates
		Homestead renovated	Olive Holmes, Associates
		Lake House renovated	Keyes Associates
		Mary Hemenway Hall demolished	
	1987	Shafer renovated	R. E. Dineen Associates
	1989	Severance, Claflin, Beebe renovated	R. E. Dineen Associates
	1991	Science Center expanded	Perry Dean Rogers
		Pomeroy renovated	Childs Bertman Tsekares, Inc.
	1992	Munger renovated	Childs Bertman Tsekares, Inc.
		Greenhouse Visitor Center	William Sloan, Associates
Diana Chapman Walsh '66	1993	Bates, Freeman, McAfee renovated	Childs Bertman Tsekares, Inc.
1993–		Cogeneration Plant	William Sloan, Associates
		Wellesley College Club renovated	Geometrics Inc.
	1993–1994	Davis Museum and Cultural Center	Rafael Moneo Studios / Payette Associates
		Jewett Arts Center renovated	Rafael Moneo Studios / Payette Associates
	1994	Founders Hall and Simpson renovated	William Sloan, Associates
	1994–1995	Whitin Observatory renovated	William Sloan, Associates
	1995	Tower Court renovated	Childs Bertman Tsekares Inc.
		Instead (Homestead) and Dower renovated	William Sloan, Associates
	1998	Campus master plan	Michael Van Valkenburgh Associates
		Clapp Library and Knapp Media Center renovated	Shepley Bulfinch Richardson and Abbott
		Hazard Quadrangle restored	Michael Van Valkenburgh Associates
	1999	Green Hall and Galen Stone Tower renovated	Childs Bertman Tsekares, Inc.
		Clapp Library/Archives renovated	Shepley Bulfinch Richardson and Abbott
		Stone–Davis renovated	Childs Bertman Tsekares, Inc.
	2000	Pendleton renovated	Childs Bertman Tsekares, Inc.
		Science Center landscape renewed	Michael Van Valkenburgh Associates
		Green Hall (Harris) Courtyard restored	Michael Van Valkenburgh Associates

This book derives from and complements an earlier anniversary publication, *Wellesley College 1875–1975: A Century of Women,* and we owe our first thanks to the remarkable editor, the late Jean Glasscock '33, and thirteen other authors of that volume. Fitted into a comprehensive historical account, its two chapters on architecture and landscape, written by Glasscock and Harriet B. Creighton '29 respectively, were necessarily succinct and summary. For some years we nurtured a conviction that these topics deserved to be treated in greater depth as well as updated, especially in light of important developments since 1975 within our discipline and concomitantly our curriculum. We finally undertook the project encouraged by increasing evidence of the College's renewed commitment to its extraordinary setting—a shift in priorities that resulted in an inspiring new master plan firmly based in history. We completed our task in a spirit of optimism and with the hope that our understanding of the College's past might likewise offer something of value to the shaping of its future.

It seems appropriate to salute here one recent endeavor of epochal importance for the future of the Wellesley campus. In the last years of his life, Walter Hunnewell secured from ten of his neighbors conservation agreements to protect the shore of Lake Waban from further development, thereby ensuring its beloved beauty in perpetuity. This was only the latest of his many services to the College next door. Not just during his three terms as trustee, he offered wise counsel and significant support to Wellesley in numerous matters regarding its architecture and landscape.

In conceiving and defining our project, we benefited from an intellectual framework that had been established by others only recently. For much of the twentieth century, campus design attracted few historians despite the massive expansion, particularly since World War II, of universities and colleges in North America. Published in 1984, Paul Venable Turner's historical overview in *Campus: An American Planning Tradition* was a welcome contribution that set forth a sophisticated analysis of building types and planning concepts. Another ambitious historical account appearing that year was written by a Wellesley alumna of the class of 1963, and it opened a wholly new field of study. Helen Lefkowitz Horowitz's brilliant *Alma Mater: Design and Experience in the Women's Colleges from their Nineteenth Century Beginnings to the 1930s* was a revelation, not only of hitherto ignored materials but also of the methodology with which to do them justice. Stylishly written and cast into a compelling narrative of the Seven Sisters colleges, this book made it clear that the development of women's education reciprocally shaped and was shaped by architecture and landscape.

To say that we have been influenced by *Alma Mater* scarcely conveys how thoroughly we have assimilated its ideas and depended on its exemplary coverage of Wellesley. That Helen Horowitz found time within a heavy schedule of her own publication commitments to read through our entire manuscript, to give us numerous helpful suggestions, and to write a preface for us adds yet a further dimension to our indebtedness.

We aspire to supplement Horowitz's accomplishment with something distinctive and illuminating, discerned from the different scholarly perspective we bring to the topic. From the earliest days of the College and throughout its history, aesthetic concepts and criteria have played an unusual, conspicuously important role at Wellesley. As architectural historians, we study these by focusing upon particular buildings and landscapes in their fullness as artifacts. We want to know them as completely as we can: their origins in the training and practice of their designers, their evolution within the latters' transactions with clients, and their adaptations of form and function to the requirements of specific programs. Our ultimate goal is to provide historically informed interpretations of these artifacts, to render meanings we believe are inherent in their aesthetic properties as well as invested by cultural contexts.

Fittingly, the impetus for our book can be situated in the curriculum and dated back twenty-five years to the establishment of the Grace Slack McNeil Chair in the History of American Art, which brought James O'Gorman to the College. Early in his tenure his students began research on Wellesley's architecture. The first was Leiliar Ann Clements Pralle, whose distinguished honors thesis on College Hall (1978) revealed to him the richness of the archival sources and predicted for her a splendid career in architectural history; its course was tragically cut short by her death four years later. Other theses on Wellesley topics followed, notably Frances Gotkowitz's on master plans (1980), Lisa Mausolf's on Tower Court (1980), Martha Folger's on the early landscape (1990), and Lori Pavese's on cottage dormitories (1995).

In addition to these, many other students' researches have contributed to our book. We are grateful to the following, who undertook independent study projects or participated in seminars devoted to the topics of the book: Caitlin Augusta (Ralph Adams Cram), Tamar Brendzel (Munger Hall), Jessica Burton (dormitories), Hannah Chung (Alexandra Botanic Garden and Hunnewell Arboretum), Salvatore De Fazio (Eliza Newkirk Rogers), Alexis Dinniman (gymnasia), Gina Ford (Stone Hall), Ellery Foutch (Eliza Newkirk Rogers and Eleanor Raymond), Sarah Gilman (Whitin Observatory), Chris Holland (Simpson Cottage and Munger Hall), Constance Jackson (College traditions), Elizabeth Kang (Jewett Arts Center), Brigid Kelly (art buildings), Sheryl Lamoureau (Tau Zeta Epsilon), Natasha Loeblich (the New Dormitories), Melissa Jordan Love (campus circulation), Diane Melish (Clapp Library; for a seminar taught by Henry Millon at MIT), Sally Meredith (Caroline Hazard), Alexandra Palmer (the society houses), Lorraine Palmer (campus restoration), Julia Rearden-Hamly (Hazard Quad), Keifsen Schleifer (technology in College Hall), and Diana Lynn Shapiro (the Science Center).

What made all their and our work possible was the bounty of the Wellesley College Archives, a treasure house taking up much of the top floor of Clapp Library. There, in a process resembling the creation of a mosaic, history can be constructed from the diverse data to be gleaned from committee reports, trustees' minutes, presidential addresses, treasurers' records, architects' drawings, engineers' blueprints, patrons' correspondence, faculty records, alumnae memorabilia, newspaper clippings, and all sorts of photographs. Guiding us through all this material, explicating its mysteries to us, and constantly divining our needs were the College's head archivist Wilma Slaight and her assistant Jean Berry. We could not have written the book without their vast knowledge, which more than once disclosed to us new facets of our topics. They met our every request, however vague or ignorant, with proficiency, admirable patience, and friendly interest. Even in the last year of our work, when the entire archival collection was placed in storage to accommodate major building renovations, they managed to conjure up references and to produce photocopies. We thank them for being our chief collaborators in this project.

In 1987 the town of Wellesley nominated the College to the National Register of Historic Places. To prepare the nomination forms the College hired Gretchen Schuyler for the buildings and Arleyn Levee '62 for the landscape. Their extensive research resulted in valuable and handy documentation that made our work easier.

Following the recommendations of the visiting committee on the landscape, appointed by President Diana Chapman Walsh '66 in 1995, the College commissioned a master plan from Michael Van Valkenburgh Associates of Cambridge, Mass. Of the six working papers that formed the basis of their master plan proposal, the second was a history of the landscape written by Professor Elizabeth Meyer of the University of Virginia. Her exemplary essay, part of which was published in *Wellesley* magazine in Spring 1997, has been an essential resource for us, and we are grateful to her for sharing this material.

What Wellesley College has been for 125 years and will be in the future owes immeasurably to the perspicacity and prudence of its trustees, who are charged among much else with the stewardship of its landscape and architecture. In these matters we appreciate fully and can bear witness to many instances of their timely attentiveness to detail as well as the importance of their long-term support and generosity.

The trustees' acceptance of the master plan proposal in 1998 was the decisive first step toward a goal to which the College would not be committed without the strong leadership of President Walsh. Speaking before many different audiences on numerous occasions, she has lucidly articulated the reasons why the special character of Wellesley's campus is a profoundly important factor in the quality of a Wellesley education. We admire her and are grateful indeed that she kindly found the time within a most demanding schedule to write the foreword to our book.

The College's decision to publish our book must be credited above all to the good services of David Blinder, vice president for resources. His vision and conviction sustained us throughout the project, and his intervention and counsel helped solve many a problem along the way. We are much indebted also to Susan M. Taylor, then director of the Davis Museum and Cultural

Center. As co-chair, with Jonathan B. Imber, of the 125th Anniversary Committee, she generously volunteered to organize the initial stages in the production of the book, and we benefited from her advice especially in planning its visual presentation.

To illustrate our text we needed contemporary as well as historical photographs. We were fortunate indeed to engage the services of one of the nation's foremost architectural photographers, Cervin Robinson. His skill, visual intelligence, and intuitive grasp of our agenda are amply evident in the color images he produced for us. To convey legibly the distinctive complexity of the campus was a challenge expertly met also by Gina Ford '97, who took time out from a busy professional schedule to produce the maps illustrating the College's history.

From the start of the project we relied upon our research assistant Elizabeth Wax DS '97, a true collaborator who also took on the task of keeping us on schedule and within budget. Among her other contributions, she patiently tracked down, verified, and coordinated a plethora of names and dates, and she has supplemented our text with the handy historical lists in the Appendix. Her good humor and common sense were invaluable.

We are greatly indebted to Susan McNally, who meticulously planned and coordinated the production of our book; Julia Collins, our extraordinarily wise and helpful editor; and Matthew Monk, whose elegant design for the book more than fulfilled our hopes. Working with this amiable team was a thoroughly gratifying experience.

It is a pleasure to record our thanks to the following persons for assistance of various sorts: Elizabeth Hope Cushing for sharing her research on Arthur Shurcliff; Elizabeth Kaiser Davis '32 for providing information from her letters home during her early years at Wellesley; Anne Knowles for helping us with maps of the Seven Sisters; Kimberly Alexander Shilland for sharing parts of her dissertation on Henry Van Brunt; Linda Vaughan for sharing her work on the history of sports at Wellesley; Melissa Webster '95 for preparing maps of the Durants' land purchases; and the architectural firm of Shepley Bulfinch Richardson and Abbott, and in particular archivist Robert Roche and librarian Katherine Meyer, for allowing and generously assisting our research in the firm's archives. For fostering and educating our interest in Wellesley's landscape, we thank Harriet B. Creighton, Stanley and Theodora Feldberg '48, Janice Lane Hunt '52, Carol R. Johnson '51 of Carol

R. Johnson Associates, Will Reed, Adel Rida, and Patrick Willoughby. We have many reasons to thank also Meg Birney, Judith Black, Nancy Bowman, Judith Brown, Maud Chaplin '56, Marie Companion, Eugene Cox, Mary Coyne MA '61, Lucy Flint-Gohlke, the late Margaret Henderson Floyd '53, Jeanne Hablanian, Sandy Hachey, Mary Anne Hill '84, Mary Lefkowitz '57, Lisa McDermott, Dennis McFadden, Marianne Moore, Rod Morrison, Del Nickerson, Alla O'Brien '42, Ann Ogletree '72, David Pillemer, Virginia Quinan, Nicholas Rodenhouse, John Rossetti, Margaret Thompson, Andrew Warren, Eleanor Webster '42, Ken Winkler, and the staff of the Mount Holyoke College Archives and of the Wellesley Free Library.

We are deeply grateful to the friends and colleagues who improved our book by checking passages and reading drafts at various stages in the writing: Lilian Armstrong '58, Rebecca Bedell '80, Jean Berry, David Blinder, Patricia Byrne, Kathryn Wasserman Davis '28, Alice T. Friedman, Margaret Jewett Greer '51, Jane Canter Loeffler '68, Wilma Slaight, Susan M. Taylor, Matthew Urbanski, Michael Van Valkenburgh, and Elizabeth Wax.

Over the years we have conducted many walking tours of the campus. This pleasurable extension of our teaching has proven also to be a significant learning experience for us, thanks to the countless visiting alumnae whose memories, insights, questions, and corrections of our mistaken notions along the way have enriched our understanding and broadened our perspective. Likewise we are grateful to the participants in the Wellesley Alumnae Association's 1999 Summer Symposium entitled "Landscape, Meaning, Memory," inspirationally chaired by Julie Moir Messervy '73.

Two alumnae deserve special thanks. Elizabeth Barlow Rogers '57 did much to alert all of us to the need for renewal in Wellesley's landscape. Walking with her through the campus on a number of occasions, we have benefited not only from her analytical skills but also from the breadth of her expertise, the results of which are nationally admired in her restoration of Frederick Law Olmsted's Central Park in New York. For Margaret Jewett Greer in her eighteen years' tenure as a trustee no expression of our admiration and gratitude seems adequate. On her frequent visits to the College her passionate interest in architecture and landscape has been manifest in numerous ways. From personally picking up cigarette butts and styrofoam coffee cups discarded on the grounds, to checking architects' drawings on site with her chalk and measuring tape (invariably finding errors, thoughtfully suggesting alternatives), to formulating policy at the highest level of the College's decision-making, she has long been an inspiration to us.

Working for many years within the architecture and landscape of Wellesley College has been a privilege and a profound pleasure to the authors of this book, which is in its entirety an expression of our affectionate gratitude to the institution we serve.

BIBLIOGRAPHY

PETER FERGUSSON
CHAPTERS 1, 5, AND 11

The most comprehensive history of the Wellesley College landscape is Elizabeth Meyer's Working Paper No. 2 in Michael Van Valkenburgh's 1998 Wellesley College Campus Master Plan (unpublished). A brief digest appeared as "Wellesley's Landscape Legacy: Master Planning for this Century and the Next" in *Wellesley*, 82, Spring 1998, 12–17, 42. We wish to extend our profound thanks to Professor Meyer for graciously allowing us to draw on her material.

Abbott, E., "Wellesley College," *Harper's Monthly Magazine* (no. 315), August 1876, 321–333.

Adams, H. B., "Letters of a Wellesley Girl," *New England Magazine*, September 1908.

Beveridge, C. E., *Frederick Law Olmsted: Designing the American Landscape*, New York, 1995.

Converse, F., *Wellesley College, A Chronicle of the Years 1875–1938*, Wellesley, Mass.: Wellesley College, 1939.

Creighton, H., "The Grounds," in J. Glasscock (ed.), *Wellesley College 1875–1975: A Century of Women*, Wellesley, Mass. Wellesley College, 1975, 265–294.

Downing, A. J., *A Treatise on the Theory and Practice of Landscape Gardening Adapted to North America with a View to the Improvement of Country Residences*, New York, 1841.

Durant, H. F., *The Spirit of Wellesley* (a sermon delivered at Wellesley on September 23, 1877), Boston, 1890.

Emmet, A., "Family Trees: Wellesley's Hunnewell Estate," *So Fine a Prospect: Historic New England Gardens*, London, 1996, 84–99.

Faculty Conference Committee, "The New College Plan and Problems," *Wellesley Alumnae Quarterly*, July 1917, 225–228.

Fein, A. (ed.), *Landscape into Cityscape: Frederick Law Olmsted's Plans for a Greater New York City*, Ithaca, N.Y., 1967.

Folger, M. "The Landscape Development of Wellesley College, 1875–1920," honors thesis, Wellesley College, 1990.

Gotkowitz, F. "The Development of a Master Plan for Wellesley College," honors thesis, Wellesley College, May 1980.

Harter, A. H., *Wellesley: Part of the American Story*, Lexington, Mass., 1949.

Hazard, C., *Some Ideals in the Education of Women*, New York, 1900.

Hill, M. B. and H. G. Eager, *Wellesley: the College Beautiful*, Boston, 1894, with an introduction by Katherine Lee Bates.

Hodgkins, L. M., "Wellesley," *New England Magazine*, 7 (no. 3), 1892.

Horowitz, H. L., *Alma Mater: Design and Experience in the Women's Colleges from Their Nineteenth-Century Beginnings to the 1930s*, Amherst, Mass., 2d ed., 1993.

Horowitz, H. L. (ed.), John Brinckerhoff Jackson, *Landscape in Sight: Looking at America*, New Haven, 1997.

Kingsley, F., *The Life of Henry Fowle Durant*, New York, 1924.

Lefkowitz, M., *Heroines and Hysterics*, London, 1981.

Levee, A. and G. Schuler, Report Prepared for the National Register Nomination of Wellesley College, Wellesley College Archives, 1989.

Olmsted, F. L., *A Few Things to be Thought of before Proceeding to Plan Buildings for the National Agricultural Colleges*, Boston, 1866.

Olmsted, F. L., "Notes on the Plan of Franklin Park and Related Matters," in C. E. Beveridge and C. F. Hoffman, *The Papers of Frederick Law Olmsted, Supplementary Series, Vol. 1, Writings on Public Parks, Parkways and Park Systems*, Baltimore, 1997.

Perenyi, E., *Green Thoughts*, New York, 1983.

Poindexter, J. and L. Sanders, *The New Wellesley*, Boston, 1931.

Pollan, M., *Second Nature: A Gardener's Education*, New York, 1991.

Rogers, E. B., *Rebuilding Central Park: A Management and Restoration Plan*, Cambridge, 1987.

Rybczynski, W., *A Clearing in the Distance: Frederick Law Olmsted and America in the Nineteenth Century*, New York, 1999.

Schama, S., *Landscape and Memory*, New York, 1995.

Schuyler, D., "The Sanctified Landscape: the Hudson River Valley, 1820–1850," in G. F. Thompson (ed.), *Landscape in America*, Austin, Texas, 1995, 93–110.

Schuyler, D., *Apostle of Taste: Andrew Jackson Downing 1815–1852*, Baltimore, 1996.

Schuyler, D., "Frederick Law Olmsted and the Origins of Modern Campus Design," *Planning for Higher Education*, 25 (no. 2), 1996–1997, 1–10.

Smith, H. N., *Virgin Land: the American West as Symbol and Myth*, Cambridge, Mass., 1970.

Warren, C., *A New Design for Women's Education*, New York, 1940.

Zaitzevsky, C., *Frederick Law Olmsted and the Boston Park System*, Cambridge, Mass., 1982.

JAMES F. O'GORMAN
CHAPTERS 2, 3, AND 4

The most important sources for the study of Wellesley's architecture are found in Wellesley College Archives.

Edward Abbott, "Wellesley College," *Harper's New Monthly Magazine*, 315, August 1876, 321–332.

"Buildings for Wellesley College," *Architectural Review*, 12, May 1921, 129–133.

Lee Ann Clements, "A New Light on College Hall," *Wellesley Alumnae Magazine*, 62, Spring 1978, 4–7.

Jean Glasscock, *Wellesley College 1875–1975: A Century of Women*, Wellesley, Mass.: Wellesley College, 1975.

Francis Gotkowitz, "The Development of a Master Plan for Wellesley College," undergraduate thesis, Wellesley College, 1980.

Helen Lefkowitz Horowitz, *Alma Mater: Design and Experience in the Women's Colleges from Their Nineteenth-Century Beginnings to the 1930s*, Amherst, Mass.: University of Massachusetts Press, 2d ed., 1993.

Harry L. Katz, *A Continental Eye: The Art and Architecture of Arthur Rotch*, Boston: The Boston Athenaeum, 1985.

Florence Morse Kingsley, *The Life of Henry Fowle Durant, Founder of Wellesley College*, New York: Century, 1924.

Charles Z. Klauder and Herbert C. Wise, *College Architecture in America*, New York: Charles Scribner's Sons, 1929.

Elizabeth Meyer, "History of the Wellesley College Landscape," Working Paper No. 2, Campus Master Plan Prepared for the Trustees of Wellesley College by Michael Van Valkenburgh, 1998.

Maureen Illona Meister, "Herbert Langford Warren: Architecture, Harvard, and the Organizations of the Arts and Crafts Movement," Ph.D. diss., Brown University, 2000.

Stephen J. Neitz and Wheaton A. Holden, *Julius A. Schweinfurth Master Designer 1858–1931*, Boston: Northeastern University, 1975.

James F. O'Gorman, *Accomplished in All Departments of Art: Hammatt Billings of Boston, 1818–1874*, Amherst, Mass.: University of Massachusetts Press, 1998.

James F. O'Gorman, "Gothic Struggle: Wellesley's Architectural Evolution," *Realia*, December 1985.

James F. O'Gorman, *On The Boards: Drawings by Nineteenth-Century Boston Architects*, Philadelphia: The University of Pennsylvania Press, 1989.

James F. O'Gorman, "Unbuilt Wellesley I: A Fragment From the Great Debate," *Wellesley WRagtime*, II, May 1979, 8–9.

George Herbert Palmer, *The Life of Alice Freeman Palmer*, Boston: Houghton, Mifflin and Company, 1908.

Patricia Ann Palmieri, *In Adamless Eden: The Community of Women Faculty at Wellesley*, New Haven and London: Yale University Press, 1995.

[Martha Halle Shackford and Edith Harriet Moore], *College Hall*, [Wellesley, Mass.: Wellesley College, 1914].

Montgomery Schuyler, "Architecture of American Colleges X: Three Women's Colleges—Vassar, Wellesley, and Smith," *Architectural Record*, 31, May 1912, 512–537.

"Stone Hall," *The American Architect and Building News*, 7, 7 February 1880, 46.

Paul Venable Turner, *Campus: an American Planning Tradition*, Cambridge, Mass.: M.I.T. Press, 1984.

PETER FERGUSSON
CHAPTERS 6 AND 7

The best published account of this period in Wellesley's history is chapter 16, "A Great Design," in Helen Lefkowitz Horowitz's, *Alma Mater*, 262–273.

"Alumnae Hall," *Wellesley Alumnae Quarterly*, 8, 1924, 68–74.

Block, J., *The Uses of Gothic: Planning and Building the Campus of the University of Chicago 1892–1932*, Chicago, 1983.

Brannon, H., "Campus Chatter," *Wellesley Magazine*, 15, October 1930.

"Building for Wellesley College" *Architectural Review*, 7 (no. 5), May 1921.

Carlson, H., "Dormitories for Wellesley College, Wellesley, Mass." *Architectural Review*, 9, 1919, 7–10.

"Collegiate Buildings," *Architectural Forum*, December 1925.

Converse, F., *Wellesley College: A Chronicle of the Years 1875–1938*, Wellesley, 1939.

Cram, R. A., "Princeton Architecture," *American Architect*, July 21, 1909, 21–30.

Cram, R. A., "Recent University Architecture in the United States," *Royal Institute of British Architects Journal*, May 25, 1912, 497–98.

Cram, R. A., "Architecture at Wellesley," *Wellesley Alumnae Quarterly*, October 1916, 1–4.

Cram, R. A., *The Gothic Quest*, New York, 1918.

Egbert, D. D., "The Architecture and the Setting," in C. G. Osgood (ed.), *The Modern Princeton*, Princeton, 1947.

Fergusson, P. J., "Medieval Architectural Scholarship in America 1900–1940: Ralph Adams Cram and Kenneth John Conant," in E. B. MacDougall, *The Architectural Historian in America Studies in the History of Art,* Vol. 35, National Gallery of Art, Washington, D. C., 1994, 127–144.

Forsyth, I., *The Uses of Art: Medieval Metaphor in the Michigan Law Quadrangle*, Ann Arbor, Mich., 1993.

Githens, A. M., "Recent American Group Plans III—Colleges and Universities: Development of Existing Plans," *The Brickbuilder*, 21, 1912, 313–16.

Githens, A. M., "Recent American Group Plans IV—Colleges and Universities: Development of New Plans," *The Brickbuilder*, 22, 1913, 11–14.

Glasscock, J. "The Buildings," in J. Glasscock (ed.), *Wellesley College 1875–1975: a Century of Women*, Wellesley, Mass.: Wellesley College, 1975, 295–338.

Goodyear, W. H., "The Memorial Quadrangle and the Harkness Memorial Tower at Yale," *American Architect*, October 26, 1921, 299–314.

Gotkowitz, F., "Development of a Master Plan for Wellesley College," honors thesis, Wellesley College, 1980.

Gowans, A., *Styles and Types of North American Architecture*, New York, 1992.

Hackett, A. P., *Wellesley: Part of the American Story*, New York, 1949.

Horowitz, H. L., *Alma Mater: Design and Experience in the Women's Colleges from Their Nineteenth-Century Beginnings to the 1930s*, Amherst, Mass., 2d ed., 1993.

Horowitz, H. L., "Smith College and Changing Conceptions of Educated Women," in R. Story (ed.), *Five Colleges: Five Histories*, Amherst, Mass., 1992, 79–102.

Horowitz, H. L., *The Power and Passion of M. Carey Thomas*, New York, 1994.

Klauder, C. Z. and H. Wise, *Collegiate Architecture in America and Its Part in the Development of the Campus*, New York, 1929.

Lanford, S. D., "A Gothic Epitome: Ralph Adams Cram as Princeton's Architect," *The Princeton University Library Chronicle*, Spring 1982, 184–220.

Mausolf, L., "Tower Court: the Phoenix of College Hill," honors thesis, Wellesley College, 1980.

"On the Buildings of Wellesley College," *Architectural Forum*, January 1932, 13–20.

Osgood, C. G. (ed.), *The Modern Princeton*, 1914.

Passanti, F., "The Design of Columbia in the 1890s, McKim and His Client," *Journal of the Society of Architectural Historians*, 36, 1977, 69–84.

Pendleton, E. F., "The Administration," *Wellesley Alumnae Quarterly*, April 1919.

Poindexter, J. and L. Saunders, *The New Wellesley*, Boston, 1931.

Schuyler, M., "The Works of Cram, Goodhue and Ferguson," *Architectural Record*, 1911, 1–112.

Schuyler, M., "Architecture of American Colleges: Three Women's Colleges: Vassar, Wellesley, Smith," *Architectural Record*, 31, 1912, 513–537.

Shand-Tucci, D., *Ralph Adams Cram: American Medievalist*, Boston, 1975.

Shand-Tucci, D., *Built in Boston*, Boston, 1978.

Shand-Tucci, D., *Ralph Adams Cram: Life and Architecture*, Amherst, 1995.

Turner, P. V., *Campus: An American Planning Tradition*, Cambridge, 1984.

"Wellesley College Central Dormitory," *The Brickbuilder*, 25, 1916, 39.

Wharton, A., "Gender, Architecture, and Institutional Self-Presentation: The Case of Duke University," *The South Atlantic Quarterly*, 90, 1991, 175–217.

Wheeler, M., "The Student Alumnae Building" *Wellesley Alumnae Quarterly*, 1, 1916, 5–6.

Whiffen, M., *American Architecture since 1780: A guide to the Styles*, Cambridge, 1992.

JOHN RHODES
CHAPTERS 8, 9, AND 10

By far the major sources were unpublished records and letters in the College Archives. Also essential to the research were the archives of Shepley Bulfinch Richardson and Abbott in Boston. For the history of the Davis Museum and Cultural Center, Susan M. Taylor and Alice T. Friedman patiently answered many questions and generously lent a variety of useful documents, including data handily compiled in class projects by the latter's students. In Chapter 9, the author's understanding of Rudolph's career and sensibility benefited from conversations and correspondence with Timothy M. Rohan, a Ph.D. candidate in the Harvard University Fine Arts Department. Among published sources, fully listed elsewhere, for these three chapters as for the book generally, the centennial history edited by Jean Glasscock was indispensable as was Helen Lefkowitz Horowitz's *Alma Mater*, the former in numerous matters, the latter more especially for the history of Wellesley housing prior to the New Dorms.

Adair, Tonja, Guillemette de Boucaud, Mary Thompson, and Amy Ralston, *The Davis Museum and Cultural Center*. Pamphlet, including interview with Moneo, published by the Davis Museum and Cultural Center, 1992.

"At Old Wellesley, New Architecture." *Architectural Forum* 98 (no. 6), June 1953, 140–145.

Bernstein, Gerald S., ed. *Building a Campus: An Architectural Celebration of Brandeis University's 50th Anniversary*. Waltham, Mass.: Brandeis University, 1999.

Brendzel, Tamar. "Separate, but Equal? The Construction of Munger Hall." Paper for Fergusson/O'Gorman seminar, 1999.

Brown, Helen M. "Wellesley's Library in Prospect." *Wellesley Alumnae Magazine* 40 (no. 1), November 1955, 7–9.

Bunting, Bainbridge. *Harvard, An Architectural History*. Completed and edited by Margaret Henderson Floyd. Cambridge, Mass.: Belknap Press, 1985.

"Controversial Building in London." *Architectural Forum* 114 (no. 3), March 1961, 80–85. [Extracts from British criticism of Saarinen's embassy, including Reyner Banham's "Ballet School" characterization.]

Crosbie, Michael J. *Color and Context: The Architecture of Perry Dean Rogers and Partners*. Washington, D.C.: American Institute of Architects Press, 1995.

Curtis, William J. R. *Modern Architecture since 1900*. Englewood Cliffs, N.J.: Prentice-Hall, 1983.

"Davis Center, Wellesley College, Massachusetts." *Casabella* 58 (no. 611), April 1994: 51–55.

Deitsch, Deborah K. "A Picture of Health: Wellesley College Sports Center, Wellesley, Massachusetts." *Architectural Record* 175 (no. 9), August 1987, 90–95.

Ehrman, Leslie. "The New Science Center." *Wellesley Alumnae Magazine* 59 (no. 2), winter 1975, 4–5.

Faison, S. Lane, Jr. "Wellesley Art Collections Re-open in New Jewett Arts Center." *College Art Journal* 18 (no. 3), spring 1959, 241–245. [With untitled review, of building per se, by Henry R. Hope, 244–245.]

Flint-Gohlke, Lucy. *Davis Museum and Cultural Center: History and Holdings*. Wellesley, Mass.: Wellesley College, 1993.

Forbes J. D. "Shepley, Bulfinch, Richardson & Abbott, Architects: An Introduction." *Journal of the Society of Architectural Historians* 17 (no. 3), fall 1958, 19–31.

Friedman, Alice T. *Women and the Making of the Modern House: A Social and Architectural History*. New York: Abrams, 1998.

Goldberger, Paul. "Architecture View: Sensuous Spaces Armored in Brick." *New York Times* July 31, 1994: 2nd sec., 30.

Guernsey, Janet Brown. "Science at Wellesley." *Wellesley Alumnae Magazine* 59 (no. 1), autumn 1975, 2–6.

Heskel, Julia. *Shepley Bulfinch Richardson and Abbott: Past to Present*. Boston: Shepley Bulfinch Richardson and Abbott Inc., 1999.

Howey, John. *The Sarasota School of Architecture: 1941–1966*. Cambridge, Mass.: MIT Press, 1995.

Kang, Elizabeth. "Jewett Arts Center: Personalities behind the Architecture." Paper for Fergusson/O'Gorman seminar, 1994.

Kelly, Brigid. "The Role of History, Money and Politics in the Evolution of Art Building Proposals at Wellesley College: 1916–1955." Independent study paper for O'Gorman, spring 1993.

Kolodny, Nancy Harrison. "The New Science Center." *Wellesley Alumnae Magazine* 61 (no. 2), winter 1977, 16–17.

Larrecq, Kathryn. "Paul Rudolph, Jewett Designer, Defends Architectural Scheme." *Wellesley College News*, October 23, 1958, 1.

Loeblich, Natasha K. "The New Dorms of Wellesley College: 1952–1994." Paper for Fergusson/O'Gorman seminar, 1994.

Loeffler, Jane C. *The Architecture of Diplomacy: Building America's Embassies.* New York: Princeton Architectural Press, 1998.

Marple, Max. "Soon-to-be-Completed Science Center an Architectural Stunner." *Wellesley Townsman*, January 22, 1976, 20.

McAndrew, John. *What is Modern Architecture?* New York: Museum of Modern Art, 1942.

Melish, Diane. "The Relationship between Client and Architect: The Wellesley College Library Reconsidered." Paper for Henry Millon, MIT, spring 1973.

Morton, David. "More Gothic than Revival: Science Center, Wellesley College." *Progressive Architecture* 59, March 1978, 70–75.

"New Architecture in an Old Setting: the Jewett Arts Center, Wellesley College." *Architectural Record* 126 (no. 1), July 1959, 175–186.

"Not Neo-Tiffany: Revivalism and Paul Rudolph." *Architectural Review* 127 (no. 756), February 1960, 78.

Paul Rudolph. Introduction and notes by Rupert Spade. With 63 photographs by Yukio Futagawa. New York: Simon and Schuster, 1971.

"Recent Work of Shepley, Bulfinch, Richardson and Abbott." *Architectural Record* 125 (no. 2), February 1959, 153–168.

Rhodes, John. "The Jewett Arts Center: A Tribute at 25," special edition of the *Wellesley College: Friends of Art Newsletter* 1982–1983: n. p.

Richardson, Joseph. "The New Dormitories." *Wellesley Alumnae Magazine* 37 (no. 1), November 1952, 6–9.

Rohan, Timothy M. "The Dangers of Eclecticism: Paul Rudolph's Jewett Arts Center at Wellesley." *Anxious Modernisms: Experimentation in Postwar Architectural Culture.* Eds. Sarah Williams Goldhagen and Rejean Legault. Montreal: Canadian Centre for Architecture and MIT Press, publication forthcoming.

Rudolph, Paul. "The Changing Philosophy of Architecture." *Architectural Forum,* July 1954, 120–121.

Rudolph, Paul. *Paul Rudolph: Architectural Drawings.* Ed. Yukio Futagawa. New York: Architectural Book Publishing Co., 1981.

Schulze, Franz. *Philip Johnson: Life and Work.* New York: Knopf, 1994.

Shapiro, Diana Lynn. "The Wellesley College Science Center: An Explanation." Honors thesis, Wellesley College, spring 1977.

"The 76th Annual Commencement and the Wellesley Weekend." *Wellesley Alumnae Magazine* 38 (no. 5), July 1954, 285–286.

"Springtime Adorns Gateway at New Wellesley Buildings." *Christian Science Monitor* 26, August 1952, 4.

Stein, Karen D. "Art World: Rafael Moneo's First American Building and Its Neighbor, the Jewett Arts Center by Paul Rudolph, Form a Cultural Acropolis." *Architectural Record* 181, October 1993, 84–91.

"Wellesley College Builds Two New Dormitories." *Architectural Record* 112, (no. 1), July 1952, 26.

Williams, Stephanie. "Labs for Ladies: Science Building, Wellesley College, Massachusetts." *Architectural Review* 162 (no. 967), September 1977, 148–155.

Wise, Michael Z. "Moneo's First U.S. Building Opens at Wellesley." *Progressive Architecture* 74, December 1993, 11–12.

INDEX